AM I GAY?

Coming Out of Cultural Christianity & LGBTQ+ Identity
Into Authentic Faith in Jesus

Garry Ingraham

Garry Ingraham

TABLE OF CONTENTS

DEDICATION

This book is dedicated to my wise, fun, faithful,

beautiful wife, partner, and best friend – Melissa.

You make this crazy life so much more

peaceful and grounded.

I love you!

PREFACE

For a long time, I have resisted writing a book about my personal story. There are two primary reasons for this: First, to be perfectly honest, I'd rather have a root canal than sit at a computer screen, typing away on a keyboard for weeks and months on end. Give me a team or church staff to share with and equip or an audience to speak to and interact with. I was made for that! The process of writing? Not so much. Quite the opposite.

Second, many books have already been published telling the stories of men and women who abandoned an identity found in the LGBTQ+ community for a new life found in Jesus Christ. Most of these books are excellent, so would there be any benefit in adding mine to the mix? Until the last couple of years, I hadn't thought so. At least, not enough to do the hard work required to write and publish a book.

When teaching and equipping, I often give several vital reasons for sharing our stories with others. When we choose to tell the truth and let other people into our past struggles, we: 1) give God the glory and credit He alone deserves, 2) give others hope for their own lives and battle against sin, and 3) take a weapon out of the enemy's hand that he's used against us. It's time for me to offer my story not only verbally but in written form as well.

Revelation 12:11 says:

They overcame him [Satan] because of the blood of the Lamb and because of the word of their testimony, and they did not love their life even when faced with death.

Peter writes in I Peter 3:15:

But sanctify Christ as Lord in your hearts, always being ready to make a defense to everyone who asks you to give an account for the hope that is in you, yet with gentleness and reverence.

Indeed, being a student of the Word is essential in sharing hope and truth with others. It is, of course, foundational. Yet, in building on the foundation of the Scriptures to communicate the hope we have in Jesus, one of the very best resources available to us is our own story and how God has radically impacted and changed our lives.

So, I have had a change of heart about completing this book, and my greatest hope is that God receives glory and that you, the reader, are filled with hope for what God desires and can accomplish in your life. I'll also be grateful for any new freedom or joy God grants me in sharing our story (mine and His).

As is true for each Christ follower: our story isn't so much about us, as it is the God who called us out of darkness into His marvelous light - I Peter 2:9. God's story is woven throughout the lives of His sons and daughters. We often don't see it amid the pain and struggle with sin, but God is so incredibly loving, gracious, and kind in our need and our grasping for meaning, love, fulfillment, pleasure, etc.— and in the end, only He can take our most significant and most shameful failures and turn them around for good. He's incredible at this.

Like me, I'm sure you're often stunned by the magnificence of how the heavens declare the glory of God (Psalm 19:1) in a cold, clear, starry nighttime sky or how a sunset shows off His creative splendor. Yet, nothing is more beautiful or powerful than how our loving Father and majestic Creator redeems broken and lost lives and sets them on a pathway of fulfillment, joy, and meaningful work for His Kingdom.

In a culture that worships self and secularism as faithfully as any other religion, we discover the truth that every human being was made for worship, and no matter how we attempt to rebel against this truth, we return by default. The only real question is, what or whom are we worshiping? The most ardent hater of Christianity still practices what they claim to despise; it's just turned toward empty and ultimately destructive things.

The worship of sex and every variety of self-proclaimed identity is where we find ourselves in the United States. With our backs turned against the God who made us, we seek meaning and a sense of purpose amid confusion, rebellion, and self-gratification. It's a path that leads toward darkness and death. I walked this path for many years until God, in His mercy, showed me a new life of surrender to Him. It allowed me to give up my futile attempts to discover and save myself.

American culture has gone off the rails. It is ever seeking to tear down norms and healthy ways of living in submission to our Creator and replace His design with the god of self and, ultimately, chaos. I am writing this book and sharing the grace and power of God's story in my life because I want you to know there's hope in Jesus – He is an anchor for your soul. He knows the proper way out of darkness, emptiness, and chaos. Authentic hope is not found in discovering and living "your truth." Rather, there is one truth, and that comes from God alone.

God doesn't wink at sin or brush it aside because sin is a hateful thing that utterly destroys and separates. Instead, Jesus paid the debt and made way for a new life, hope, and victory. I want this book to encourage you to keep asking, seeking, and knocking (Matthew 7:7-8), discovering the God who loves you in the midst of it all, working, waiting, and longing for you to surrender and find your new life in Him.

A favorite quote by Max Lucado says this:

God loves you just the way you are, but he refuses to leave you there. He wants you to be just like Jesus.

I hope and pray this book meets you where you're at, and through telling my story and God's story in my life, you'll be encouraged in what God deeply desires to do in your own life.

Finally, I believe it would be an enormous loss if my book were read as a story that the reader never connects with personally. If my account doesn't lead to your introspection and discovery of fresh areas of need or for Jesus to move more deeply and heal more fully, then telling my story hasn't been of much value.

Now, the working out of your story and mine may be radically different, but the root issues of human struggle with sin and self are often the same, just expressed differently – maybe quite differently. As a means of helping readers connect with their own story and consider possible areas of need and healing, several questions will be asked at the end of each chapter. I encourage you to prayerfully engage with these questions to get the most out of this book. Ask God if there are ways you still need healing at different points of your childhood stages of development or the years that followed.

Blessings over you in your reading and contemplation. May the Holy Spirit guide you.

INTRODUCTION

I t feels pretty ironic to me that I, of all people, would brag about the goodness of God amid our struggles, but I now believe in His goodness with my whole heart.

Many years ago, those kinds of statements about God's goodness would've pissed me off. Anytime I heard Romans 2:4, where the Apostle Paul writes, "*It is the kindness of God that leads us to repentance,*" my feeling wasn't one of comfort but an angry, disgusted sense of contradiction. I couldn't understand how those words could be applied to a God who was silent to my pleading and prayers.

Where was He when I was being abused as a young boy? Where was He when every school day felt like an exercise in familiar and fresh ways of shame and rejection? How could a good God allow such evil in the world, and too often in His Church, to thrive?

When I read about God's mercy or kindness, I would think, what a load of crap. His goodness felt contradictory and untrue amid my struggles. God seemed to be anything but merciful. Yes, I know He sent Jesus to die for our sins, but what about...?

I'd go off on some frustrated accusation of injustice that I had grown accustomed to laying at God's feet. Of course, this was all my own private internalized conversation. No one knew what I was thinking or the attitude of my heart toward God. I believed no one was ever supposed to wrestle with these thoughts, and I certainly didn't believe anyone in my church would have answers.

At that point, there was a substantial emotional disconnect for me because I often felt as if God simply refused to do anything to lift the pressures, temptations, desires, and struggles that we go through as boys, girls, men, and women. Where *was* He?

God seemed wholly detached and disconnected from me. As a young person, I often felt like nothing more than a mere pawn on His cosmic chess board - moved around anywhere and in any way that suited His purpose for that moment in history. At best, I thought I was nothing to Him. At worst, I thought He hated and despised me. So, over time, as my bitterness and judgment grew, I returned the favor.

I still recall those sharp, crippling emotions as I type out these thoughts. I remember all my feelings of anger and rage—even raw hatred toward God and His church. Though I was blind to it then, I have looked back through the lens of the last couple of decades and see so clearly that the Lord has been utterly merciful, showing numerous times that He never left or abandoned me. It's incredible how, in our blindness and rebellion, we can be so sure of utterly wrong things.

He's shown me how, just as Jesus said, the Lord continually stretches out His hands to an obstinate and disobedient people (Isaiah 65:2 NIV). That indeed described me as obstinate and disobedient. I was also wounded, broken, blind, and ignorant of so much truth. I grew up mimicking a form of godliness but without the power of His life within (II Timothy 3:5).

Much like the nation of Israel in the Old Testament, whom God continually invited to come and be comforted, to find safety, to be blessed in the Promised Land, which He provided for them, He invites all to yield and surrender to what is good and wholesome. He desired them to find their blessings solidified, strengthened, and extended over time through their worship of and fellowship with Him.

Hindsight and having new eyes to see far more reveal truths I was once blind to, stumbling around in my attempts to free myself and find meaning and purpose through self-effort. What a futile waste! I remember the darkness of my bitterness and hatred fueled by woundedness, sin, and demonic strongholds. Isolation and secrecy never lead us anywhere good. They never produce health.

As Christians, we have a real issue with rarely or never sharing our stories or only cherry-picking little bits and pieces of the narrative that we're comfortable with others knowing – only the good stuff. Frankly, that has so little value. But God can do incredible things when we are willing to share the whole truth of our story honestly: the depth of the pain, the depth of the addiction, and the depth of the depravity, rather than yielding to the temptation to sanitize the truth. Nobody wants others to know how messed up we were (or are).

We Christ-followers need to stop censoring our stories. Others desperately need to know the truth – the whole truth. We need to be fully known and loved, regardless of what we've done or what has been done to us.

Of course, I'm not arguing for oversharing. We don't have to be too detailed to be specific and clear about where we've been or what we've struggled with. We share a complete account for the sake of others and our benefit.

It is impossible to experience being fully loved without first being fully known. Otherwise, in our minds, we have a line that goes like this: *Sure, they may like or even love you now, but if they knew you, the real you, they wouldn't want anything to do with you.*

When we share only the cleaned-up, respectably whitewashed story of what our life once looked like, people can't relate to it because they think they're so much worse than that. Or that they're so much more broken than that. This is too often the falsehood we project because we are so intent on casting a better image than simply and honestly revealing the messy version of ourselves that other broken people can relate to.

Andrew Comiskey, founder of Desert Stream Ministries and author of the Living Waters program, refers to this projection of our lives to others as "the good-false self." The good-false self needs to die. For most of us Christians, it is one of our biggest idols.

When we're willing to share our whole story, we also benefit and discover greater freedom. That was certainly true for me when I shared my testimony at the church for the first time. It had become my second chance at a family. I'll share more about how God used this church to impact my life later.

Throughout this book, I hope to emphasize the value of sharing our authentic stories. The following is an example from my mid-thirties.

One day, after many months of walking in the light with my small men's group, I was sitting in the office of the counseling pastor. We talked about the freedom Jesus gives and how I was no longer bound to pornography, chronic masturbation, or sexual encounters with men when the senior pastor happened to peek in.

"Hey," he said to my counseling pastor. "For my message this week, I'm discussing freedom in Christ. I'd like someone to share a related testimony to help people connect with the lesson. Know anyone?"

There was hardly a pause. My counseling pastor glanced at me, brows raised, a grin playing on his lips.

My heart drummed against my ribs. This was no coincidence. This was God at work.

"Um, tell me more," I said.

The senior pastor and I discussed how my testimony might fit into his lesson. I'd been walking in victory, obedience, and light and living this new life in Christ, and while I'd never shared my story in public before, I sensed an urgent need for others to know it. This was a watershed moment. Nearly a thousand adults would be present between the two Sunday morning services.

My mouth went bone-dry.

But I knew in my heart it was the right decision. Excitement and terror streaked through me at the same time. I later asked my mentor if she might pray with me. She and her husband were my small group leaders and had a gift for discernment. After we prayed together, she looked me straight in the eyes and said, "Garry, I believe this is an opportunity for you to take a weapon out of the enemy's hand."

Though her statement resonated with me, I had no idea how right she was. I hated how strong Satan's influence had been in my life and how I had allowed him to manipulate and distort my thinking. Since I was very young, his lies have captured my heart for too many years. Whatever could break the power he'd wielded against me needed to be done. I labored over my testimony... trimming, trimming, and trimming again until I got it right. I only had a few minutes to share a lifetime of trial and error.

Delicate though this event was, something powerful happened.

I rose before the congregation and named specific sins that had controlled my life. Inside me, something monumental shifted.

I want to share the importance of that with you later in this book, but for now, let's start at the beginning.

Revealing our authentic story to become truly known... perhaps for the first time, is what the apostle John in I John 1:7 calls walking in the light:

But if we walk in the light as He [God] Himself is in the light, we have fellowship with one another, and the blood of Jesus His Son cleanses us from all sin.

Real freedom isn't found in carefully managing who knows certain things about us while tenaciously guarding the worst stuff to take to our graves. Rather, absolute freedom is found in letting go of control and image management, no longer caring who knows because the God of the universe knows everything, and despite it all, He still wildly loves us. He's made a way to reconcile us to Himself and His family through Jesus' sacrifice and our surrender to Him. Regardless of where we have once been or what we have done, He invites us to walk a new path with Him: the narrow way.

Enter through the narrow gate, for the gate is wide and the way is broad that leads to destruction, and many enter through it. For the gate is small and the way is narrow that leads to life, and few find it. Matthew 7:13-14

This is what I hope and pray for you as you read this book. Don't become so overly fixated on my story that you miss what the Holy Spirit wants to say to you about *your* story. He wants to meet you in your unhealed areas to restore your life. He is waiting to guide you through the narrow gate and walk beside you along the narrow way.

Your story may be similar to mine or radically different, but this is where you'll discover the freedom, purpose, and joy of joining with the Father, Son, and Holy Spirit and turning the ashes (and successes) of your past into incredible eternal value.

As you are about to turn the page and open up the first chapter, I want to mention Chapter One. This chapter contains relevant background on my parents and what they brought into their marriage and child-rearing. The simple truth is, for both good and bad, we are profoundly impacted by the environments we grow up in, especially in how our parents relate to one another and us as their children.

To foster a better understanding of ourselves, more profound healing, and even greater compassion for our parent(s), it is essential to understand our personal history, and often that of our parents and grandparents, at least in part.

So, let's get started.

Chapter 1

FOUNDATIONS – MY FATHER AND MOTHER

My parents weren't big on preserving and passing along our family history. Mom was forty-two when I was born, which left me with little opportunity to make memories with my much older grandparents. They passed away when I was a child. However, I know some critical details about how my parents were raised. As human beings, our experiences, especially our choices, profoundly impact our lives and future generations. Perhaps this glimpse into my parents' upbringing will shed some light on my personal story.

My father was born in 1922. His family lived in the farmland and forests of upstate New York. At seven, the Great Depression hit and lasted ten years of his life, from early childhood to his teenage years, until 1939. A year or so before the economic crash, my grandmother left her husband and her children for another man who was an alcoholic. Of course, this was a severe crisis for my grandfather, compounded only by the chaos of economic hard times, high unemployment, and job uncertainty. Dad was six when he and his siblings were doled out to various relatives. Unfortunately, at least in Dad's situation, he was forced to live with an aunt and uncle who had no interest in being caregivers. They made sure he knew how unwelcome he was.

Dad recalled them being rather highbrow—prim and proper—making him feel like a fish out of water even more. Of course, he was grateful to have food, a roof over his head, and clothes on his back, but he desperately wanted to return to the home he'd grown up in with his family. Instead, he was forced to adjust to new and emotionally cold surroundings, separated from everything familiar to him, and was left searching for identity and validation from cold, uninterested caregivers.

I can only imagine the pain and confusion that went through his mind and heart at such a vulnerable young age. Divorce was rare back then. Nothing like today's modern divorce culture, where marital breakups are just as common as staying together, maybe more so. In today's society, hearing about something like this garners little more than a yawn. Children born out of wedlock are *passé*, assuming they survive the womb at all. However, back then, it was shocking and shameful for a family to go through a divorce. Shame wasn't only reserved for the person who walked out but also for the abandoned spouse and innocent children.

My grandfather somehow pushed through it all and maintained his stable job for decades, although he had no idea how to juggle work and family as a single parent. This led him to conclude that his kids would be better off spread out to other relatives until he could get his life back together. During this time, perhaps a couple of years later, Grandpa married again. To his credit, he wanted to bring his children back home. He finally did so, and while it was good to be reunited, there was one glaring difference from their earlier lives: they had a different mother.

I remember Dad occasionally commenting on how much he appreciated his stepmother caring for children that weren't hers. But he also mentioned that things changed when she started having biological children. She cared for my father and his original siblings out of responsibility, and they each felt it. A child deserves to be truly loved, and their instincts allow them to sense when they aren't.

Dad missed out on the feeling of unconditional maternal love, and he missed his natural mother.

I don't know how many years Dad spent in this confusion and loss. Eventually, his biological mother returned without the guy she'd run off with. Though she lost the man, she had gained a child and returned home with a new son from the extramarital relationship.

Around this time, one of Dad's siblings became ill with polio and later died. Dad rarely spoke of her, but when he did, his face brightened, and his eyes watered with obvious sadness and affection. This tragedy must have added even more to his sense of loss and confusion.

When Dad's mother returned to the area, his father and stepmother (my grandfather and step-grandmother) had two children. In many practical ways, they also wound up raising a new young son from the extramarital affair. Dad was still connected with his mother (my grandmother), but this extended family unit was an unexpected and odd situation. For example, my grandmother and step-grandmother buddied up and talked on the phone for long periods. As a boy, I remember our phone connected through a party line. This allowed several households in our rural neighborhood to share the same phone line. It might sound a bit wild for those of us living land-line free and glued to our cell phones, but back then, with a party line, a phone call between two people could be heard by any household within that group of neighbors if they happened to pick up the phone.

Mind you, proper etiquette dictated that if somebody *did* pick up the phone (those in conversation would hear a unique *click* when this happened), those talking were supposed to wrap up the call so somebody else could use the line. In those days, if our party line was in use, you could bet your bottom dollar it was Dad's mother and stepmother gabbing away.

Later, they learned that the man my grandmother left her husband for had died, and because she'd become close with her ex-husband's new wife, her new child was raised right along with my dad and his siblings. This boy grew up, fell in love with, and married one of the girls from the same home, as they had no biological connection.

Dad was a middle child stuck in the middle of this mixed family. His mother had a new child from a different father, and his stepmother had two children. As you can imagine, within this unique family unit, Dad didn't exactly experience the kind of structured familial love that children long for and were created for. From what I know, my father's basic needs were tended to. Still, due to the broken home in his pivotal childhood years—the abandonment from his mother and subsequent harsh circumstances—Dad was deprived of a healthy, secure attachment. Rather than thriving in a reliable, loving, consistent home, he resorted to simply surviving. Those early deprivations impacted his spirit in some very significant ways.

Knowing where he came from and the man he later became makes me so thankful for my father. He has so many outstanding qualities: a strong work ethic, self-sufficiency and handiness with tools, and a love of the outdoors–especially fishing and hunting– that he passed on to me and my siblings. And more importantly, he was always faithful to his wife and took his faith in Jesus seriously. Dad read through the Bible from cover to cover each year.

I once saw an old picture of Dad when he was ten or eleven, kneeling in the grass, playing the guitar, and singing, and it was such a surprise. I'd never once seen him playing an instrument, let alone sing. Mom explained that when he was young, music and guitar were something he loved right up until the day he quit. One of his sisters had confided to Mom that their other siblings used to gang up with other kids in the neighborhood and bully Dad over his music. One day, Dad had enough. He never picked up his guitar or sang again.

That story is a natural anchor point in understanding my father. Growing up, he had so many disappointments and hurts that he pulled inward, isolated, and became highly self-sufficient. He avoided any circumstances where he could fail and be shamed or mocked. Knowing this makes me terribly sad.

It's so contradictory to today's culture, where society regards any form of discomfort as an existential crisis, with every disagreement as a micro-aggression. This is the opposite of my father's childhood era when nobody cared about emotions, especially kids. During the Great Depression, life revolved around necessities. If you're unaware, upstate New York is cold in the winter. In the worst of it, the temperature dips well below zero degrees. While this can be fun for kids with snow days and recreation, adults are stuck with heating the house and feeding themselves and their families. It was a time of little luxury–not nearly enough to acknowledge emotional sensitivities or pain. Simply surviving took all a person's energy and resources. You did what you had to do and hoped for the best. A child's emotional state and circumstances are at the bottom of the priority list. Counseling was nearly nonexistent, highly suspect at best, and usually negatively regarded. Dad did what all children did in those situations: he detached himself, shoved down his emotions, put on his big boy pants, and survived the worst.

As a result, Dad became a wizard at making good use of anything. With materials like scrap wood and metal, he could build a barn, shed, or home addition and build it well! He could re-purpose almost anything. He had to. Learning to make do with what he had forced him to think outside the box. It's funny because I never believed I had anything in common with him as a kid. However, I'm sure I inherited (or learned by observation) some of Dad's frugal and ingenious creativity.

One of my favorite memories of Dad was his laugh. I loved to hear him laugh! He had the best laugh when he was comfortable and unconscious of himself. But sadly, this was rare. On those occasions he wasn't on guard – perhaps at a picnic or playing cards with friends – he'd sometimes burst out in a contagious roar. For me, those memories are both delightful and odd at the same time because I rarely ever recall him *being* happy. My childhood images of him revolve around frustration, heavy-handedness, or brooding over something.

His headaches probably didn't help the matter. For as long as I can remember, Dad had severe headaches, often full-blown migraines. Medicine would sometimes take the edge off, but not much. He attributed these to a head injury he sustained as a young boy, but I wonder if there was more to it ... not just physical, but emotional. Perhaps even spiritual?

Neither of my parents finished high school, which limited the kind of work Dad could find. A desk job would've killed him anyway, so not surprisingly, he discovered that he was skilled at operating heavy equipment. No one wore ear protection back then, so the nature of this work only aggravated his headaches even more. Without a doubt, it impacted his hearing later on.

Everyone, including me, had assumed and adopted the notion that Dad was an introvert who didn't enjoy being around people. However, as I grew older and experienced remarkable healing and freedom in many areas of my own life, I suspect the opposite was true of him. He may well have been an extrovert struggling with severe shame and rejection. The losses from his early childhood onward would have prompted anyone to retreat inward and isolate themselves from others. Back then, it was rare for churches to teach about the soul-level healing available through the power of the cross. Forgiveness of sin and eventual eternity in heaven? Yes. But very little on the revelation that Jesus *wanted* to bring healing to those deep places of pain and loss in our lives – today, in this life.

There was no teaching in Dad's boyhood church that Jesus not only has the power to rescue us from the consequence of our sins - hell, but His blood can also save and heal us from the power of sins done against us. Dad was never taught that grace is available to heal the wounds we carry. It saddens me that he missed out on that aspect of the Gospel. He progressed and changed over time, softening and becoming more compassionate later. As the youngest in our family, I know I benefited the most from this change in his temperament.

Recently, I had an opportunity to visit with and minister alongside a much older cousin of mine who has been pastoring and overseeing churches for decades. My cousin, with his wife in the front seat, drove us to a ministry event and shared an idea he'd become fascinated by. An idea he hoped he could get my input on regarding my parents, particularly my father.

My mother and my cousin's mother were sisters. He recalled many visits our families shared—mostly playtime with my siblings before and after I was born. He remembers Dad being a scary figure he never wanted to cross as a boy. As he drove, he recounted when Dad laid into him for taking a walk with my sister without permission. He also remembered when one of my brothers got a little mouthy with my dad ... the next thing he knew, my brother was picking himself off the floor. Dad did not tolerate the slightest disrespect.

While he recounted these memories, my cousin would glance back at me in the rearview mirror. His wife had been chiming in from time to time with whatever tidbit her husband had missed in his storytelling, and together, they explained how every year after Mom and Dad began the winter habit of flying to visit me in Arizona, their flight always required a lengthy layover at an airport near my cousin. This gave the four of them a chance to see each other and catch up on all the various family details.

Then my cousin said, "If you're okay with it, I'd love to get your perspective on something."

"Of course," I responded. "Anything."

"I'm wondering if my perception about Uncle Bob is accurate," he continued. "I felt like each year, your dad was changing in a good way. He seemed more and more gentle and humble. The man I knew from childhood, when my family would visit your family, was rough and angry. But now, especially when they'd speak about you, even your dad would break down and tear up over what you were going through, how far you were from God. In later years, he'd remark on how He was working in your life and how much you were responding to Him."

I was thankful my cousin shared his thoughts and how, year after year, he'd witnessed the changes God wrought in Dad's heart, particularly regarding me. Through this conversation, God gave me a gift, a reminder of the growth between Dad and me. But I'll come back to those details a little later.

"Without a doubt," I told my cousin. "Dad changed a lot during those years. He and I became much closer. God was at work."

This conversation reminded me of another observation a dear friend and mentor had made regarding my parents. During one of their extended visits with me in Phoenix, they said, "I love that even into their seventies, your mom and dad are both so teachable and still growing in Christ!"

Sentiments like that were significant to hear, yet such a far cry from how I grew up. In truth, Dad's anger issues and detachment were rough on my young mind. I'm reminded of Paul's exhortation to fathers – *Fathers, do not exasperate your children so that they will not lose heart.*—Colossians 3:21

I needed so many things from him that, at the time, he didn't understand how to give. These were things he had not received himself as a child. How can a father pass lessons of value on to a son when he never received those himself? Thankfully, in Christ, I have seen how God can take an unfathered man and build an awareness of what's needed in the lives of his children.

Regardless, Dad and I developed a solid relationship through the years—one I'm deeply thankful for. Today, I'm honored to be my father's son. I'm honored that Dad and Mom were both committed to God and one another. They were married for 68 years during a rapidly changing era that saw many couples around them divorcing and breaking their commitments to one another. Dad was a remarkable man in so many ways. He chose to stay and fight for his marriage and family, which is what I most admire about him.

Dad once told me that when he was young, he and his buddies sometimes gambled with one another while playing cards. Over time, they progressed to betting on racehorses. He recalled how excitement would overcome him as he watched horse races – the intense rush of possibility, followed by the emotional crash of losing, and a fresh dollop of hope that he could be the winner next time. To Dad's credit, he recognized these intense feelings led many people into addiction, often losing everything they had. He didn't want to wind up like that, unreliable and unstable. He found the strength to change, to walk away and never gamble again.

On several occasions, Mom and Dad shared how, before I was born, they used to have friends over for parties and card-playing – drinking and smoking were commonplace. During this season of their life, a new pastor (who had recently started preaching at a church nearby) stopped at their home for a visit and invited them to church the following Sunday. Mom had grown up attending church, and Dad had also made a profession of faith at some point in his teen years. But by this point, neither of my parents had been to church for years. The Lord used this pastor's visit as a spark to draw them back to church. Again, they stepped up and allowed God to change their lives. Hosting and attending parties centered around alcohol became a thing of the past. This was not without consequence. A number of their friends lost interest and pulled away.

Some months or years later, that same pastor asked Dad to consider becoming a deacon at their church. Dad was humbled and honored by the request but also convicted. He'd stopped drinking long before but had not yet been able to give up his cigarette habit. He prayed and read Scriptures regarding the qualifications for serving as a deacon and elder within the Church. After years of being a two-pack-a-day smoker, he quit cold turkey and never picked up a cigarette again. He wanted to serve as a deacon with a clear conscience. I believe this attitude of surrender and obedience were essential ingredients that God used to soften and shape him into a far more gentle and compassionate man as he aged. Dad never minimized the truth of God's Word. Instead, he grew in his capacity to show grace and patience as others, and I stumbled and failed along the way.

Just as Dad experienced awful tragedy as a child, Mom had her own early traumatic experiences.

She was two years younger than Dad, five years old at the start of the Great Depression. Her father died unexpectedly — various family members have given different explanations—but his death was sudden, leaving five little ones and a wife behind. This would be a massive loss for any family at any time, but for the sole breadwinner, husband, and father to die during such a widespread national economic crisis, it was a tragedy that destabilized and traumatized them for years to come. His death completely devastated my mother. She loved her father dearly and felt the pain of his absence for many years. But as mentioned, back then, times were far less sensitive than now. Despite the devastation, Mom and her siblings were expected to go to school and forge through life as if nothing had happened. After all, everyone was living through tough times in that era, and even the death of a parent did not afford any special allowances.

Mom recalled a day after her father's death when she came home from school to find her mother sitting in the same rocking chair as when she'd left, riddled with grief and shock over the loss of her husband and family provider. Not only did my grandmother have four children to feed and care for, but she also had a newborn baby. Grandma struggled to meet her infant's most basic needs, sinking deeper into a severe depression of her own. They had never been well-off financially, but now they had no source of income. My grandmother had no idea what to do.

Grandma's sister lived in the house next to theirs, and after a few weeks of my grandmother's depression, my great-aunt had enough of it. One morning, she burst through the door carrying the new baby in her arms and demanded my grandmother get up. She handed Grandma her crying baby and gave five essential reasons why she needed to start functioning again — calling each of her five children by name and insisting they needed their mother to get up off the rocking chair and be their mother again.

And that was that. It was just the kind of verbal slap in the face Grandma needed. She snapped out of her listless depression and assumed her motherhood duties again. Of course, the crushing grief and loss were still constant companions, but Grandma was no longer paralyzed because of them.

However, regarding finances, Grandma had no choice but to apply for welfare. Oh, how she hated it! But there was no other way to feed her children. If you didn't know, back then, welfare was radically different than it is today. Mom recalled the unannounced home visitations from welfare like one might remember a bullying or harassment encounter. By design, visits were unbelievably shameful. Whenever a welfare worker came out to ask questions and inspect homes, they would enter the house like they owned the place and snoop around as if they had a search warrant, opening up cupboards, closets, etc. They rifled through everything and anything to make sure food wasn't stashed away somewhere in secret. These experiences undoubtedly stole away the final remnants of Grandmother's dignity– a sacrifice she made for her children. Despite this help from the state, a summer garden plot for produce, and consistent effort in being frugal, feeding all five children remained a constant struggle for Grandma.

And so, Mom often felt the sting of want and the hollow of deprivation. She told me about a secret little place she'd often escape to for reprieve from the cruel circumstances. When poverty overwhelmed and loneliness settled in like a virus, Mom would grab a little bread from the bread drawer—usually a piece from the stale heel— and run out the back door. Across the yard, up a hill, into an overgrown hedge row between hayfields is where she made a private clearing between trees. Nestled between the berry briars and vegetation, she would hide away, undisturbed beneath the branches, and hug her knees to her chest. This is where tears could fall freely, without correction or scolding by her mother or any other adult. This was a place where she could be free– a place where she could feel her broken heart, miss her father, and mourn his passing.

That wasn't her only grief, unfortunately. Although she was only a young girl, she had to contend with unwanted advances from a local married man. This creepy guy was insistent Mom was going to be his girlfriend. When his obsession with her became clear, Mom did everything she could to avoid him. This pedophile was even bold enough to show up at my grandmother's house asking for Mom. Back then, without a father, no one was around to protect a vulnerable girl like my mother. Somehow, between hiding under the bed or escaping to the hedgerow, Mom managed to stay away from this guy.

At the age of twelve, Mom was forced out of her home, which wasn't necessarily terrible, though it did upend everything she ever knew. Grandma was told by the state that since her daughter was twelve, she was old enough to work and could no longer live at home. That is, as long as the household was to continue receiving welfare. Welfare was how the family ate. So, Mom went to live with an acquaintance from the family, just as Dad had. But unlike Dad, who lived with relatives who didn't want him, Mom had the good fortune of moving in with Mrs. Edwards. Mrs. Edwards was a kind, delightful woman who looked after Mom and provided room and board. In exchange, Mom helped her out with chores around the house. There was one caveat, however: Mr. Edwards. He was an unruly, awful man, but Mrs. Edwards ensured Mom steered clear of him and never left her alone with her cantankerous husband.

Mom once told me how Mr. Edwards hung a line of twine from the ceiling so it dangled directly over the middle of the bathroom tub. A little metal weight had been tied on the end of it, and it hung approximately two inches above the tub's surface. This was how Mr. Edwards measured the hot water usage. If water touched the bottom of the weight, that was too much. Because Mom never knew when Mr. Edwards might inspect the water level, she took great care with her baths and never once risked a frivolous use of hot water.

Mrs. Edwards ended up living to a ripe old age, and I had the privilege of accompanying my mother on nursing home visits and meeting her several times as a young man. She loved the Lord. Her faith and kindness helped provide a solid footing for my mother during otherwise unstable and uncertain years of her life, and I'm grateful for that.

Like Dad, Mom had much to contend with early on. They longed for stability, safety, and normalcy when they met through mutual friends. Neither of them had any big ideas or grand visions of greatness. They both just wanted life to make sense.

As they spent more and more time together, their relationship evolved. Ironically, neither of them ever professed any breathtaking spark of romance or intense head-over-heels love igniting between them. They just made sense together, and it felt safe. For them, that was enough. They could borrow $5.00 from my dad's best friend, pay the Justice of the Peace, and get married.

Mind you, Dad's father, and especially his stepmother, were horrified at the idea of Mom and Dad marrying so quickly, but two months was all it took for my parents to know they wanted to be together. After they tied the knot, they moved in with Dad's father and stepmother until they could afford a place. They were highly motivated to make that happen sooner rather than later.

At the very least, my parents' union had an unstable beginning, but their marriage survived for sixty-eight years. Dad took his final breath in 2010, at the age of eighty-eight, in my living room. He and Mom had been living with us for several years, and I took time off work to care for him in hospice. His daughter and two sons also cared for him and spent lots of time at our home, helping and saying their goodbyes. It was a profound time for us as siblings—at once peaceful, beautiful, and heart-wrenching. A time of goodbyes and free-flowing tears. A time not of regret but of love - while hating the encroaching inevitability of separation – even temporary separation, knowing we would see Dad again in heaven.

Caring for aging parents is not without its challenges, nor is it without its joys. I'm honored that Melissa and I got to be there for my parents as they stepped out of this life and into the next.

Mom lived another five years after Dad passed. Those years were precious. She lived long enough to meet her grandsons and spend lots of time with them since we all lived together under one roof. She was so grateful to witness the fruit of God's radical, everyday redemption, far beyond anything I could ever imagine.

Even as Mom grew older and frail, it wasn't unusual for her to talk about her father in longing terms. Although she stepped into heaven at ninety-one and her father died when she was only five, she still missed him. She longed for the day she'd be reunited with him in heaven, along with her mother and siblings. However, as the day neared, she spoke most about how much she wanted to see Jesus for the first time. She wanted to see the One who had given everything for her.

Though my parents had grown up around Christianity, they never knew the healing power of Christ at a young age. For them, the church rightly showcased the blood and power of Christ for salvation, the forgiveness of sin, and eventual life everlasting in heaven, but little else. They carried a lot of unresolved pain, not knowing that Jesus wanted to bear it for them.

My parents lived with me for several years before Melissa and I met and would continue to do so until their passing. I praise God for my wife, who was able to sacrifice our independence as newlyweds enough to allow my elderly parents to live with us ... but to be fair, I did make a sacrifice of my own when she brought her two cats along.

Thankfully, Dad lived long enough to see my first son enter the world and get to know him. Mom lived longer and helped us welcome our second son two years later. How she adored our boys! Since Mom lived with Melissa and me the longest, she had a front-row seat in observing the train wreck of my life come to complete restoration by Jesus. Piece by piece, He took all that Satan intended for great evil and transformed me/us into a witness of His grace. He alone could save and rebuild a life that was in shambles, completely lost.

During our many conversations, Mom listened intently as I explained my experience. Jesus had helped me grow whole again. The freedom I enjoyed came only from learning to open my many places of shame and loss and give them to Jesus, along with sharing those places with some trusted others in His body. Through my sharing, Mom began to recognize her own need, her pain, and her loss, allowing it to come into the light more fully. She hoped that maybe Jesus wanted to meet her in her decades-old places of shame, regret, and wounding. More than hope, she began to believe.

I'm amazed and invigorated by the fact that both my parents were teachable. They pressed more into what God had aligned for them until He called them home. Mom, in her mid-eighties, even asked me to set up an appointment for her with a particular female counselor at our church. After her first appointment, Mom told me she could share things she had never spoken of. Together, her counselor and Mom took areas of need to the Cross and invited Jesus into those broken places. Mom allowed Him to gather up some of the shattered pieces of her soul and make her new again.

It had a profound impact. Mom was at peace. I witnessed the release she felt from all that weight of sin and shame carried around for decades. It was a sensation she hadn't fully experienced before. A greater wholeness. Forgiveness. Freedom. Hope.

Within these pages, I've offered little more than a thumbnail sketch of my parent's stories, but I hope it sheds light on their struggles. Neither of them experienced the kind of nurturing, secure home life God intended for children, and it reminds me of a statement a colleague once made during a lecture more than ten years ago. She said, "God's original intention for children was for them to be born into perfect families."

This was such a simple yet profound statement of truth–so much so that I don't remember anything else from her teaching. I've often pondered that thought: There are no perfect people ... no perfect moms or dads, and no perfect children.

What we do have is a perfect God who is nearby and deeply interested in us. We have a God who's made a way for us to heal, a way for reconciliation through His own broken body. The kind of life my parents came out of, and their ongoing openness and progress of growth and transformation, is all the evidence I need. It shows that it's never too late in this life to surrender. It's never too late to embrace a life of humility and change.

For my parents, this realization and growth came later in their lives. They entered marriage and parenting with very broken ideas and expectations. From this, they formed their own broken experiences. Behavior management was the only form of parenting they knew. A child's emotional needs were never considered, not when their parents' focus revolved around behavior. In their generation, children were to be seen and not heard.

Years ago, the idea that a child has an interior life wrought with emotion didn't even register as an area of importance for parents, not even for many Christian parents. The idea of parenting or shepherding a child's heart was non-existent – at least in practice. Two of my siblings left home a couple of years before adulthood. One of them hated how poor our family was, resenting how we always just barely scraped by. He had big plans and wanted to start his own life and business, and he did. The other went into the military, where he was able to finish high school. Both were highly motivated to leave our home because of our father—his anger, controlling nature, and rigid religious beliefs and practices.

For my parents, fun was a waste of time. As such, our home was a place rife with rules and lacking in Christian virtues like compassion, patience, love, and kindness. Is it any surprise my siblings and I spent as much time away from the house as possible? Walks in the woods, fishing, and exploring, among other mischievous activities. For me, mischief usually included something of a sexual nature—searching out pornography or sneaking off with neighbor kids that we were supposed to stay away from.

As the youngest child, luckily, some of the rougher edges of my parents' child-rearing skills were softened through time and four preceding offspring. However, my particular and significant disadvantage was that both my parents were content with the notion that their procreation in this world was finished. At forty-two, Mom discovered I was in the works. This was not a happy revelation for either of my parents.

As we conclude this chapter, you'll soon turn the page to Chapter Two and start reading my story. But before you do, one final thought: I don't know about you, but I wouldn't say I like it when someone tells (or even hints at) the end of a book or movie. I have violated this personal rule only while reading the *Lord of The*

Rings as a teen. During Gandalf's battle with the Balrog in the Mines of Moria, the tumbling Balrog, in one last attempt to avenge himself, snapped his fiery whip around Gandalf's ankle and dragged the wizard into the abyss to certain death. As a young man, I was so horrified at this impossible turn of events that I couldn't bear to read any further. Not if Gandalf was dead! I quickly flipped toward the end of the book and scanned for his name without reading the content. I found his name, to my immense relief, reading just enough to know he had survived. At that point, I could return to my reading of Tolkien's brilliant trilogy without despair. *Phew*!

As such, I've tried not to delve too deeply into my personal story in this chapter, but I hope this glimpse will prompt you to continue with me to the pages ahead. There, I'll share how my parents' brokenness from their childhood bled into my youth and my life. Now, you have the gift of a peek forward and know the outcome of my relationship with them. You can peruse the following chapters, knowing there is hope and restoration.

Hope is vital. Having a sense of direction can help spur us on to what lies ahead. Hopefully, you will find encouragement as you read. In your journey, whether you're a mom or dad agonizing over a child/children or you're a Christian leader looking for a resource for those in your care, maybe you will relate. Most especially if you're struggling with your pain and addiction, desperate for God to meet you right where you are.

The good news is that God wins in the end for you and me. He also has given us a solid prophetic foundation for knowing the outcome of our futures. He wants us to be with Him: us, His followers and children. Journey with me as I share some of my struggles and His victories within these pages, and I pray it will help you in whatever way you need it most.

Questions for Self-Reflection / Journaling / Group Sharing

1. What was your parents' upbringing and childhood like?

2. How might their own experiences, both positive and negative, have influenced the way they parented you?

3. What were the cultural and societal factors that may have influenced the way your grandparents raised your parents?

4. How might these factors have shaped their beliefs, values, and behaviors as parents in raising you?

5. What cultural and societal factors influenced your parents' parenting style during childhood?

6. How might these factors have shaped your beliefs, values, and behaviors?

7. What were some of your parents' sacrifices and efforts to provide for your well-being and upbringing?

8. How can you appreciate and acknowledge their dedication and love, even if you sometimes feel frustrated or misunderstood?

Chapter 2

THE IMPORTANCE OF
MOTHER – AGES 0-2

A child experiences enormous physical and cognitive development during the first two years of life. Physically, a baby is born with the ability only to control their head and limbs. By the end of the first year, they can sit up, crawl, and sometimes even walk. In the second year, the child continues developing gross motor skills like running and jumping.

Cognitively, a baby is born with only the ability to react to stimuli. However, over time, they can recognize familiar faces, understand simple commands, and begin to use gestures to communicate. In their second year, a child continues developing their language skills and will start understanding more complex concepts. They will also show signs of memory, problem-solving, and imitative behavior.

In this time of growth, social and emotional development are essential aspects of a child's life. While it may appear that beyond the obvious physical advances, very little happens during these first two years of life, nothing could be further from the truth. During this pivotal time, children are designed to begin forming secure attachments to their primary caregivers. They develop a sense of self, and they start to understand the emotions of others—none more so than that of their mother.

Ergo, some of what we go through on our life's journey is inevitably a result of our relationship with our moms. I'll get to my own experience shortly.

Research shows that an infant's primary need for their mother during the first stage of development is her presence and responsiveness to their needs. When a mother responds to her child's cues for food, comfort, and playtime, her actions allow the child to feel a sense of security and consistency, which becomes essential for the child's overall well-being. The gift of a mother's nurturing and comforting presence remains a crucial and necessary framework for her children's later healthy attachments. This allows children to gain and fortify trust, which will later form the foundations of their future relationships.

The concept of attachment between a mother and child is a well-established psychological theory extensively studied and supported by research. The idea of attachment, first proposed by John Bowlby in the 1950s[1] and several other authors subsequently (Ainsworth, Wall, Waters 1978; Cassidy, 1989; Sroufe 1989)[2,3,4], states that infants have an innate need for a close and secure relationship with their primary caregiver, usually their mother and that this attachment is essential for their emotional and social development –

For an everyday, accessible book on attachment and its influences, see Clinton and Sibcy's *Why You Do the Things You Do: The Secret to Healthy Relationships.* (2006)[5].

When a mother is not present for her child's needs – physically or emotionally – deep gaps form in a child's psyche. This deficiency can affect how they relate to others for the rest of their lives.

The mother/child relationship also plays a crucial role in her little one's cognitive development. Their bond provides a rich language environment and engages children in interactive language communication. Research shows that children exposed to more language-rich environments at home have better language outcomes[6]. In addition, research shows that mothers who are sensitive and responsive to their infant's cues are more likely to have emotionally secure, confident, independent children and have better social skills[7].

Can you see the design in the dynamic there? A purpose exists within that design, and when followed, it delivers the best results. But what happens when the design goes awry, as it often does? Or furthermore, when a child or infant senses they are not wanted?

When my parents found out they were pregnant, there were tears alright, but not of joy and celebration. Mom was forty-two, and Dad was forty-four. They were tired, overworked parents of four. The thought of a fifth mouth to feed weighed heavy on their shoulders like an anvil—all the long, sleepless nights with a newborn to look forward to—dirty diapers, spit-up, teething, and temper tantrums. The idea of starting the parenting process all over again was almost more than my parents could bear.

The *idea* of parenthood can often be daunting, whether it's our first time, our last, or anywhere in between.

However, in my mom's circumstance, all her angst dissipated after I was born. Throughout my childhood, she often recounted stories of sitting up with me at night while everyone else was asleep. Her eyes would glimmer with love and fondness as she recalled wrapping me up in a blanket and snuggling into me with a hug. In those early years, we lived in a very rustic and poorly insulated cabin in the woods, and on windy upstate New York nights, it wasn't uncommon to see tiny, powdery flakes of snow blowing through gaps in the wall-board.

I had a strong attachment to my mother at this youthful stage, more so than anyone else. While Dad leaned more into an angry, distant demeanor those days, Mom was far more relationally open and available. She was the primary one to meet my needs. It was well known that my dad never changed a diaper. Even when Mom was sick with the flu after giving birth to my older sister, Dad's idea of helping with diaper changing was to put his daughter on the hospital table and roll her over to Mom. Times were different back then when it came to gender roles.

* * *

How does all of this tie into a Christian worldview?

When we understand the bond between a mother and child reflects God's love, we know the design in place by our Creator. Mothers are given the primary role and responsibility of caring for and nurturing their pre-born and newborn children throughout the first stages of their development. It's one of the many reflections that reveal the unique and beautiful way a woman bears and reveals God's Image. A woman who is genuinely in touch with these truths sees the role of motherhood as a high calling from God and a way to serve and glorify Him – even in the frequently mundane wash, rinse, repeat cycle of motherhood.

Let's talk about the earlier phase of life – the unborn, or pre-born, stage of development. In this modern day, many would have us believe this stage of life doesn't matter—in fact, many declare it isn't life at all, giving zero consideration for what occurs in the womb before birth.

Did you know that evidence shows babies in the womb can perceive and respond to different types of stimuli, such as light, sound, and touch, as early as twenty-four weeks of gestation8? Several studies on fetal development show that unborn babies can hear and respond to voices and music, indicating they have some auditory awareness9.

Furthermore, research has shown that pre-born babies can and do respond to touch. One source for this information is a study published in *Infant Behavior and Development* in 2017 titled *Fetal Behavioral Responses to the Touch of the Mother's Abdomen: A Frame-by-frame Analysis* 10. The study examined the effects of gentle tactile stimulation on the heart rates of pregnant women and their pre-born babies. The results showed a significant increase in the baby's heart rate in response to the tactile stimulation and fetal responses to maternal touch and voice using ultrasound imaging. The results showed that the fetuses responded to motherly touch by moving and exhibiting facial expressions, indicating that they could perceive and respond to the touch.

Another piece of evidence is that pre-born babies can exhibit different behaviors, such as hiccups, sneezing, and even smiling 11,12. This indicates they also have some level of motor control and can experience other internal states.

These studies prove how prenatal experiences can impact the developing pre-born child. For example, research shows that babies exposed to stress in utero are more likely to be anxious and have behavioral problems later in life 13. High antenatal maternal anxiety is related to ADHD symptoms, externalizing problems, and stress in eight-and nine-year-olds. Studies also show that babies exposed to certain types of music or speech in utero are more likely to be familiar with and respond to those sounds after birth14.

Pre-born babies are conscious, aware, and affected by the environment around them before birth, and prenatal experiences can and do impact their development. Here are a few examples of the many studies that support these assertions:

DeCasper and Spence (1986)15 found that prenatal maternal speech influences newborns' perception of speech sounds. It found that newborns could distinguish between their mother's voice and the voice of a stranger, indicating that they had some level of auditory awareness before birth.

Lecanuet et al. (1996)16 found that unborn babies could distinguish between different types of music, indicating that they had some auditory perception before birth.

Hepper et al. (1992)17 found that pre-born babies could distinguish between different odors, indicating that they had some olfactory perception before birth.

DiPietro et al. (1991)18 found that pre-born babies preferred a familiar touch, indicating that they had some tactile perception before birth.

Van den Berg et al. (2010)19 found that pre-born babies exhibited a stress response to loud noise, indicating they were affected by the environment before birth.

Granier-Deferre et al. (2005)20 found that pre-born babies exposed to a specific melody in-utero could recognize it after birth, indicating that they were affected by the environment before birth.

These studies prove that unborn babies can perceive and respond to stimuli and exhibit other behaviors and that prenatal experiences can significantly impact their development.

Over the years, I have witnessed times of prayer with a few people in which a presenting root issue, deep emotional turmoil, or negative experiences seemed to connect back to a sense of disruption in their pre-birth experience. We would invite Jesus into that gap, sense of loss, fear, or whatever the case was. While there was usually a release and restoration of calm and peace during that reckoning, I wondered if that person's memory could be rooted as far back as pre-birth. How could that even be possible? Then, a friend introduced me to Dr. Verny.

In his book, *The Secret Life of the Unborn Child*21, Dr. Thomas Verny, M.D., draws from two decades of medical research to offer a glimpse of the growing sensitivities and awareness a baby experiences as they develop in their mother's womb. His studies show that by at least five months of age, a pre-born baby can hear and sense the environment around them outside of their mother's body. I highly recommend reading this book, but I'll share a brief story that stood out.

A child he calls Kristina was a seemingly healthy and energetic baby at her birth. However, rather than moving toward her mother's breast, she would turn her head away each time her mother tried to feed her. The doctor concluded she might be ill, but Kristina devoured a formula bottle when they took her to the nursery. Concluding her earlier behavior was an anomaly, Kristina was brought to her mother again in the morning. Again, Kristina turned her head away from her mother's breast.

In an attempt to decipher the cause of this, the doctor thought of a simple experiment that might help shed light on what could be the cause of Kristina's behavior. He asked another patient of his if she would be willing to try breastfeeding Kristina, and she agreed (remember, this was many years ago).

Kristina quickly latched onto the woman's breast, hungrily feeding. The doctor sat with Kristina's mother the next day and explained what had happened. He asked if there had been any severe illnesses during pregnancy. There wasn't. He pondered a moment, perplexed. Another question was forming in his mind. He asked point-blank if she wanted the baby, and that's when the issue surfaced.

"No, I didn't," the young woman said. "I wanted an abortion. My husband wanted the child. That's why I had her."

Dr. Verny stated that was news to her doctor but, obviously, not to Kristina.

In a straightforward and primitive way, Kristina showed signs of rejecting her mother because somehow, while she was in the womb, she sensed her mother's total lack of desire for her.

There are many studies (not just anecdotal stories) that Dr. Verny includes in his book that support this essential need and process of bonding with a mother while her baby is still in utero. Reading *The Secret Life of the Unborn Child* sparked questions about my experience.

I don't know how many months into her pregnancy my Mom felt that she did not want another child or if it somehow affected me. I do know my Dad was never happy about having another kid. Perhaps after I was born, he managed to come to terms with this new reality of a fifth child and managed not to project his dissatisfaction. I don't recall overt rejection from Dad, but rather, a hands-off, detached, and distant attitude. This, of course, left me to be raised by my mother.

* * *

One of the teaching topics our ministry has developed is entitled *Parenting Kids to Thrive in a Sex-Saturated Culture.* Whether speaking to parents or equipping pastors and Christian leaders, we speak to raising children from two essential perspectives – the need to prepare for *prevention* and *recovery*. These two distinctions are significant when training parents or expectant parents. I would love for more pregnant parents (and couples who are not yet pregnant) to participate in parenting classes that speak to a biblical view of sexuality and identity. While mothers (or planning-to-be-mothers) are often more interested and engaged in the topics related to raising healthy and secure children, fathers and future fathers are less invested. They tend to assume this is the stuff their wife needs to pay attention to and that his role as a father will pick up at some point in the coming years of his child's life. But it's never too early for dads to actively participate in their child's healthy development – even before birth.

We need to help both parents prepare for preventing (or minimizing) adverse childhood experiences by understanding how they can play a vital role in developing their child's well-being and healthy emotional fullness. Children thrive when they experience fun, joy, safety, acceptance, love, stability, boundaries, and balanced discipline. When they learn that God made them for a significant purpose and they understand that *who they are* as a boy or girl has deep meaning, they can value the gift of their biological design and gender. When a child understands they were made with great intention and purpose, and that is paired with a warm, loving sense of belonging, the world's allure and Satan's lies are far less compelling than when a child feels empty, confused, and purposeless — left to figure out life on their own. In this vulnerable condition, plenty of people will gladly step in and disciple kids, just not in any godly or helpful way.

Some of my earliest memories occur after we moved from our rustic cottage where I was born to a new property – with twenty acres, a trailer, and an old three-story barn directly across the country road from Dad's father and stepmother. It's where I first learned to ride a bike and first learned to swim. It's where I encountered my first hornet's nest and suffered a vicious attack from dozens of the little devils, which resulted in my terror of stinging bugs throughout childhood. It's the place where I not so cleverly licked the ice that had formed on our gas tank one morning, only to find my tongue fastened onto the frosty metal while I panicked and screamed until Dad appeared and set me free with a quick jerk, as he slipped on the ice while holding me. It's where I started school and learned what bullying was—how easily boys could hate me and how indifferent men could reject me. A place where I realized just how much words can hurt—words like *sissy*, *queer*, and *faggot*. A place where I developed a loathing for gym class and its pecking order, where the *real* boys would be incessantly pointed out to me.

It's also where I was first introduced to pornography and experienced sexual abuse. I'll explain more about that in the next chapter.

The pre-birth experience and the 0-2 stage shape a baby's development. A healthy prenatal environment and positive maternal mental health during pregnancy can set the foundation for a child's healthy development. At the same time, a mother's responsive and nurturing care during the 0-2 stage is vital for attachment, emotional regulation, and healthy development. A lack of consistent and responsive care during this stage can result in attachment and developmental issues that can have long-lasting effects on the child's life. Therefore, providing a nurturing and supportive environment during both the pre-birth experience and the 0-2 stage of development is crucial for a child's lifelong physical and emotional well-being.

Questions for Self-Reflection / Journaling / Group Sharing

1. What are you aware of in your story of conception through birth?

2. What was your relationship like with your primary caregiver, typically your mother, during the first two years of your life?

3. Are there any recurring patterns or themes in your current relationships that may be related to your early childhood experiences?

4. Do you see any opportunities in which you can use your insights about your early childhood experiences to deepen your relationship with God and others?

5. How might these situations have shaped your view of God's love and care for you?

6. How might God be inviting you to heal and grow in these areas?

1 Bowlby, J. (1958). The nature of the child's tie to his mother. *International Journal of Psychoanalysis*, 39, 350-373.

2 Ainsworth, M. D. S., Blehar, M. C., Waters, E., & Wall, S. (1978). Patterns of attachment: A psychological study of the strange situation. *Hillsdale, NJ: Erlbaum.*

3 Sroufe, L. A. (1989). Relationships, self, and individual adaptation. In R. V. Kail (Ed.), Advances in child development and behavior (Vol. 21, pp. 241-271). *San Diego, CA: Academic Press.*

4 Cassidy, J., & Shaver, P. R. (2016). Handbook of attachment: Theory, research, and clinical applications (3rd ed.). *New York: Guilford Press.*

5 Clinton, T., & Sibcy, G. (2006). *Why you do the things you do: The Secret to Healthy Relationships.* Thomas Nelson Incorporated.

6 *Caring relationships: the heart of early brain development.* (n.d.). NAEYC.

7 ScienceDirect.com. *Sensitive Responsiveness:*

8 Moon C. The role of early auditory development in attachment and communication. *Clin Perinatol*. 2011;38(4):657–669

9 Hepper PG, Shahidullah BS. Development of fetal hearing. *Arch Dis Child Fetal Neonatal Ed*. 1994;71(2):F81–F87

10 Marx, V., & Nagy, E. (2017). Fetal behavioral responses to the touch of the mother's abdomen: A Frame-by-frame analysis. *Infant Behavior & Development*, *47*, 83–91.

11 Ustun, B., Reissland, N., Covey, J., Schaal, B., & Blissett, J. (2022). Flavor sensing in utero and emerging discriminative behaviors in the human fetus. *Psychological Science*, *33*(10), 1651–1663.

12 Whitehead, K., Laudiano-Dray, M. P., Meek, J., & Fabrizi, L. (2019). Event-related potentials following contraction of respiratory muscles in pre-term and full-term infants. *Clinical Neurophysiology*.

13 Van Den Bergh, B., & Marcoen, A. (2004). High antenatal maternal anxiety is related to ADHD symptoms, externalizing problems, and anxiety in 8- and 9-Year-Olds. *Child Development*, *75*(4), 1085–1097.

14 Cirelli LK, Jurewicz ZB, Trehub SE. Effects of maternal singing style on mother–infant arousal and behavior. *J Cogn Neurosci*. *2020;32(7):1213–1220*

15 DeCasper, A. J., & Spence, M. J. (1986). Prenatal maternal speech influences newborns' perception of speech sounds. *Infant Behavior & Development*, *9*(2), 133–150.

16 Lecanuet, J., & Schaal, B. (1996). Fetal sensory competencies. *European Journal of Obstetrics & Gynecology and Reproductive Biology*, *68*, 1–23.

17 Hepper, P., McCartney, G., & Shannon, E. (1998). Lateralized behavior in first-trimester human fetuses. *Neuropsychologia*, *36*(6), 531–534.

18 Fetal neurobehavioral development. (1996, October 1). *PubMed*.

19 Van Den Bergh, B., Mulder, E., Mennes, M., & Glover, V. (2005). Antenatal maternal anxiety and stress and the neurobehavioural development of the fetus and child: links and possible mechanisms. A review. *Neuroscience & Biobehavioral Reviews*, *29*(2), 237–258.

20 Granier-Deferre, C., Bassereau, S., Ribeiro, A., Jacquet, A., & DeCasper, A. J. (2011). A Melodic Contour Repeatedly Experienced by Human Near-Term Fetuses Elicits a Profound Cardiac Reaction One Month after Birth. *PLOS ONE*, *6*(2), e17304.

21 *The Secret Life of the Unborn child*. (n.d.). Book by Thomas R Verny | Official Publisher Page | Simon & Schuster.

Chapter 3

THE IMPORTANCE OF FATHER – AGES 3-6

If the church building doors were open, our family was there – Sunday morning, evening, and usually midweek. As a child, I found services boring. Between the organist and the hymns, our congregation's musical production fell somewhere in between a funeral score and a shrill, tone-deaf choir. I don't know what we would've sounded like without Mrs. Reese. She sat near the front, inside the aisle, and was the only one capable of reaching the high notes... sort of. I remember her high-pitched voice like it was yesterday.

As a highly sensitive boy, I noticed things that I doubt most boys typically pay any attention to. One Sunday in particular, after church service, I stood near my Dad and watched other members banter and bounce around, each of them eager to say goodbyes, weave through the aisles, and exit out the back of the building. While Dad spoke with those passing by, he gripped my shoulder—not a loving touch of paternal care, but a cold stay-where-you-are gesture more like a stiff poke or prod. As a kid, this was about as far as his physical affection toward me went. I remember this instance well because his mechanical touch annoyed me even at six or seven. The rejection was so palpable that I ducked away from his firm, bony fingers just as a looming elderly man named Mr. Adams shuffled past me. He had survived a stroke some time ago and now walked/lurched with a cane. I didn't understand what had happened to him. In his post-stroke condition, he was just big and frightening to me. As one side of his body didn't function well, he clumsily turned toward someone else he wanted to greet and smacked me square in my face with the back of his good hand, raising it to greet the other person.

I'm sure I gasped. My cheek stung. But Mr. Adams didn't even notice. I rubbed my face, thinking men are just oafs. I was young and highly impressionable, and even something as insignificant as my father's cold touch and Mr. Adam's unintentionally clumsy slap shaped my outlook on men – and not for the good.

Now, those encounters may seem silly and minimal on the surface. Still, for a vulnerable boy who already felt like he didn't fit in with (or was even wanted by) his own gender, these minor circumstances stacked one on top of another over time and had a cumulative effect.

It is important to note here (and I'll repeat this truism more than once) that an individual's *perception* is the lens through which they interpret everything around them. We often make assumptions based on our perception of what feels and seems true to us. These perceptions are often faulty and sometimes altogether incorrect. Mainly as a child, without much self-awareness, we can believe our perceptions are spot on - not even questioning our conclusions. This internal processing based on our assumptions can lead to gross over-generalizations.

My perceptions and assumptions resulted in judgments and hostile generalizations of an entire gender: my own. Simple incidences such as these can occur countless times within a month or year. During a child's growth, his internalized anger, disappointment, and even disgust of his gender can prompt him to detach and reject the primary sources he needs to navigate a healthy and whole sense of himself and others.

Again, perception is everything in the eyes of a child. Personality and temperament also influenced how I perceived all of my interactions.

* * *

Back in my boyhood home, it wasn't unusual for Dad to lose his cool over something that wasn't working right. Maybe one of our small farm animals – a calf, cow, or goat wasn't responding the way he wanted; he couldn't find a tool he needed, etc. His favorite default expletive in these situations was always, "Shit!"

I can't tell you how many times I heard that word and experienced his associated anger. More importantly, I never recall him correcting himself, apologizing, or acknowledging his sin.

Looking back, life felt full of contradictions - *do as I say, not as I do*. This pattern left a lasting impression on my childhood self, and it wasn't a good one. It's just one example of the many common ways the Christian principles my parents professed seemed to contradict their actions. That's confusing for a child, and the convictions we once believed rock-solid become flimsy and malleable.

Of course, my parents weren't unique in their struggles to uphold their faith and live it out consistently. We all struggle with this, and frankly, kids are the ones who see and experience our inconsistency more than anyone else. The thing I wish my parents had done differently is to come back to us, acknowledging where they had blown it and asking for our forgiveness and God's forgiveness in front of us. I never witnessed that kind of humility or personal correction, so our family's firmly held beliefs did not feel so strong.

On the outside, our family checked off all the boxes for Christian living: we went to church regularly, sang hymns, listened to sermons, read our Bibles, prayed, and sometimes had family devotions. But for me, something still felt like it was missing. In hindsight, I can honestly say that witnessing Dad's outbursts of anger that were never backed up with an acknowledgment of wrongdoing profoundly impacted my value of the gospel and faith. I couldn't see how either could make much of a difference in life. It also diminished my view of men.

However, as the old saying goes, the apple doesn't fall far from the tree. I also have had chronic issues with expressing anger. Outbursts, complete with internal (and sometimes verbal) cussing, are not beneath me at times. We live in a fallen world, and it takes concentrated effort to maintain a godly walk consistently. My boys have witnessed some of my episodes themselves over the years. While my initial instinct is to regroup privately, confess my sin through prayer, and move on, there's a greater responsibility in the balance. From my experience with my father, I know it's vital for my boys to hear my apology and confession of sin. They also must see my change of heart and spiritual growth in these areas of weakness and sin.

I share this because raising strong sons and daughters with a sense of morality is essential. An engaged, warm, and strong father and walks with God are vital to their life journey. A father doesn't need to be Superman, but he does need to understand and practice shepherding the hearts of his children. He needs to live out his beliefs and acknowledge them when he fails. Part of what makes a home feel truly safe to kids is their parents' outward acknowledgment and addressing of issues. Face every problem head-on. Let your children see that adults must work through issues as children do and that we all grow when we do the hard work rather than sweep our sins, failures, or problems under the carpet.

* * *

When it comes to a father's presence in their children's lives, their involvement is crucial for their child's healthy development. It's even more imperative during the early ages of two through six. Studies show that children with present and invested fathers also tend to have better cognitive, social, and emotional outcomes than those without.

One of the critical ways fathers contribute to their children's development is through play. Rough-and-tumble play, in particular, has positively impacted children's social and emotional development1. This type of play, characterized by physical activity and roughhousing, allows children to learn about boundaries, develop self-control, and build self-esteem. Fathers are particularly well-suited to engage in this activity, as they often have more physical strength and energy than mothers—a perfect design from our all-knowing Creator.

In addition, fathers as role models are also more apt than mothers to encourage risk-taking2. This can play a crucial role in the development and growth of children. When children are exposed to new challenges and appropriate risks, it can help them develop skills and competencies such as:

1.Problem-solving. Children must find a solution when they face a challenging situation or obstacle. This can help them develop problem-solving skills and critical thinking.

2.Decision-making. Children learn to make decisions when presented with different options and consequences. This can help them build their confidence in making choices and help them develop a sense of autonomy.

3.Resilience. Children who take risks and experience failure learn to cope with disappointment and setbacks. This helps them build resilience, a valuable skill for navigating life's challenges.

4.Faith-building. When children can see and experience parents stepping out in faith to obey and follow God, it builds their faith and trust in Him. They rely on God to lead and shepherd them as they grow and move toward adulthood.

Of course, moms and dads can both provide these opportunities. Still, there is something constructive about an attuned father's masculine voice and presence that offers the assurance and courage needed for their sons and daughters to take healthy risks.

Research shows that fathers involved in their children's lives tend to have children who score higher on intelligence and academic achievement measures3,4,5. Because God has created men and women differently, fathers often provide children with a unique and necessary stimulation and learning experience different from what mothers can offer. For example, fathers may be more likely to take their children on outdoor adventures or engage in problem-solving activities, which can help to develop children's cognitive skills.

Beyond cognitive support, fathers aid in their children's emotional development. Children with involved fathers tend to have better emotional regulation and are less likely to experience anxiety or depression6. Fathers are intended to provide children with a sense of security and stability, and they can also function as fundamental role models for emotional expression and regulation – especially for their sons7,8,9.

However, it's worth stating that for many dads to model healthy emotional expression and regulation, they likely have some personal internal work. Perhaps it's best to start by meeting with a pastor or counselor about one's history, should any of these areas be a struggle. Without doing this inner work, our wives and children must experience the unhealed sides of our emotions.

* * *

Another study published by the Institute for Research on Poverty found that children with involved fathers tend to have better emotional regulation and are less likely to experience anxiety or depression10.

Research supports the claim that rough-and-tumble play, in particular, positively impacts children's social and emotional development. A study published in the *National Library of Medicine*11 found that rough-and-tumble play between fathers and children is positively associated with children's social development, including their ability to form friendships, share, and take turns.

Fathers involved in their children's lives tend to have better mental health and are less likely to experience depression. For example, a study published in the *Contributions to Management Science* found that fathers who reported high levels of involvement in their children's lives also reported better mental health and less depression12.

Children with involved fathers are also more likely to have better relationships with their peers, have higher self-esteem and better academic performance, and are less likely to engage in risky behavior such as drug use and early sexual activity 13.

For additional resources on this topic, please see the following:

•**The role of father involvement in children's later mental health.** *Journal of Adolescence*. This research demonstrates the positive correlation between father involvement and children's mental health outcomes14.

•**Child poverty.** According to the U.S. Census Bureau's recent report on income and poverty in 2014, children who are born in father-absent homes are four times more likely to suffer from poverty than children born in married homes15.

•**Preventing crime and poverty.** Today, nearly 25 million children have an absent father16. According to the professional literature, the father's absence is the most important cause of poverty. The same is true for crime. Those in intact married families are the least likely to commit delinquent acts of all adolescents 17.

•**Numerous benefits of fathers in the home.** Research shows that a father's absence affects children in multiple unfortunate ways, while a father's presence makes a positive difference in the lives of both children and mothers18.

Furthermore, children who grow up with involved and supportive fathers are less likely to experience mental health issues, poverty, criminal behavior, and imprisonment.

* * *

I recall running away from my mother when I was young, perhaps as young as three. She was furious with me about something I did or didn't do, and her reaction frightened me. I knew enough to recognize a spanking was imminent. I ran into my parents' bedroom, where my dad was, and ran right up to him. He scooped me up. I don't recall what he said, but his tone was humorously sympathetic. We could both hear Mom rushing down the hall after me. But instead of intervening or helping Mom settle down, he handed me off to her. I don't recall the events after that, but I remember my emotions, even from a young age. The lack of protection from Dad, and even from Mom in that situation, felt wrong. There's a reason this very early memory has lingered all these years with so much clarity.

The memories that stick with us the most are those that have either strong positive or negative emotions associated with them. As the adage goes, people won't always remember what you say or do, but they'll never forget the way you made them feel. Again, what impacts us profoundly about a painful memory isn't necessarily the actual event or even the intention of the person doing us harm or withholding good (sometimes even tremendous hurt is entirely unintentional). But often, it's the way we *perceive* it and process it.

I guarantee the way Dad saw that situation was very different from how I felt about it. He knew I would be punished for whatever I did, but that would be quick in his world, and it would be over. It felt very different with my limited understanding (not to mention the fear of my looming punishment). Looking back, I think it was about trust. I felt a diminishment of trust in him at that moment. I don't remember ever running to him for protection again.

In his book *Healing for Damaged Emotions* 19, David A. Seamands wrote, "Children are the best recorders of information and the worst interpreters of information."

Melissa and I often refer to this quote while teaching because it is so profoundly true. Kids need someone (ideally Mom and Dad) to help them sort out their thoughts and feelings – truth from error. As parents, we must gently and consistently mine our kids' hearts to understand better what they are feeling, questioning, doubting, and struggling with.

My dad never knew the importance of understanding my heart or shepherding and guiding the unseen turmoil within me. I wish he would have attempted to help Mom settle down before handing me off to her. I wish I would have seen him as an advocate in various situations. This was just one of many instances where I felt unprotected and left to figure life out alone.

A Father's Influence on Sexual Behavior

Fathers also play a crucial role in helping to shape the beliefs, views, and, ultimately, the sexual behavior of their children. While discussions about biblical perspectives on sex and identity are typically reserved for the third stage of development, it's never too early for moms and dads to begin helping their children understand a simple, positive framework for how each boy and girl or man and woman has been given the priceless treasure of God's image. This image is uniquely expressed through a child's masculinity or femininity and is revealed according to His created design of intentional, binary biology.

Regarding modern culture, we, as parents, can help our children build a solid foundation of common sense, natural law, and resilience. This is vital to prepare youth for their eventual encounter with a world gone off the rails in rebellion against God. Children rely on parents to set boundaries and enforce them.

Nothing could be more critical today than a father highlighting God's design for two genders and designating that boundary as part of God's order.

Over and over, research shows that children with supportive, solid relationships with their fathers are less likely to engage in hedonistic sexual behavior20,21,22. They are also more likely to delay sexual initiation. This type of engaged paternal influence helps older children value God's design and respect the gift of sex as it was intended to be within the covenant commitment of marriage. This influence can help steer children away from sex before marriage and empower them to avoid risky sexual behaviors with damaging repercussions, such as pornography, unplanned pregnancy, abortion, sexually transmitted diseases, sexual addiction, and the hidden but genuine damage to the soul that occurs whenever we engage in sex outside of God's exclusive design for marriage (I Corinthians 6:18).

Boomerang Effect

When fathers are engaged, their well-being is also positively impacted. God ordained blessing and well-being over parents who put their children before themselves. Loving our kids by providing a whole-enough reflection of God's love and value of them prepares them for the world and gives them a sense of worth. It also fulfills us as mentors and accentuates the reflections of our Heavenly Father inside us.

Aside from spiritual wholesomeness, even secular studies show that fathers involved in their children's lives have better overall mental health23. This is likely because fatherhood provides men with a sense of purpose and fulfillment as sons under the authority and blessing of their Heavenly Father. Intentional and loving fatherhood also helps men develop stronger relationships with their wives, children, and others.

In fact, not only are fathers intended by God to play a vital role in their child's well-being during the three-to-six-year stage of life (and beyond), but they are essential in their child's life starting at conception. Harkening back to *The Secret Life of the Unborn Child*, Dr. Verny makes this statement about fathers:

It also makes sense that our new knowledge would enhance the father's part in pregnancy. A relationship with a loving and sensitive man provides a woman with an ongoing emotional support system during pregnancy. And if, in our ignorance, we have disrupted this delicate system by rudely excluding the man, now that we have discovered – or more accurately, rediscovered – just how vital emotional security and nurturing are to a woman and her unborn child, he can finally be restored to his rightful place in pregnancy.

It's almost shocking but refreshing to read such a statement. As it turns out, men aren't merely sperm donors after all. Just as mothers have an essential and unique meaning in raising children, so do fathers. God created the mom and dad roles as providers in the rearing of children and designed it from conception to adulthood (and even beyond). Following this design is essential for raising secure, well-adjusted, happy children who become confident and productive adults.

God designed fathers to love and sacrifice for their wives and families (Ephesians 5:25, Colossians 3:21), but we know that concept is under devastating attack today. The family structure that God established at creation is no longer promoted or even supported in the secular world. Caring for the innocent and most vulnerable is no longer a given. Abortion, among other things, has radically damaged our national value of life, most especially toward the innocent and vulnerable. In her essential book for the times we're living in, *Them Before Us,* author Katie Faust outlines how far society has shifted from basic primary care of children first to a varied and widespread commodification of children for the sake of adults' wants and desires.

Godly men and fathers must lead the way in repentance of sin and exploitation. They must restore what it means to be a strong man made in God's image as protector and servant-leader. I'm reminded of the instruction and command given by God:

You shall, therefore, impress these words of mine on your heart and your soul, and you shall bind them as a sign on your hand and as frontals on your forehead. You shall teach them to your sons, talking of them when you sit in your house, walk along the road, lie down, and rise.—Deuteronomy 11:18-19

Men who are sold out to Jesus and His purposes are desperately needed. Women need these kinds of faithful, committed men as husbands, and children need these kinds of engaged men as fathers to rise and be present and invested in guiding and preparing the next generation for Kingdom purposes.

* * *

We need to learn how to reframe our experiences when we're young. The only way that can happen is when a wise and loving person listens and responds to us with love and truth. That doesn't mean horrible things didn't or won't happen. They have. They will. But the ability to view something that happens to us from different perspectives and invite Jesus into any abuse, rejection, abandonment, or neglect allows Him to bring inner healing. This does not negate what happened to us or erase all the pain, but it lets Him help us reframe our sense of God and ourselves. This reframing will enable us to walk in new freedom, unshackled from the weight and prison of painful experiences and the way Satan tries to define us through them.

In hindsight, it would have been meaningful to me even if Dad had merely attempted to ask Mom what had happened and why she was so upset. But honestly, given my Dad's background and how he was treated growing up, a response like that would have been the furthest thing from his mind.

Because of the healing God brought to my rebellious and bitter heart in my twenties and thirties and how my mom and dad softened and grew in their love and pursuit of Jesus, my parents and I became very close, dear friends. I'll explain more about that later on, but I want to acknowledge that there are no perfect parents – myself included. Melissa and I are fortunate to have two boys who quickly forgive when we confess how we have sinned against them in one way or another. And we are prayerful and hopeful that our confession and request for forgiveness heal a fresh wound quickly, preventing the infection that can otherwise trouble them for years and even decades.

* * *

Andrew Comiskey, founder and director of Desert Stream Ministries, writes in his flagship program, Living Waters24: Restoring Relational Integrity Through the Broken Body of Christ, "When a boy reaches the age where he begins to separate from Mom to form a greater connection with his father, he all too often turns into a void. No safe, strong, and loving father is present – far too often, no father at all. Often, boys grow into men who are either ambivalent toward their father or hate him outright."

As husbands and fathers, men have abandoned their post and broken their vows – true in the world and too often true in the Church. The issue isn't only with those men who have married and sired children, only to emotionally or physically abandon their families. Nationally, we see an increasing hostility against the beautiful and necessary institution of marriage as a stabilizing building block of life, communities, and society in general as God designed it. Young men and women have bought into the lie of forgoing marriage and children to pursue personal achievement.

Anonymous hookups, friends-with-benefits with no attachments, and shacking up without vows have become preferred to the monogamous life-long commitment between one man and one woman, let alone procreation and rejoicing in children as gifts from God (Psalm 127:3). We live in an age when a baby in the womb is viewed by many as a parasite or tumor to be destroyed and extracted at will, rather than a tiny image-bearer of God - a life to be celebrated, nurtured, and protected.

We must re-educate our young men, both culturally and spiritually. Many men today have the undeveloped emotional maturity of a child due to their upbringing and godless indoctrination. That immaturity was certainly true of me well into my thirties, but that changed in the company of men with a heart for God, one another, and me.

Twenty years ago, I attended a weekly men's group where we went through two John Eldredge books, *Wild at Heart* 25 and *Waking the Dead*. During this time, I read about an idea that both fascinated me and brought clarity to something I had not previously understood or had the slightest concept of. In chapter four of *Wild at Heart*, Eldredge writes about the wound that most men carry. This wound, picked up sometime during childhood, usually strikes directly against a man's sense of masculinity.

Eldredge writes, "*Masculinity is bestowed. A boy learns who he is and what he's got from a man or the company of men. He cannot learn it in any other place. He cannot learn it from other boys, and he cannot learn it from the world of women. From the beginning, the plan was that his father would lay the foundation for a young boy's heart and pass on that essential knowledge and confidence in his strength... Femininity can never bestow masculinity.*"

I needed my Dad's good initiative toward me. I was designed (as all boys are) for his attention, direction, correction, love, and delight. But he was distracted by many other important and necessary things: providing for his family, house projects, church, caring for our farm animals, etc... But I needed him to awaken and call forth something within me—my boyhood and budding manhood. Instead, that essence lay dormant and unrecognized by me for many years. I will explain more about that later.

Often, a father can bridge his son's life, connecting him to the world of men and boys, but my dad was aloof and isolated. He had no masculine community to connect me with. Unless there was a couple that he and Mom spent time with together, he didn't have any friends.

In my fear and rejection of masculinity, I over-identified with women and girls and, as a result, marinated in the feminine throughout my developmental years.

* * *

Fathers Needed!

While teaching and preaching at churches and events around the country, I often make a statement like: "From my perspective, fatherlessness is the single most significant factor that sustains the mass-scale erosion of general well-being, the emotional and psychological instability of younger generations, and full-on chaos throughout most of American society today."

Yes, in addition to fatherlessness, many other destructive factors involve the instability of children, marriage, and society. But this single core issue cannot be overstated in its originating magnitude and devastating, ever-expanding impact.

I am so grateful that my mom and dad stayed together when many husbands and wives in our extended family were divorcing. But fatherlessness does not only occur through divorce and abandonment. Fatherlessness is often an issue in seemingly intact Christian families, too. Dad is physically present but too preoccupied with his job at the church, his career, hobbies, addictions, etc. Sometimes, his wife and their kids only receive whatever crumbs are left over after he focuses on his many roles and responsibilities outside and around the home.

I'm often reminded of tragic lyrics from a song by Harry Chapin recorded in 1974:

Cats In The Cradle

[Verse 1]

My child arrived just the other day.

He came to the world in the usual way.

But there were planes to catch and bills to pay.

He learned to walk while I was away.

And he was talkin' 'fore I knew it, and as he grew.

He'd say, "I'm gonna be like you, Dad,

You know I'm gonna be like you."

[Chorus]

And the cat's in the cradle, and the silver spoon.

Little boy Blue and the man on the moon.

"When you comin' home, Dad?"

"I don't know when, but we'll get together then.

You know we'll have a good time then."

[Verse 2]

My son turned ten just the other day.

He said, "Thanks for the ball, Dad, come on, let's play.

Can you teach me to throw?" I said, "Not today

I got a lot to do." He said, "That's okay."

And he walked away, but his smile never dimmed.

It said, "I'm gonna be like him, yeah.

You know I'm gonna be like him.

[Verse 3]

Well, he came from college just the other day.

So much like a man, I just had to say

"Son, I'm proud of you, can you sit for a while?"

He shook his head and said with a smile.

"What I'd really like, Dad, is to borrow the car keys

See you later, can I have them, please?"

I've long since retired, my son's moved away.

I called him up just the other day.

I said, "I'd like to see you if you don't mind."

He said, "I'd love to, Dad, if I can find the time.

You see, my new job's a hassle, and the kids have the flu.

But it's sure nice talking to you, Dad.

It's been sure nice talking to you."

And as I hung up the phone, it occurred to me.

He'd grown up just like me.

My boy was just like me.

[Chorus]

And the cat's in the cradle, and the silver spoon.

Little boy blue and the man on the moon

"When you comin' home, son?"

"I don't know when, but we'll get together then, Dad.

We're gonna have a good time then."

* * *

I want to close with a story. Perhaps you've heard this one already. I have listened to it several times, and it always strikes me as poignant and sad. I have found several slightly different versions on the Internet, but this is the gist:

Several years ago, a prison chaplain devised an idea he thought could encourage the male prisoners he spiritually cared for. With permission from the warden, the chaplain contacted a greeting card company to ask if they would provide him with 500 Mother's Day greeting cards for prisoners to send back home.

The company agreed, and the day came when prisoners were allowed to pick a card from the designated table. They were enthusiastic and anxious to take advantage of the opportunity to send something home to their mothers. The event was so successful that more cards were requested and supplied.

The chaplain noted that Father's Day was close at hand. He contacted the greeting card company again, and they were happy to help. They started with another 500 Father's Day cards, anticipating the possibility of more being requested.

As before, the table was prepared with cards to be picked, filled out, and mailed back to their fathers. Only this time, rather than long lines of men who wanted to send a card to their mom for Mother's Day, not a single man showed up to get a card for their father.

We saw earlier that statistically, when fathers are absent from the home, boys are at a far higher risk factor across several measurements, including incarceration. I think it's pretty safe to assume that those men who wanted to send a card to their mother had some emotional attachment to her, whereas their lack of connection with their father was also apparent.

Questions for Self-Reflection / Journaling / Group Sharing

1. From a Christian perspective, what does it mean for fathers to "train up" their children? How have you experienced this kind of guidance in your life? What did you experience?

2. Children need different interactions and styles of play with mom and dad. Was your dad engaged in physical play with you? Did you experience fun rough and tumble interactions with him? How did the presence of this interaction (or lack of it) impact you?

3. In what ways have you seen the adverse effects of absentee or uninvolved fathers in the lives of those around you or in your own life? How has this impacted your views on fatherhood?

4. How can we cultivate a culture that values and supports fathers actively involved in their children's lives? What role can the church play in this effort?

5. What biblical examples can we look to for guidance on the importance of fathers in the family unit? How can we apply these lessons to our own lives and relationships?

6. In what ways have you seen God's love reflected in the love of a father figure? How can we better understand God's fatherly love through our experiences with earthly fathers? Or, has your experience with your earthly father tainted your ability to experience the love of your Heavenly Father?

7. How can we pray for and support fathers struggling to balance their roles and responsibilities within the family? How can we encourage and empower fathers to be the best parents they can be? How do you specifically need encouragement as a father?

1 Ginsburg, Kenneth (2007) The Importance of Play in Promoting Healthy Child Development and Maintaining Strong Parent-Child Bonds. *The American Academy of Pediatrics:*

2 Zero to Three. (2023, June 27). The Daddy Factor: How fathers support development | *Zero to Three.*

3 E. Flouri and A. Buchanan, "The Role of Father Involvement in Children's Later Mental Health," Journal of Adolescence 26(2003): 63–78

4 A. Sarkadi, R. Kristiansson, F. Oberklaid, and S. Bremberg, "Fathers' Involvement and Children's Developmental Outcomes: A Systematic Review of Longitudinal Studies," *Acta Paediatrica 97* (2007)

5 W. J. Yeung, G. J. Duncan, and M. S. Hill, "Putting Fathers Back in the Picture: Parental Activities and Children's Adult Outcomes," *Marriage & Family Review 29*, Nos. 2–3 (2000): 97–113:

6 Garfield, Yogman, "Fathers' Roles in the Care and Development of Their Children: The Role of Pediatricians." *The American Academy of Pediatrics* (2016)

7 Amato PR, Rivera F. Paternal involvement and children's behavior problems. *Journal of Marriage and the Family.* 1999;61:375–384. doi: 10.2307/353755.

8 Coley RL, Medeiros BL. Reciprocal longitudinal relations between nonresident father involvement and adolescent delinquency. *Child Development.* 2007;78:132–147. doi: 10.1111/j.1467-8624.2007.00989.x.

9 Harris KM, Furstenberg FF, Marmer JK. Paternal involvement with adolescents in intact families: *The influence of fathers over the life course.* Demography. 1998;35:201–216.

10 Involved fathers play an important role in children's lives. (2020b, April 23). *Institute for Research on Poverty.*

11 Freeman, E., & Robinson, E. L. (2022). The Relationship between Father–Child Rough-and-Tumble Play and Children's Working Memory. *Children (Basel), 9*(7), 962.

12 The impact of fatherhood on men's health and development. In *Contributions to Management Science* (pp. 63–91).

13 All4kids. (2023). A Father's Impact on Child Development. *Child Abuse Prevention, Treatment & Welfare Services | Children's Bureau.* .

14 Murphy, H. (2002). Book review. *Journal of Adolescence, 25*(3), 352–353.

15 Walt, Proctor (2015). Income and Poverty in the United States: 2014. US Department of Commerce.

16 *Effects of fatherless families on crime rates [Marripedia].* (n.d.).

17 *Effects of family structure on Crime [Marripedia].* (n.d.).

18 National Fatherhood Initiative®, a 501c3 Non-Profit. (n.d.). *Father absence statistics*. National Fatherhood Initiative.

19 Goodreads. (n.d.). *Goodreads.*

20 Alleyne-Green, B., Grinnell-Davis, C., Clark, T. T., Quinn, C. R., & Cryer-Coupet, Q. R. (2014). Father involvement, dating violence, and sexual risk behaviors among a national sample of adolescent females. *Journal of Interpersonal Violence, 31*(5), 810–830.

21 Grossman, J. M., Black, A. C., Richer, A. M., & Lynch, A. D. (2019). Parenting practices and emerging adult sexual health: The role of Residential Fathers. *The Journal of Primary Prevention, 40*(5), 505–528.

22 Fathers Respond To Teens' Risky Sexual Behavior With Increased Supervision. (2009, May 9). *ScienceDaily.*

23 FCS3321/FY1451: The Impact of Fathers On Children's Well-Being. (n.d.).

24 Living Waters Guidebook | *Desert Stream Ministries.*

25 *Wild at Heart's Amazon page.* (n.d.).

Chapter 4

THE IMPORTANCE OF PEERS – THE PRETEEN YEARS, AGES 6-11

I stared into the open doorway of the huge yellow bus. At age five, it appeared like a gaping mouth, its steep upward steps like teeth, taunting me inward to an unfamiliar and scary place. I could not bring myself to step up. Leaving the familiar surroundings of home and Mom had riddled me with anxiety for weeks.

Today was the moment of truth. But why hasn't God answered my prayers for help? I wished He would somehow direct my parents to give me another year at home before starting school. Where was the fearless, extroverted toddler who loved greeting strangers, chasing angry geese, and climbing trees? Somehow, I'd lost my curious boldness at the thought of a new environment. The first days of school were supposed to be exciting. At home leading up to it, though, my stomach tightened and ached whenever my family mentioned kindergarten. It was an idea so foreign and cold that I couldn't bring myself to dwell on it – except to pray for relief.

Only now, there was no escape.

The bus driver glared at me with an impatient sigh. My three older siblings prodded me from behind.

"Come on, get in!" one of them huffed.

I thrust my hands out on either side of me, grasped the doorframe, and burst into tears. It was my last-ditch effort to thwart the horrors awaiting me.

Several kids were already waiting on the bus and witnessed my outburst, pressing their gawking faces to windows. Homes along our long rural route relied solely on the school bus for transportation, and our stop was one of many.

From behind, my older brother grabbed me beneath my arms, pressed a knee to my back, and shoved me up the steps. All at once, I found myself stumbling down the aisle, red-faced, eyes streaming, nose running, trying to find a seat and hide behind the backrest in front of me. Kids prodded and laughed, but it would have been worse if my two brothers and sister weren't on the bus.

The seats were empty, but I was blocked when I attempted to squeeze in or sit on the aisle. Kids were saving open spots for their friends and didn't want a bawling baby sitting beside them. It all happened in seconds, but as I worked my way down the aisle, finally, one kid allowed me to stumble over him to the window seat. The bus lurched forward. I felt a new tightness in my gut and a wash of anxiety as Mom waved goodbye from the driveway, and then we were out of sight.

So, within seconds of my first day of school, I managed to plaster a giant L for Loser on my forehead that only my peers could see. Unsurprisingly, the months and even years that followed would be a textbook case of childhood bullying. Thus began my experience of one of the nastiest sub-cultures known to man – the twice-daily school bus ride. Back then, in the rural country, the school bus carried students from kindergarten through high school, with only one adult to referee, whose primary focus was not running the thirty-foot vehicle full of minors off the road. In the realms of kid-dom, when it came to the confines of the bus, the further down the aisle you went, the seedier the crowd.

To this day, I still experience a pang of apprehension (though mild now) when a yellow school bus passes by. My wife and I can share a laugh about it now. While I'm sorting through negative memories, Melissa (as a homeschool mom) daydreams about stuffing our boys through the bus's backdoor and waving them off to school for a day to herself. It's all about perspective.

Courage and rescue were frequent topics of prayer for me. As I forced myself to school each day, the notoriety of my bus performance spread. If a boy was unaware of my weakness from the bus, I unwittingly ensured he knew about it with my non-athletic ability during recess and gym class. This was only elementary school, but there was still a pecking order – especially in PE. It only took a week for the much cooler jocks and team captains to determine I wasn't quality teammate material. Throughout school, I remained one of two or three kids who were never chosen for a team until we were the very last options.

One afternoon in first grade, an older neighbor boy asked me to come over and play on the bus ride home from school. This was a boy other boys respected, and it was a rare delight to be invited to spend time with him. He seemed kind and genuine, too. There would also be other neighborhood boys to peruse his tractor magazine collection. Now, I couldn't have cared less about looking at pictures of tractors, but I couldn't pass up an opportunity to be one of the boys.

That day, I hurried off the bus, changed into outside clothes, and trotted to his house. My heart raced with anticipation. Social settings and peer interactions were not my forte. My mind fired off in a hundred directions of what ifs—how the other boys might shame or mock me.

Anxiously, I knocked at his front door, and another kid opened it. Several other older boys were behind him, including the boy who'd invited me, all gathered around the kitchen table examining something.

"Hey, come here," the boy from the bus said, waving me over.

On the table was a magazine, but not one with tractors. It was his dad's hardcore porn. I learned the kid's parents were away, and he'd rifled through his dad's secret stash and pulled some out for all the other boys to ogle. My eyes widened. I'd never seen anything explicit before. I'm sure I had a stupid look because the others around me burst out hysterically as the pages turned. So many emotions swirled around me—confusion, repulsion, intrigue, guilt—so that my stomach clenched. But I couldn't look away from those glossy pornographic pages. Not just naked images but various sexual acts between men and women on full display. I'll never forget those intense moments when my innocence was stripped away.

One image, in particular, captured my attention and is seared into my memory with crystal-sharp clarity. A woman in various poses spread across several pages holding a whip. As a naïve young boy, the whip seemed so odd and out of place that I didn't know how to process it. My images of women were maternal and nurturing, but this—this was extreme and bizarrely captivating. Even as I write about this memory, these many years later, those images remain clearer than I would like.

At that young age, I was already struggling with so much. Adding the introduction to pornography only confounded me further and complicated my brain's natural processing. But it wasn't just magazine porn that I was exposed to that day. It was sexual abuse. Some of the boys started imitating sexual acts with each other. But beyond that, my memory is entirely black. I can't say how far the abuse went or how long it lasted, but I know I walked home that evening held captive by a more significant confusion and shame than usual - a much more broken little boy.

* * *

One day in second grade, during recess, a new game caused our classroom to erupt with commotion. Different groups of kids competed and bantered excitedly, but I retreated under a long table against a wall. There I sat quietly with my legs beneath me, watching the commotion from the safety of my obscurity and wishing I could escape it all. Familiar feelings of shame and self-contempt for that shame crashed through my young heart and mind. And then ... a strange and random thought popped into my mind. I beseeched Satan and propositioned him: "If you will make me a witch, I will serve you for the rest of my life."

At the tender age of seven, I thought the only thing that could give me power was witchcraft. I had no idea where this thought came from, though I suspect it was partly fueled by my growing sense that God didn't care about me or my struggles. But I don't know how I could have ever viewed the idea of bargaining with evil as a good idea. It does, however, highlight how desperate I felt. I know I longed for the power to get away and never return.

The source of this idea was undoubtedly from the pit of hell. In retrospect, I think I had come to such a point of questioning and hopelessness—and since no real answers had come from the Church or God, maybe Satan was my only hope... perhaps he would step in and do something. Remember the quote from Seamands, "Children are the best recorders of information and the worst interpreters of that information."

By the way, I later repented to God and renounced that horrible, misguided agreement. Part of what made my school experience so acutely painful was that I was susceptible and aware. I picked up on everything around me. I can now see that part of what I perceived as a curse in my youth became a strength in adulthood. That is the beauty of how God works through each of us, though we can't always see it that way at the time.

* * *

Growing up in the country, Mom and Dad had little concern about where I was, even when I was only five or six. It was God's country, and bad things weren't supposed to happen in beautiful rural settings. Often, I went for walks alone in the woods, to a creek, a pond, or the river, letting my imagination run free with make-believe worlds and safe spaces. That was before the abuse and porn robbed me of my innocence. Even after, I still took walks and wandered all over the countryside, but my thoughts and imagination became polluted with sexual thoughts, explicit images, and overall dirtiness. I don't remember if it was before or after the abuse, but one afternoon, on a particularly perfect day, I crossed my grandparent's field to visit a pasture and creek I knew well.

The sun was bright, and the temperature and humidity were almost surreal. Typically, this region is one of the cloudiest in the country. The moisture in the summer can make everything feel wet and sticky. But not on this day. I felt the strong, southerly breeze on my skin. It playfully tugged at my hair, filling my lungs with fresh, clean air.

As was my habit when walking through the mature hay field, I carefully pulled on the stalk of a tall, green shoot of grass (a field full of them - soon to be cut, bailed, and stored in the local farmer's barn as winter food for the cows) until a tender shoot slipped out. As I walked nearly chest-deep in the grass, I chewed the soft blade to the end and pulled another.

At the far end of the field, my siblings and I trod a path through a patch of weeds and wild grass. A barbed-wire fence at the path's end kept cows in their expansive pasture. It was an idyllic spot because it opened to a wide but shallow valley hemmed in on one side, far in the distance by our familiar river and fishing holes. I stood still for a few minutes and looked out over the valley – scattered cows grazed, wildflowers danced in the breeze, and the creek below gurgled, all while that warm, strong breeze sailed around me. It was beautiful. But something else lingered. Highlighted and contrasted by all I was taking in was an even more profound and especially acute sense of aloneness.

If I had not been taking all this in and feeling it so intensely, I would find it hard to believe that such a young boy could even have the capacity for what I'm describing. But it was there—my thoughtful awareness of the beauty around me. I was sad, feeling utterly alone. Yes, I had my family. But I had so many feelings and so much doubt and fear going on inside me all the time that no one knew about. I didn't understand it as a kid, but I believe that internal separation and not feeling known by anyone was the primary source of my loneliness.

Weeks later, that memory faded into the background and became replaced by new experiences and memories. It's fantastic how in God's existence—His I AM-ness— He isn't bound by time the way we are. I believe every moment (even our history) is as present to God as you are while reading these words. He uses these moments in His great wisdom to help shape and guide us. Although the memory of that beautiful/lonely experience faded, in a strategic moment, the day before my thirty-ninth birthday, God brought that memory up during group prayer time. More on that later.

* * *

After the sexual abuse encounter, I was so ashamed that it took me two or three weeks to confide in my mother. We were outside at the time, hoeing and pulling weeds in the vegetable garden, and I blurted out something. I could no longer contain it, though I don't remember exactly what words I used. Mom, in her shock, stood bolt upright with a loud gasp. She just stood there looking at me, tightly gripping and twisting the handle of her hoe. A moment later, she let her tool fall in the row between the carrots and tomatoes and quietly instructed me to keep working. She disappeared into the house, presumably to speak to Dad, and ten or fifteen minutes later, she returned with very stern orders that I never play with those boys again. And that was it. Problem solved.

Except, it wasn't.

Adult-me has wondered what went through my mom's mind in those moments. Did it bring her back to her pre-teen abuse - to that married guy who'd stalked her?

We each deal with our brokenness in different ways, but I'm so grateful that Mom later sought counseling for herself and invited Jesus into her wounded places through prayer. For her, that appointment didn't happen until she was in her eighties, but better late than never, as it is never too late to accept Jesus and His healing grace for all of us. I wish Mom hadn't had to juggle to suppress her wounds for so much of her life. I wish the Church had taught about freedom from such things when she was younger. Regardless, Jesus sustained her all those years and brought a greater degree of freedom in the latter years of her life, for which I'm grateful.

Of course, in my boyhood days, all my Mom and Dad knew to do was to try to protect me going forward. They ensured I disconnected entirely from those boys, but they didn't understand the damage already done. My sense of shame and dirtiness, and feeling like a disappointment to God, only festered and grew over time, as did my prematurely awakened sexual curiosity.

Effects of Porn

Even in the middle of nowhere, porn is accessible. Porn opens the doors where doors are meant to be sealed. It promotes an unhealthy perception of sex and confuses young minds too ill-equipped to process lewd acts and unnatural behaviors. I've had the privilege of speaking with and getting to know several other adult men who, similar to my own boyhood experience with porn, have had their struggles too.

Many of these men suffering from porn addiction have shared with me that, at some point during their youth, they sensed where they might find pornography. I believe this knowledge is often demonically-sourced. The accounts have been too numerous, too coincidental, and too detailed to be only mere happenstance.

During a formative period in my own family, my Mom and Dad suffered what I'd call a rough time navigating the throes of parenting headstrong children. However, that greatly impacted me and my perception of my parents at the time. Dad was used to barking orders until everyone fell in line, but that technique wasn't working anymore. As a result, there was a period of very heavy-handed discipline being dished out at home. It ignited a lot of conflict.

I wanted the fighting, yelling, and war of wills to stop. Dad thought he could continue to solve everything by loud intimidation and, at times, physical punishment, but those tactics don't work well with strong-willed, older children. In those moments of parental aggression, I hated my father. I was also frustrated that I was too young, weak, and powerless. Instead, I would storm outside to escape the family conflict and pound away at anything within reach in our backyard.

Even though the harsh treatment wasn't dished out in my direction, it drove a wedge in my heart that separated me from Dad and Mom. Long after the dust settled from these episodes, and even after this tough season seemed to pass, my heart weighed heavily from harboring judgments against my parents. These and other situations caused me to pull back emotionally and detach from Dad.

Psychologists and mental health professionals refer to this reaction in children as defensive detachment. It can occur due to repeated negative experiences with one or both parents. Children who experience neglect, abuse, criticism, or instability in their family environment may develop defensive detachment as a coping mechanism to protect themselves from further emotional harm.

For example, a child with a parent who is **consistently** angry, critical, or unpredictable may begin to emotionally distance themselves from that parent to avoid the feelings of hurt, fear, or confusion that come with interacting with that parent. This detachment can manifest as a lack of attachment or affection, avoidance of interaction, or a general disinterest in the parent.

Children may also detach from a parent as a form of self-preservation if they feel their needs and feelings are consistently ignored or dismissed by that parent. This detachment can create a cycle, as the child's emotional distance may further erode the relationship and contribute to an unstable or unhappy family environment.

It's important to note that defensive detachment can affect a child's emotional development and relationships1. Therapy may be necessary for addressing defensive detachment. Often, a child needs a place to work through their experiences and learn healthier coping mechanisms for dealing with stress and trauma. Release of unforgiveness toward our parent(s) can also be essential in recovering from defensive detachment.

More Boyhood Struggles

Let's talk about the woes of gym class that I hinted at earlier. It's one thing to deal with the conflicts at home and escape to school each day for a reprieve. When school is just as bad, if not worse, a child has nowhere else to turn to be at peace and be a child. The elementary school coach was more of a drill sergeant than a caring mentor who wanted his class to succeed. If he were still around today, I suspect he'd be brought up on child abuse charges for his particular methods. For example, I'll never forget the day I shuffled onto the gymnasium floor only to find two thick ropes dangling from the rafters like something out of a medieval gauntlet.

Instantly, my heart sank. I knew whatever torture awaited couldn't be good. When Coach made it clear that each of us was to climb up the rope to the top and back down, a giant lump formed in my throat, and I could hardly swallow. Heights would be the death of me! I hate heights even to this very day. How could I get Coach to understand this debilitating fear and excuse me from the exercise?

Stiff-jawed, I watched all the jocks scurry over for their ascent. Moments later, Coach blasted his shrill whistle, and the frenzy of athleticism began. Some boys reached the top, some struggled, and only got halfway. And, of course, there were the usual couple of kids who barely got off the floor. Thank God for them. When my turn rolled around, there was no way to stall, nowhere to run. My pulse pounded in my ears. I had no idea what to do or how to do it. My arm strength was more like a girl my age. The coach offered no coaching or instructions, so I was on my own.

Approaching the closest rope, I stood on my toes, reached as high as possible, wrapping my little hands around the rough, thick fibers, and stared upward at the goal. It might as well have been Mount Everest. So high. It would be impossible, but I knew I had to give Coach something. With all my force, I tried lifting myself off the ground. My feet and legs wavered, and my arms trembled. I had no idea how to use my legs and feet to stabilize myself.

So, ten inches off the ground, I just hung there.

"Move, Ingraham!" Coach bellowed in the background. "Get up that rope NOW!"

Flushed, I dropped to the floor, wiped the sweat off my face, reached around the rope, and tried again. Snickers echoed from the boys around me, all watching my ineptitude. I wanted to pull myself up that rope and prove to everyone—especially myself—that I could do big things. I was every bit as much a boy as the rest of them.

But I couldn't move. Rope fibers cut into my hands, sweat rolled down my face, and sinuses burned behind my eyes. I couldn't cry, though—not in front of all of them. It would only make me more of a target than I already was. I would *not* repeat the first day of school episode from the bus!

Worse still, in that moment of weakness on the rope, when I could've used a trusting mentor to rescue me from a humiliating scene, I had nothing more than an ape of a man throwing out berating comments like gloved fists, with me being his punching bag.

This kind of physical education ritual went on several times a week. Every class became a reminder that I was a failure, that I was not authentic boy material—if I didn't feel it myself, Coach made sure to reiterate it for me so I never forgot. He zeroed in on my weaknesses like a guard dog smells fear. Day by day, week by week, my inhibitions stacked up and pressed down on my shoulders. The desire to disappear intensified.

But what could I do? I couldn't excuse myself from gym class. I had to show up and take whatever Coach dished out. In those emotionally exhausting situations, the only possible solution was the only defense mechanism a child has, which is to detach and disconnect. I did the best I could. As a result, shame at my lack of self-preservation grew, as did my anger.

* * *

Now that we're discussing anxiety-riddled situations let's talk about the locker room experience. It's hard to describe what I felt back then, even as an adult with a skilled vocabulary. As a thin, under-developed boy, getting naked and showering with other boys felt like a violation. I had already figured out I was attracted to guys, and in the locker room, I felt like I had a neon sign on my forehead alerting everyone to this fact. As early as age eight or nine, I became aware I was more interested in the bodies and builds of boys than girls. When I found porn, I was more drawn toward men than women. My mind was haywire with thoughts of uncontrolled bodily responses—like, what if I got an erection while I was undressed around the other naked boys?! Gradually, I began to understand that anxiety trumps sexual attraction on any given day. My severe stress levels in those locker room situations were a kill switch for any hormonal engines beginning to rev.

There was no way of avoiding the locker room, so I would either not change or be discreet—changing clothes while the other boys were in the shower, then slipping out as if I had already showered and headed to class.

This routine worked pretty well until Coach decided to police the locker room.

Like TSA at the airport checkpoints, Coach stood outside the locker room door and inspected us as we exited. Forcing back a rough swallow, I attempted to slide past him.

He grabbed my shoulder, held me in place, and examined me. "What do you think you're doing? Did you even take a shower?"

"Yes," I lied.

"Bull!" Coach roared. "You stink, Ingraham! Get back in there and get washed. Don't even think of skating out of here beforehand. I'll be standing right here to make sure. And hurry it up!"

He huffed and backed me through the door, his hand firmly on my shoulder.

I didn't know what to do or what to say. I just froze up.

Back inside the locker room again, Coach announced to everyone that I still needed a shower. I cringed in my sneakers. There was no avoiding any of it now. Most of the boys were done and heading back to class, but a few lingered. I plopped down on the bench before my locker and tried to muster up the courage to undress. The shame and fear that rattled up my spine at that moment threatened to paralyze me. It was almost too much to bear.

My only consolation was that Coach had returned to inspect other boys and wasn't towering over me. Undoubtedly, he'd be back soon, so I let that anticipation motivate me to move. Quick as a flash, I undressed, rinsed so my hair was wet enough to be convincing, redressed, and fled the scene.

* * *

"Where are you, God?"

"Why don't you make any difference in my life?"

"Why aren't you helping me?

Do I even matter to you?"

"Why did you make me like this?"

"What even am I?"

As a boy, I internalized all these thoughts and questions but didn't dream of discussing them with anyone. Who would I ask? There was nobody. How could that even be? Why was a little kid dealing with this shit alone when he was supposed to live in a Christian home?

I have no doubt my struggles were obvious. Anyone with one eyeball and two brain cells to rub together could see I was treading a sea of issues. With no one to talk to and no help, my only resource was anger. Anger became my superpower, and I wore it like armor. Not only did it shield me from the hurt, but it also seeped into my bones like poisonous vitality. It strengthened me and let me detach from the pain, and I grew to rely on it more and more each day.

One year, right before Halloween, when I was probably eleven or twelve, I stumbled on an old black taffeta dress in my mother's closet. I don't quite recall what I was doing there, but possibly I was searching for costume ideas. I pondered over that dress, thinking it looked just like the one worn by the Wicked Witch of the West in *The Wizard of Oz*.

And that was enough to spark my interest and curiosity. I made a black pointed hat from construction paper or something and donned that dress and hat throughout our neighborhood for trick-or-treating. Believe it or not, my parents let me stay in full witch costume for a Halloween party at our church for two years.

As harmless as that may seem and understandable in the spirit of the season, the truth is that dress became more than just a costume for me. On the rare occasion that no one else was home, I'd pull out that dress from my mom's closet and put it on, looking at my reflection in the mirror fastened to the back of the bedroom door. Each time, I was surprised at how intensely I enjoyed the sensation of being someone else. That had been my wish for years – to be someone else. Empowered with a new identity, I pretended to be a powerful witch. Fantasy became my escape, and, as a teen, I spent more and more time lost in my imagination.

Once, during one of my "dress rehearsals," one of my aunts visited my mother. It was nearing Halloween again, and I had the bedroom door closed but not locked. All at once, my aunt spoke to me from the other side of my door, and the knob began to turn. Horrified, I glanced down at the black dress. I couldn't possibly get it off before the door opened. I leaped in front of my door and pushed my body against it.

"I'll be right out," I called, feigning casual indifference.

But it wasn't enough. My aunt turned the knob and pushed from the other side.

I stood firm.

And so it went, this battle of the door, with both of us pushing against it with all our might.

Anger seeped from my pores like sweat. Why wouldn't she just leave me alone? My mother must have suspected what I was doing and made a thing about it with my aunt. Why else would she be invading my privacy? Intent to shame me, no doubt.

When my strength waned and I was forced to surrender the door, my aunt flung it open and barreled her way in.

There was nothing left to do and certainly nothing to say. I fell flat on my bed and buried my red face in the comforter, bracing myself for whatever abuse was on the menu.

"Oh, what a cute little girl," my aunt crooned. "What's your name, little girl? Is it Sally?"

On and on she went, humiliating, shaming, and harassing me until she eventually ran out of things to say. It felt like an eternity as I lay still and silent, like a corpse on the bed, counting in my head the seconds that passed as a means of some distraction. Eventually, she left the room, returning to wherever my mother was.

I quickly shut the door and pulled off the dress, mortified on many levels. Perhaps the biggest reason was my aunt's inability to be discreet. This was the aunt you shared with only when you wanted the news to travel at the speed of light. Family reunions would feel even weirder than usual after this.

I put that dress away for good that year after Halloween. No, it wasn't entirely because of my aunt's shame fest. I think I knew that it was getting a grip on me. I liked the feeling of pretending to be a woman, a witch. I liked it too much. The dress made it all seem more real – easier to be in the role. I don't know what eventually happened to the dress, but it remained in my memory as a symbol of power, both mystical and magical, and I'm sure that also played a role in why I was drawn to it.

The dress and associated fantasy also represented the start of a long period in my life when I deeply wrestled with who I was. On the one hand, I knew I was a boy, but because of my lack of acceptance in the world of boys and men, I didn't feel like a real boy. The fact that I was sexually and romantically drawn toward men rather than women only added more evidence against me being a real boy. But on the other hand, I knew I wasn't a girl either. So, this left me in a complicated place of belonging or lack thereof. Fitting in nowhere left me feeling like a neutered, genderless thing – some third, broken category I couldn't explain and could find no explanation for. Wearing that dress helped me feel more connected with some gender, and for a growing kid longing for identity, it empowered me.

There is no doubt that if I were growing up today, in our present environment, I would not only experience same-sex attraction, but I'd deal with gender dysphoria and transgenderism, too. Thank God there was no language or popularized confusion masquerading as science back then. During that vulnerable time in my life, consumed with my self-hatred, anxiety, and desire to escape at nearly any cost, I would have been swallowed up by all the false promises and lies disguised as diversity and inclusion today in almost every corner of society.

* * *

I didn't understand it then, but as I look back over my childhood years into my thirties, I developed a severe and problematic pattern. I dealt with my issues and the inevitable hard times of life by avoiding them in any way possible. Rather than digging in to face problems, to learn and grow from them, and to earn the resilience that comes as a result, I found a way to escape every chance I got.

Often, escape came in the form of fantasy—books, clothing, role-playing games, and the constant hunt for pornography, resulting in chronic masturbation.

Other times, I would make sudden, sweeping changes in my life, a pattern that may have started when my parents pulled me and two other siblings out of the local public school. In fourth grade, I was enrolled at a Christian school in a town nearby. Before that change in schools, I listened from the kitchen as Dad and Mom were around the corner in the living room, quietly discussing the possibility – the pros and cons of such a move. Even back then, they were concerned about how the public school influenced and affected their children with an anti-Christian viewpoint.

I could hardly believe that I might escape the school I was in and all that went along with it. But the decision was made, and the day came when we showed up for our first day at the Christian Academy. Unfortunately, we still had to ride the bus to the public school and then wait in a room for another smaller bus to pick us and a few other kids up for our trip to the new school. But at least I was done with gym class, the coach, and the all too familiar bullies who seemed to roam the halls of the public school constantly.

My first day at the Christian school was a hopeful one. Being around Christian students, being taught by Christian men and women dedicating their lives to the education of boys and girls... it all sounded like a dream come true. Maybe God had heard my prayers. Maybe He was coming to my rescue!

The school was in the basement of a Baptist church, which doubled as open-space Sunday school rooms every weekend. The basement transformed into a room filled with brightly colored slide-out dividers – one divider between each student's tiny desk - Monday through Friday. The long room was painted a bright white and lit by rows of fluorescent ceiling lights. The dividers were alternately painted red and blue – an intentionally patriotic theme.

I quickly learned there was very little instruction given. For each subject, students were expected to read the history, story, examples, or instructions written in their workbook and answer the questions or respond. If we had questions or needed help, we would put a little American flag or Christian flag (depending on what we needed) in a hole drilled into the top of our divider. When a monitor was free, they would come to our desk to see what was required.

After reading through a section of the workbook and answering the questions, the student got up, went to the table in the middle of the room with the answer key, and checked their answers. For a kid who had never read an entire book up to that point and struggled with basic reading and comprehension skills, this was an incredibly frustrating way of learning, but I felt like I had to fumble my way through. I quickly became aware I was falling behind the other kids my age. So, in trying to improve my performance, I started using the answer key as a way to not only check my guesses (few of my responses were real answers) but also to see the correct answer to as many unanswered questions that were still ahead. This way, I didn't have to read entire sections. Of course, I wasn't learning anything, just guessing and cheating to get the answers.

I quickly ran into problems with the adults running the show. They assumed I was a problem child who refused to complete his homework and constantly lacked focus. In a word – obstinate. No one bothered to ask or figure out what was happening to me. Instead, the mantra "delayed obedience is disobedience" was a constant refrain I grew to hate, as the statement was often directed at me.

Most of my interactions were with women who helped out at the school – they were called monitors. Several men were also involved in the school's leadership – the church pastor, principal, and school supervisor. I would have given anything for one of these men to recognize that I was struggling and needed a father figure or masculine guide. I needed a well-grounded man to offer more than Scripture verses to highlight my shortcomings and failures. I needed coaching and mentoring – someone to show interest in me as a boy –someone who viewed me as worth pouring into. Instead, I was constantly running afoul of the rules and order.

Entering puberty at the Christian school only increased my sense of shame and self-hatred. It seemed that nothing in life could lift my spirits for long. When I discovered masturbation (though I didn't know what it was called), this became a frequent means of self-comfort and escape. I put up my American flag several times a day to request to use the bathroom – taking longer than expected for a boy simply emptying his bladder.

During these years, constant sexual thoughts, the frequent hunt for and use of porn, and masturbation to cope with negative emotions and emptiness only multiplied and intensified my shame. I recall doing chores outside in June, July, and August, even pushing our old hand mower around our lumpy yard to cut the grass and weeds for hours in the summer heat and humidity while wearing long pants and multiple baggy shirts. Mom and Dad couldn't understand what I was doing. They constantly told me to wear shorts and a T-shirt, but even with sweat pouring down my face and body, I refused to wear less clothing.

I didn't realize until decades later, during an inner-healing prayer time, that I was attempting to cover my shame. I now know that using clothes or excess body weight can often be an unconscious avenue of self-protection and hiding. We may be trying to prevent further abuse, especially sexual abuse, or an attempt to wall off people from getting too close – either to hurt us or to see us for the disgusting person we feel we are. The latter was true for me.

* * *

School, school, school. Have I mentioned how much I hated school? I hated it with every fiber of my being, in every possible way. Not one particular school but the whole experience of it. I was terrible at sports, as well as schoolwork. I didn't excel at *anything*. That is anything except shame and fear. I lived my life afraid all the time. I was painfully self-conscious and brimming with self-hatred. That kind of unhealthy existence stunts a child's social interaction and growth.

It wasn't until I returned to college as an adult that I discovered the joy of learning. I even received affirmations from professors- that was a new experience. One professor in particular once complimented me on a writing assignment. I remember thinking, "You've got to be kidding me. I'm doing something well that's worth commenting on?"

Later, after preparing and delivering a speech in his class, he caught me afterward and asked if I had ever considered teaching.

"You've got a gift of communication," he said.

I knew he was talking to me, but I was still half-tempted to look behind me, just to be sure. Those words of encouragement made me want to work more diligently, especially in *his* class. They sparked an even deeper enjoyment of learning. Perhaps there was more to me after all.

After winning more of these simple and intentional affirmations, I couldn't help but think back on my grade-school experiences, both public and private. Would it have been so hard back then for teachers to impact my life positively? To look at me and see something worth investing in or someone they could offer a word of encouragement to—especially at the Christian school?

It was much smaller than a public school, maybe around eighty students, and I liked that difference quite a bit. It wasn't all that bad to start with. There was a regular chapel service, and I was moved early to raise my hand and accept Jesus as my Savior. It wasn't the first time I prayed the sinner's prayer, but every time

I said the words, they came out hollow. By then, porn and masturbation had become my primary form of coping and self-medication. Deep down, I knew it was wrong, and I hated myself after giving in repeatedly, but I couldn't stop. Each time I failed to resist the temptation, I became disgusted and frustrated with myself– which was often. My self-inflicted punishment was biting the back of my hand as hard as I could. Sometimes, my hand would bleed or turn black and blue along my teeth marks. But no one ever seemed to notice it. Cutting wasn't a thing back then. If it had been, there's no doubt I would have used that behavior to both punish myself and provide a relief valve for my internal frustration and self-hatred.

As a result of my easily distracted mind and impulsive behavior (I probably had undiagnosed ADHD back then), I was constantly getting into trouble. I'd receive demerits and accumulate many negative consequences for my infractions. It left me feeling like I could never succeed or improve. So why bother? I managed to frustrate nearly everyone without deliberately trying to be bad—this stagnated state of being often felt like an anchor, pulling me deeper and deeper into failure. Failure can suffocate, leaving us desperate for anything resembling oxygen, regardless of how tainted it may be.

So, my time at the Christian school became more frustrating than in public school. Maybe my expectations were too high. Undoubtedly, part of my negative recall of the school has nothing to do with the school. Instead, it was the harsh reality of all the unaddressed and unhealed areas of sexual and relational brokenness. Not to mention all the unanswered questions about who I was and if God loved me. It certainly didn't clarify any of my sexual confusion. These questions and many others were a constant din in my head. Add in the fact that my mind had been polluted with sexual thoughts, desires, and abuse since the age of five or six. It's no wonder I was completely lost. A young child cannot begin to process these internalized secret struggles effectively, and little did I know they were shaping my entire development.

It's possible that private schools could have turned out differently. Maybe it could've been an excellent experience. However, I again found myself at the bottom of the male pecking order. I was over being in that bottom-tier status, so I didn't bother trying to fit in with them. I made my place among several girls who adopted me into their clique. We hung out every day during lunch and breaks, and it was great in one sense because it felt a lot safer than having no one in public school. But it didn't help me grow as a young man. It wouldn't be until much later that I learned how vital being around other boys would be to my development. I needed to learn to navigate the rough waters of maleness—to forge a place among my gender and understand myself in their company. That doesn't happen for a young boy in the company of girls.

Thus, my early life patterns of staying with the girls continued. I marinated in the world of the feminine because it felt like my safety net and, on some level, it was more interesting. It fell in line with my search for belonging. Is it any wonder that I was experiencing same-sex attraction? Girls weren't a mystery to me at all. I was with them all the time – at home, church, school. It led me to over-identify with the feminine – taking on a type of false feminine rather than embracing and enjoying my God-given boy-ness. In crucial ways, I identified more with girls than my gender. Boys, on the other hand, were not only mysterious but unreachable. They frightened me and intrigued me at the same time. I held both a level of fascination and contempt for my sex.

This dichotomy was reinforced through various negative experiences. Not only with boys but even with Christian men. A particular example comes to mind. I was eleven then, and my current Sunday School teacher was Mrs. Peterson. She was the best I ever had. Not only was she kind, funny, and beautiful, but she acted as if she liked the kids in her class. One Sunday, Mrs. Peterson asked if I would like to join her and her family for an upcoming weekend at their camp on a nearby lake. I was so excited. Mrs. Peterson's daughter, Sarah, was a couple of years younger than me, but we got along great.

The problem was, as often happens in upstate New York, it rained most weekends. That weekend, we could barely get outside. Saturday afternoon, we were visited by a particularly torrential downpour. Mr. Peterson had gone to town, and Mrs. Petersen was taking a nap, so it was just Sarah and me in the family room of the small lake cottage. Sarah happened to be learning how to crochet but was still pretty new to it.

Little did she know I'd become proficient at crocheting. Over the years, my aunt would visit when I became ill and teach me how to use hooks and yarn. I learned how to make everything from potholders to blankets. So, when Sarah struggled with the crochet needle, I showed her a thing or two, and we crocheted together.

Mr. Peterson walked in the door about that time, shaking off the rain, and glanced at me. I thought he might be grateful I was helping her. Instead, his face contorted into a sneer of contempt.

"What are you doing?" he bellowed at me, obviously shocked that a boy would touch a crochet needle and yarn, much less give a girl some assistance.

I pushed the yarn and crochet needle into Sarah's hands while her mouth hung open.

"You've got to be kidding me!" he spat, yanking off his wet boots. "What's wrong with you? Are you a boy?"

He was so loud and persistent that he woke up his wife. She opened and stepped through the bedroom door. Quickly, she attempted to redirect her angry husband with questions about the store. It took several attempts, but she distracted him until he stomped off into the bedroom for a hot shower.

I was shell-shocked, just sitting there. I didn't understand the tirade from my Sunday School teacher's husband. I didn't know what to do. Mrs. Peterson busied herself in the kitchen, humming an old worship song as if nothing had happened. I couldn't wait for the weekend to be over.

I'd buried the event down deep by the time my parents picked me up that Sunday evening. They could tell something was wrong with me, but I shut down and refused to say more than a word or two. It wouldn't matter anyway, so why bother?

Same-Sex Attraction

Over the years of walking out a journey of healing with God and the last couple of decades of ministry to others, I am convinced that a common cornerstone of same-sex attraction is when admiration for others of the same sex morphs into envy. This kind of envy occurs by comparing ourselves to others and coming up short (often coupled with self-hatred). Envy often becomes sexualized (especially in our current sex-saturated culture) through fantasy, masturbation, or sexual experimentation with someone we envy. Once envy becomes sexualized, any time we compare ourselves to someone of our gender and feel deficient, it can trigger sexual desire and temptation. This attraction can become solidified to the point of feeling innate and immutable. This is why, for so many people, it feels authentic and makes complete sense to believe the *born that way* explanation.

Beginning around puberty, while at the Christian school, I secretly idolized and envied several older boys. Meanwhile, self-hatred was a constant, gnawing companion. Typically, envy is triggered by something we perceive we don't have or don't have enough of. It could be another guy's muscular body, athleticism, how they carry themselves and exude confidence, or how others gravitate toward them. For women experiencing same-sex attraction, envy can be connected to another woman's appearance, her perceived strength, career, or business success - or even the envy of greater security and safety that men possess - resulting in a desire and pursuit of becoming masculine. But I believe, generally speaking, sexualized envy is a much more common driver for men than women.

After a few years, I begged my parents to put me back in public school. The fact that the Christian school cost a lot of money and we were struggling financially became the deciding factor. Not knowing what else to do with me, my Dad and Mom agreed. The next day at the private school, I told one of the leaders I wouldn't be returning, and he insisted I talk to the principal about it.

Upstairs, in the principal's office, I was motioned to sit in a chair across the desk from him. He sat in his office chair, looking at me, resting his elbows on the desk. Both hands joined together as each finger on his left hand touched the tip of his fingers on his right hand, just under his chin and stern face. I once again took notice of his well-manicured, unusually long fingernails for a guy – that was an oddity that I often noticed with him. He was dismayed at what he had already been informed of: my decision to leave the school.

Finally, he broke the silence. "Will you pray with me about this decision?"

"No," I said. "My mind's made up. I'm leaving."

He peered at me with a frown and handed me his Bible. "Turn to Psalm 66:18 and read it out loud."

I obeyed. "If I regard wickedness in my heart, the Lord will not hear."

The principal used this verse to explain why I wouldn't pray—I had sin in my heart. Well, that was a duh moment for me – of course, I had sin in my heart. I had sin *everywhere*. I wish I could have told him how being at his so-called Christian school had done nothing to improve the sin in my life or my heart. I wanted to tell him how being there only made me feel beaten up and weighed down. I wish I asked him where his God was when I needed Him most and why He hadn't cleansed me of my dirtiness.

But I didn't. I couldn't. I just bottled up everything I was feeling and sat there. A moment later, I left in silence. It was the last time I'd seen this man, but it wouldn't be our last communication—more on that later in Chapter Fifteen.

The Value of Peer Bonding

Peer relationships allow children to practice and develop social skills such as communication, cooperation, and empathy. For example, children with positive relationships with their peers are more likely to engage in prosocial behaviors, such as sharing and helping others.

Several factors can influence the development of positive peer relationships, including a child's social skills, personality, and experiences. Children who are more extroverted and have strong social skills are more likely to have positive peer relationships2. Similarly, children with positive experiences with peers are more likely to have positive peer relationships in the future3.

Unfortunately, as you've already read, my childhood is not one filled with experiences and stories that highlight the value of peer bonding. Instead, mine is the opposite. The adverse effects of that lack in my life were abundantly clear. But my story didn't end there. God has been faithful in bringing me back to some of those core needs at the right time, through the right circumstances, to fill the gaps in my heart and soul. Through whole-enough connections with godly brothers later in life, He restored what had been broken and undeveloped in me. I'll share more about how that happened later.

Still, the way God has naturally wired us for maternal love, paternal love, and meaningful connection with friends are all part of our ideal healthy development throughout childhood. As we've seen to be true of both the mother/child and father/child relationship, the peer stage of development is part of the very basis of what God designed us for. We need a healthy community. He designed us for relationships. Our sphere of connection expands beyond mom, dad, and siblings into the lives of other young people our general age, preparing us for greater individuation and finding and navigating friendships in adulthood.

Positive peer relationships are one thing, but the pendulum can also swing in an unhealthy direction - what happens when a child succumbs to peer pressure? It can result in negative experiences that have lasting effects into and even throughout adulthood. Peer pressure can lead children to engage in substance use, sex, extreme risk-taking, or violence. When peer pressure is so severe that it turns into bullying, children who become victims perceive peer relationships as negative experiences – and this is exactly how I processed and perceived them. This social deficiency fosters lower self-esteem and increased risk for mental health problems.

As you have read about me living through this third stage of development, I fell into the negative category. My severe lack in these core stages of development—the way God wired us and intended for us to form healthy relationships—had a detrimental effect on me and my growth, both naturally and spiritually. As a Church, it also means we have some extra work to do in reaching, properly educating, and walking with our young people regarding God and His body.

I was so unformed throughout my twenties and well into my thirties. Outwardly, I was a man with all the working equipment, but inwardly, I remained a lost little boy. I was a husk of a man. I needed older brothers and godly spiritual fathers to help find, activate, and stir up the true masculinity in me and show me that it was good. I needed what every boy, and many men today, still need – the company of godly men to impart what John Eldredge describes as "an essence - something like food" through their presence, time, vulnerability, love, and correction.

With all this chapter has pointed out about necessary peer bonding, it behooves parents, educators, and other adult caregivers to find creative and varied opportunities for children to interact with their peers positively. One size does not fit all. Each child will be different. But by encouraging positive social behaviors and addressing negative peer experiences, we instill a sense of community and belonging for our children.

Fatherly Guidance

My boys and I have regular conversations and check-ins about how their hearts are doing. This includes discussions about whether they struggle with faith in Him, etc..... Also, gentle, non-shaming questions about how they are handling their curiosity, sexual thoughts, porn, and masturbation. Some of these questions need to be asked at age-appropriate levels. But it's never too early to help your kids become comfortable by asking loving questions for the sake of shepherding their hearts.

I highly recommend that parents open up this line of communication with their sons and daughters. One of the things I've reminded my boys over the past several years is that sex is designed and blessed by God. Sex is His wonderful idea. When experienced within the boundaries He created it for, sex is an amazing and beautiful gift – a gift through which a husband and wife bond together even more deeply, not to mention how new life is created.

I let my boys know very bluntly that they will be curious about sex, and at some point, they will find themselves incredibly curious about scantily clothed or naked bodies. For example, I warn them that when a friend tries to show them porn on his phone, I caution them not to give in to their curiosity because they can never unsee it afterward. And to let me know if a friend tries to show them such things. This caution has already been tested, and my boys didn't take the bait – but in our sex-saturated culture, opportunities for lust and sexual sin abound.

We don't keep our kids in a bubble. We want them to be prepared for real adult life, but because of what happened to me, I also know the value of preserving and enjoying innocence for as long as possible.

I have made a point to share different aspects of my own story with them and my struggles – especially how God, in His mercy, brought me through my addictions and sin patterns in ways I once never thought possible. They must understand that we all face challenges and temptations, regardless of age. I want them to be prepared for what they are up against. I want them to understand the gravity of what it means to ignore God's design and the destruction that road leads to. The damage to our souls is not worth it. We may sin in isolation, but the effects of sin do not stay in isolation. We damage those closest to us through ripples of guilt and shame.

While Satan and his kingdom are always on the prowl, seeking someone to devour (I Peter 5:8), I believe, in his perverted evil, he craves to rob the innocence of children at the earliest possible ages.

That said, I'm amazed at the grace God has shown me. I'm forever grateful for how He woke me out of my stupor and gave me a fresh start – a new beginning. As Christ-followers, we have become new creations (Galatians 6:15, II Corinthians 5:17). With His strength and new life, I could experience this much-needed formation of peer bonding, even as a thirty-something man. While this process naturally and usually occurs between ages six and eleven, it's never too late to discover and enjoy it. God is not limited in His power and plans to rescue us from broken places. He offers healing for the various fractures of our hearts at any age. Melissa and I often say, among many other things, the Church is our second chance at family. We'll discuss that in more detail in Chapter Eleven.

Questions for Self-Reflection / Journaling / Group Sharing

1. What are some things that have prevented you from opening up about your painful peer experiences in childhood?

2. How can you overcome these obstacles and take the risk of sharing your story?

3. How can you support and encourage others struggling to share their experiences?

4. How can your past experiences help us learn to open up to others in our lives today?

5. Who are some people in your life that you trust and feel safe talking to about anything?

6. How can you identify safe and supportive people to share your stories with?

7. How can you create a safe and supportive environment for them to share their stories?

1 Smyth, T (2021) A Defensive Attachment Response Self-Perpetuates. *Psychology Today.*

2 Berdan, L. E., Keane, S. P., & Calkins, S. D. (2008). Temperament and externalizing behavior: Social preference and perceived acceptance as protective factors. *Developmental Psychology, 44*(4), 957–968.

3 Parker, J. G., & Asher, S. R. (1987). Peer relations and later personal adjustment: Are low-accepted children at risk? *Psychological Bulletin, 102*(3), 357–389.

Chapter 5

PUBERTY, ATTRACTION, & SEXUAL INTEREST – AGES 12-17

As much as I wanted out of the Christian school, bouncing back to public school resolved nothing. The education certainly wasn't better. I don't remember seeing any of my old bullies from several years before, but there were undoubtedly new ones. I must've still had the target on my forehead, though, because it didn't take long for them to find me.

I managed to venture outside my comfort zone by joining the swim team. My build wasn't suitable for the sport, but it was a far better option than football or basketball. Also, one of my brothers had been on the swim team a few years before, and there was an element of familiarity. Trying to branch out past myself, my parents, and my familiar isolated home environment somehow prompted me to take a risk and attempt something new.

Because our family never had extra money, my swimsuit was bought at a nearby Salvation Army thrift store. After scrounging, I found a halfway decent suit two sizes too large, which thankfully had a pull string that could be tightened.

On the first day of swim practice, my twelve-year-old scrawny body seemed delayed compared to other boys in the locker room. I hurriedly changed, still cringing at the thought of being seen naked. I tightened up that drawstring as best I could. The suit's excess material bunched up in the front like I was wearing my father's swim trunks. I felt as ridiculous as I looked. Chlorine assaulted my nose and sinuses until they stung. My bare feet slid and sloshed over the drenched tiles.

Everything about the moment was uncomfortable. But I was there, and I was determined to try.

Bolstering as much confidence as possible, I joined my team poolside. They gave me a once over, their gazes lingering on my oversized shorts. Giggles and whispers permeated the air. But I remained determined, folding my arms over my skinny chest and waiting for the coach's instructions (a different coach than the drill sergeant from former years.)

The whistle blew, quick and shrill, from the coach's mouth. The team came to order, ready to warm up with laps. We formed lane lines, and after the first two lineups dove into the water and swam their lap, it was my lineup's turn. Alongside several other boys, I swung my arms anxiously at my sides. I was okay with swimming, but diving? That was another story. I'd never been good at form. Rather than jumping off and stretching long and thin into the water, my arms and legs tended to flail about and curve into my body like a pretzel. Would this time be any different? Could I resist the urge to crumple when it was my turn to dive in front of other boys I already felt anxious around?

But I was determined. Besides, these weren't just other boys anymore. They were my team! Teammates stuck together and encouraged each other, right? I stared down at the pool's surface, now choppy from all the activity, and assumed the diving position. In my mind, I believed I could make it work...

FLOP.

My body hit the water in an awkward splash that pierced my skin. More a fall than a dive. As if that wasn't humiliating enough, the force of the water pushed my swim shorts down to my ankles, and all the boys along the pool edge had a front-row seat for the spectacle.

Naked in front of them again. I couldn't catch a break. Water flooded my nostrils and thankfully hid my tears as I snatched my shorts back into place before rising to the surface for air.

I emerged to find my teammates doubled-over in stitches, pointing and calling out to make sure everyone in the vicinity knew what happened. There were no girls around, and typically, most boys couldn't care less about being naked in the boys' locker room, but they made a big deal about this. About me. They didn't have to sense my discomfort; it was apparent, and they pointed it out. My earlier determination evaporated, along with whatever confidence I'd strung together to show up with, and I groaned.

Coach frowned sympathetically and told me to change. I bolted for the locker room, dressed, and never returned.

Now, you may be thinking, "What's the big deal? So, you were embarrassed, Garry. Everyone experiences embarrassing moments as kids and adults."

And that's true. However, for me (and others going through similar crises), my struggles were too daunting for what I was equipped to handle, and these feelings of *othering* from the boys and men around me stacked up over time and pushed me to the edge. They ungrounded me. I had no idea where my place was. Even though my home and family were familiar, I didn't feel like I fit in or belonged anywhere. That feeling radically changed when I was nineteen. I will share more about that in Chapter Nine.

Thank God, today, I can laugh at those awkward memories. I burst out several times as I wrote this. But it sure wasn't funny at the time. It was emotionally crippling. Maturity and healing get us through what feels like impossible circumstances. Kids need to know it gets better, and it's up to adults to ensure they know this. There is no better way to help children understand that life is bearable and seemingly insurmountable difficulties and temptations can be overcome than by sharing what God has brought you through – how He rescued your life (age-appropriate content, of course). This helps provide a foundation to build a godly life. To learn from Jesus and accept healing from our Heavenly Father.

I'm reminded of a concept I heard many years ago that said something like this ... "Because Satan knows our history and our particular wounds and vulnerabilities, he delights in tempting people around us (those we know well and even total strangers) to deliver another blow or poison arrow to that painful, wounded place – essentially tempting people to do what has always been done to the struggling one – reinforcing the lie, the accusation, the sense of worthlessness – whatever the thing is that's deeply wounded within."

Sometimes, it isn't always the situation that's so bad (like my swimming experience). The repetition of the same theme/s reinforces a larger and profoundly negative narrative, often over the years. You can learn a lot by observing and considering the behavior of various creatures God created.

When I was a young boy, we had several different farm animals. Chickens were a favorite – both for their eggs as well as meat. But as a little boy, one thing I learned about chickens surprised and horrified me. On the rare occasions that one of them was wounded in some small way (usually flying or running into something sharp

– a piece of wire sticking out of a fence or coupe, etc.), invariably, one of their tribe would notice it – a speck of blood, or broken skin under their feathers. That one would start pecking at the small, insignificant wound, and it wouldn't stop. The wounded chicken would often run into a corner trying to protect itself. The other chicken would make a specific excited clucking sound that hurriedly attracted the rest of the chickens. If we didn't catch what was going on soon enough, the flock would peck the one chicken to death.

Similarly, Satan loves to do this to people, especially children. To alert others to weakness or vulnerability and then tempt others to peck at the wound until it becomes bigger, more painful, infected, much more severe, even life-threatening. But with people, an attack usually targets and crushes the inner person. We often don't notice an emotional wound, so it's assumed that everything is okay when, inwardly, nothing is okay.

The idea applies perfectly to my foray into swimming. As part of my decision to return to public school, I took a risk and joined a team sport that had only previously offered bad experiences. But I did it anyway, hoping a new experience could be different and help me connect with other boys better and healthily. This was an excellent thing that I was attempting to do. Still, without an awareness of how much the enemy of my soul wanted to shame and discourage me back into my hole of isolation, I had no determination or courage to persevere through the first challenging experience. That sound and needed lesson would be learned later in life when I was no longer dominated by fear, shame, and anger.

When we stick our neck out to try a scary thing again, only to get the same negative results as in the past, a message is reinforced: *You idiot, don't ever do that again! This is what happens when you take a risk or try something new.*

Those words were going through my head—my inner voice scolding me for trying. Reinforced negative experiences can be powerful when we listen to and agree with them.

Proverbs 13:12 *Hope deferred makes the heart sick, but desire fulfilled is a tree of life.*

Both physical and psychological bullying had been regular experiences in my first round of public school, from kindergarten through third grade, and I was constantly afraid of it every day. It was rare that anyone used a backpack or a bag to carry books from class to class. As a relatively small and scrawny kid, I had difficulty carrying my textbooks like the other boys did – with my hand looped under the stack, held low at my side, pressed against my left hip. Instead, I could carry them more easily in my arm, with the books held against my chest rather than at my waist, but that's the way girls carried them. When walking the hallways from class to class, other boys frequently mocked me for holding my books like a girl. Embarrassed and ashamed, I practiced at home - carrying them the *right* way. The books were much more unsteady in my hand at my side, but I was determined to make it work.

With their entourage of two or three other dutiful followers, young tyrants often looked for their favorite kid(s) (easy targets) to torment on the bus, the locker room, the lunch room, and the hallway between classes. I was always braced for name-calling, mocking, getting shoved, tripped, and knocked down on the floor. As I started carrying my books *like a boy*, they were already unsteady in my grip. Among the din of kids in the halls on the way to class, familiar troublemakers would sneak up behind me. They'd kick the bundle of books at my side so they scattered. Laughter and name-calling ensued.

Then, of course, there was the matter of the combination lock on my assigned hallway locker. I don't know if you, my reader, had struggles with this crazy thing, but over and over again, I was shown how to open the lock, but it always took several attempts to get it right... no matter how long I used the same locker. One kid, in particular, harassed me mercilessly while I attempted to open my locker. There were days he was waiting for me – leaning against the far wall across from my locker, before or after school. The ridicule and physical bullying were paralyzing to me – paralyzing on the outside, but rage built on the inside.

Finally, after weeks and months of this, he picked the wrong day to mess with the wimp. He came up behind me as usual. I turned and exploded in anger, shoved him back, and shouted a tirade of frustration. The bustle of kids transferring to other rooms paused, aware of the commotion. Not seeing anything all that exciting, they resumed their migration. I approached him with my fists clenched, ready to let one fly.

He tripped and fell over his own feet while backing away from me. Lying on the floor, he thrust his hands out and yelled, "What the f***! You don't have to get so mad!"

Then he took off.

At that moment, I realized, in a way I had never understood before, he was a weakling and coward. I never had trouble with this guy again. I wish I could say the same for others. Although I had a big win with this guy, I still lived in fear of others.

For me, returning to public school in the seventh grade was just another kick-the-can-down-the-road avoidance of pain and discomfort. My grades were terrible. I traded homework and studying for nature walks and fishing whenever I could get away with it. Sadly, I'd hidden pages of porn in all my favorite haunts like little idols scattered over the countryside. Every chance I got, I'd steal away from home to make my ritualistic pilgrimage to one or more of these locales to pour over my stash. Addicts always feel more secure when they have an extra stash or two in multiple places.

* * *

In his book *Attachment and Loss (1980)*1, Bowlby discusses the importance of attachment for adolescent development, asserting that despite what many have believed, the need for attachment does not diminish in adolescence but becomes more complex. He proposes that adolescents undergo a process of detachment from their parents, in which they begin to separate from their parents emotionally and physically to form their identities. However, he also argues that this process of detachment does not mean that adolescents no longer need or value attachment to their parents. Instead, he believes that adolescents continue to need attachment to their parents, but in a different form than they did in childhood.

According to Bowlby, youth are in a period of transition and turmoil during adolescence as they try to balance their desire for autonomy and their need for attachment. Adolescents must develop a sense of self-identity and independence while maintaining attachment to their parents and other significant adults. This can be a real challenge!

Some of the specific challenges boys and girls in this age range may face include:

•Puberty: This can be a difficult time for youth as they experience some physical changes that can be uncomfortable or difficult to understand. Hormonal changes can also cause mood swings, acne, and other challenges.

•Social pressure: As youth enter their teenage years, they may feel pressure to conform to societal expectations and fit in with their peers. This can be incredibly challenging for youth who think they do not fit in or struggle to understand their identities.

•Mental health: Studies have shown that youth aged 12-17 have a higher risk of developing mental health issues such as depression, anxiety, and eating disorders. They may also be at risk for substance abuse and self-harm behaviors.

•School and academic pressure: As youth move through their teenage years, they may feel pressure to excel academically and to prepare for college and the workforce. This can be challenging for youth who struggle with learning or are uncertain about their plans.

•Family dynamics: Family dynamics can also be challenging for youth in this age range as they navigate growing independence and autonomy while dealing with conflicts or changes within their families.

•Technology and social media: The rise of technology and social media can also present challenges for youth in this age range. They may struggle with cyberbullying, sexting, and the pressure to present a perfect image online.

Specific to boys between 12-17

•Physical development: Boys in this age range will continue to experience physical changes such as height and muscle mass growth and the development of secondary sex characteristics such as facial hair and a deeper voice. Boys may also experience an increase in the production of hormones such as testosterone, which can affect their behavior and emotions.

•Cognitive development: Boys in this age range will continue to develop their cognitive abilities, such as memory, problem-solving, and abstract thinking. They may also develop a more complex understanding of the world around them and become more interested in exploring and understanding abstract concepts.

•Social-emotional development: Boys in this age range may begin to experience a broader range of emotions and struggle with anxiety, depression, and loneliness. They may also form stronger relationships with their peers and become more interested in romantic relationships. Some boys may also begin to explore and question their identity.

•Behavioral development: Boys in this age range may begin to take more risks and engage in more risk-taking behaviors such as substance use and risky sexual behaviors. They may also become more independent and may begin to assert their autonomy. Boys may also develop a greater sense of morality and become more interested in social and political issues.

Specific to girls between 12-17

•Mental Health: Studies show that girls in this age range have higher rates of depression and anxiety. One study found that girls are more likely than boys to internalize symptoms such as depression and anxiety2.

•Body Image: Studies show that girls in this age range are more likely to be dissatisfied with their bodies and engage in disordered eating behaviors3.

•Attraction: Romantic and sexual attraction typically develops during early adolescence, and several factors, including genetics, environment, and socialization, can influence it.

* * *

Never having lived anywhere but Upstate NY, I took the lovely area for granted. I was born into a farming, gardening, hunting, fishing, and even trapping family, so outdoor activities and animals were part of everyday life. We lived off the land for the most part—between the deer and fish we brought home, our vast vegetable garden, and our chickens and barnyard animals. Knowing how to preserve food by canning and freezing ensured we had food over the cold winters until we could plant in the spring and harvest again during summer and fall. Ironically, my mom was the most patient and quiet hunter – she usually shot a deer yearly – whether the guys did or not.

The older I grew, the more I appreciated the legacy and knowledge my parents passed on to us. Because of them, I know I can provide for myself and my family in various ways that many people do not know today. Upstate New York was the only home I knew – lush and green in the summer, often brutal in the winter. I knew nothing else than that way of life. But I also felt alone in this vast, open, beautiful landscape. Loneliness gnawed at me all the time. I longed for a friend. But the only kids in the neighborhood who were close to my age were ones I wasn't allowed to be around (nor did I want to), and older ones involved in weekend drug and drinking parties – and I didn't want anything to do with them. This is about the time I met Victor.

I was probably thirteen, and Vic was a couple of years older. He and his parents moved down the road from us and started coming to our church. We would see each other outside in the neighborhood, and one day, he asked me to play catch with him. Before long, we were riding bikes together. We caught fireflies after sunset and played hide-and-seek in the dark until my mom or his would call us in for bed. He was different from the other boys. Before long, Vic and I were hanging out regularly at his place or mine after school.

Together, we found countless places to hike, bike, and explore around the farmlands and forests surrounding our homes. It was a boy's paradise in many ways, but had become dull and meaningless. However, with a new friend, these familiar places became fresh possibilities for play and exploration.

Victor and I spent several days a week hanging out together. It's difficult to describe the feeling of having a friend of my own gender. I had friends who were girls at school and church, and I was grateful for them. But a boy also needs his own kind to play with and be around. A boy comes to know himself and who he is better when in a relationship with other boys. Finally, I had a friend who was a boy in my neighborhood. I was experiencing the feeling of being liked and laughed with (instead of at) by another boy.

Until I started homeschooling, Vic and I went to the same public school, but we rarely saw each other there because he was two years older. Unlike me, as a natural athlete, he liked playing scholastic sports and stayed after a day of classes for practice and games. Because of that, feelings of inferiority plagued me. It was so effortless for Victor to be a boy and do boyish things, as it was for most boys. Why was it so hard for me?

I began playing the comparison game again, losing to Victor on all counts. What had started as a fun and easy friendship now grew complicated. But it wasn't because of him. It was me. When Victor made a new friend or talked about friends at school or on a sports team, my jaw would clench with jealousy. I didn't understand what it was at the time. I just knew whatever I was feeling felt miserable. I couldn't figure out why he needed other friends when he had me. Of course, today, I see the apparent unhealthiness and control involved in these assumptions and inner wrestlings, but I was blind to it then.

I was too naïve to realize how far the pendulum of my heart had swung. Over the years, I'd somehow prevented myself from relating to boys and men in a way that initiated an internal construction of self-protection and guardedness – a starvation diet, emotionally. Peering through the lens of Attachment Theory, I can now see that I had been operating out of an Avoidant Attachment at that time. Not because I wanted it, but rather as a means of avoiding the pain associated with many past occurrences – rejection, abuse, shame, etc.

Concerning Victor, the sharp pangs of jealousy and envy superseded the dull ache of loneliness. These strong, painful emotions festered inside me, and I hated it. Without my understanding or consent (in the language of Attachment Styles), the pendulum of my heart managed to dislodge itself from its well-secured place of independence and self-protection as used in Avoidant Attachment. From there, it swung right past Secure Attachment (healthy) to Ambivalent Attachment (the emotionally needy, don't-leave-me relationship style).

My heart, which had been starving for love and relationship for a long time, was now firmly unbudgingly in the camp of the Ambivalent Attachment. It was too late to wish it back to its old, familiar, self-protective hiding spot. Nor could I disconnect myself from this place of overwhelming emotion. So, what was I supposed to do now?

With no one to open up to, I sucked it up, stuffed it down, and muddled my way through. I continued my dependency on porn, fantasy, and masturbation to check out and escape... even for moments. No Man's Land on my own, as usual.

Envy is a strange and powerful emotion. It can seductively and quietly arouse such personal negativity and desire for what we do not have or *perceive* we do not have that we let all logic slip away. In this unexplored emotional territory, my envy soon turned into sexual attraction toward Victor. Vic and I would briefly talk or joke about sexual topics. On a particular day, we snuck into a neighbor's garage. He was eager to show me something he'd discovered by chance earlier that week.

Since the side door was unlocked, we snuck in and found the calendar of naked ladies on the garage wall. Victor snatched it, stowed it under his shirt, and we beelined for the woods. We pored over it with fascination, as any teenage boy would do – dry-mouthed and hearts pounding.

Typical in many ways, but certainly not innocent. Something happened that day... something that tragically took our friendship in a dramatically different direction than the fun and trusting relationship it had been. It opened the floodgates, and most of what we discussed after that experience was sex. We made up sexual stories to tell each other, eventually leading to masturbation. Teenage hormones marinating in stolen porn and sexual curiosity ripened to the point of greater sexual exploration with each other. Boundaries were crossed. And with it came a whole lot of guilt and shame. With it came the reality that our friendship could never be the same as it was before. We'd stashed the calendar in the woods and found ourselves gravitating toward its hiding place repeatedly, sometimes alone, sometimes together. Of course, I had other hidden porn as well, and I showed all of it to Victor. *Returning like a dog to its vomit.* (II Peter 2:22).

Victor and I were horrified at the thought of our families ever finding out about what we were doing. We vowed never to say anything to anyone. Sometimes, we managed to skate around our sexual sin and spend time together doing other things. But when we have willfully opened the door to lust and feed it often, it's a formidable foe to battle, and most times, we find ourselves fornicating again. This happened off and on for several years. For me, it strongly reinforced my same-sex attraction. For Victor, it was sexual release, but he remained attracted to the opposite sex.

* * *

I was only at the public school for maybe a year and a half. As mentioned, my aunt and uncle pioneered homeschooling in New York State. In the late 1970s, they almost lost their children due to pulling them from the public school system. My uncle had been a teacher at the school. My aunt was a nurse, and they had four children. They were concerned with the agenda they saw happening in public schools and didn't want their kids exposed to it five days a week.

Can you imagine? Public school must have been like Sunday school back then compared to today's environment and culture. Still, my aunt and uncle picked up on it and decided to homeschool their kids. They did the best research they could before the internet age, using library resources on homeschool curricula. But shortly after they pulled their kids out of school, the state sued them for custody and took them to court. It was a very tense case – impossible to predict the outcome. My uncle's attorney was unsure the judge would rule in their favor and was concerned that child protective services would take the children away from their loving and nurturing home.

Ultimately, the judge ruled in the family's favor, breaking open the possibility of homeschooling in New York. Many families reached out to my uncle and aunt and traveled long distances to get time with them, learning how to teach their children at home best. Back then, homeschool resources were scant compared to today's wide range of options.

Once, during a visit between our families, my uncle and aunt encouraged Mom and Dad to educate me at home – to try it at least and see if it didn't provide some improvement over what I'd been receiving. After some deliberation and prayer, my parents agreed. After seventh grade, I was done with public and private education. I began home education.

Our families became more intentional about visiting one another regularly to guide my education. They provided Mom with input and advice on what I should read and what curricula to work out of.

This was a massive relief for me because I no longer had to deal with the ridicule and bullying or my constant anxiety and fear of what would happen to me at school day after day. The downside? Yet another decision reinforced an unconscious pattern: when circumstances get hard, quit and move on to the next thing.

I often joke (sort of) that homeschooling comes in two different packages - excellent and rigorous homeschooling and lax and undisciplined homeschooling. Our boys and many family friends receive exceptional home education. I, on the other hand, got the fly-by-the-seat-of-your-pants version.

But to be fair, that's only kind of true. And it's mainly because I was so difficult to teach. But somehow (bless my mom!), we made it through. One of the tragedies of my past educational experience was that I had grown to despise books and the overall experience of learning. The truth is, I was barely reading anything. In my estimation, books were filled with word after word of boringness. I was woefully below where I should have been for reading skills and comprehension.

For this reason, I am incredibly thankful that I began homeschooling. My uncle lit a spark in me to see reading differently. He loved books and had shelves lining the living room walls in their old rustic house, especially classical literature.

He was wise in the way he introduced me to a new genre. He knew how to naturally draw me to the point that a book would completely captivate me. He introduced me to C.S. Lewis's writings: *The Chronicles of Narnia*, *The Great Divorce*, *Screwtape Letters*, *The Space Trilogy*, Tolkien's *The Hobbit*, *The Lord of The Rings*, and *The Silmarillion*. At the time, I was most naturally drawn toward fantasy, but my uncle also made sure I read some of the stories of faith and missions and a few books by Mark Twain. Both my reading and comprehension improved significantly in a relatively short period. Until then, the only book I had ever finished was *Charlotte's Web*. I know - ridiculous. But, during my public-school years, I was passed along from one grade to the next, regardless of competency.

With my uncle's encouragement, curiosity, and guidance, homeschooling became my most enjoyable educational experience out of the three, as well as the most effective and meaningful. I began homeschooling in eighth grade and continued through completion. I finished when I was just 16.

Around sixteen, I developed a massive admiration for an older cousin who was in his early twenties. He didn't treat me like a child. He talked with me meaningfully and listened to what I shared as if he valued my perspective. This felt very new to me. I loved whenever I could get time with him, which was too seldom. Looking back, I think life would have been very different if I'd had regular time with a man like this – an older brother or father figure who took a genuine interest in me, or if my dad had been a little bit like this when I was young.

My cousin introduced me to *Dungeons & Dragons*. He didn't play himself, but some of his other college friends were into it. This was the same period I learned I liked reading, especially fantasy. Having saved up money from a summer job, I found a place that sold the game and bought it. I was immediately captivated. My life felt aimless and meaningless to me. I felt stuck and desperately wanted to escape. I wanted to go somewhere, anywhere. Do something exciting. See other places. But we lived very meagerly on Dad's salary and couldn't afford much beyond necessities.

Along with pornography and a blooming sexual addiction, *Dungeons & Dragons* became another form of escape. I was also curious about and drawn toward sorcery and the occult. I always felt that my interest was not good, but I felt captivated by anything new that offered some escape. I set up an old tent in the summer weather under some trees just outside our yard, and this was my place to imagine and plan. Ironically, I couldn't find anyone to play the game with, so I was always the dungeon master, creating worlds and setting up the rules for how things worked. It didn't matter that this was meant to be a game for multiple players. I spent hours every day pouring over game ideas and worlds scribbled on graph paper, preferring to escape into a make-believe world rather than live in reality.

Meanwhile, our pastor invited my brother and me (enrolled in Bible school) to a two-day event – *Basic Youth Conflicts,* taught by Bill Gothard. At least we were in an event center with a couple of thousand people. As a kid from the simple life of farms and small country towns, I was mesmerized by the event's scope, the building's size, and the crowd. The teaching lasted for hours both days, but it was so good and more relatable to my struggles than general Sunday morning preaching. I was eager to scribble notes as fast as possible, taking in everything I could absorb and following along in my thick hardcover manual.

By the end of the second day, I thought I'd never be the same again. I felt as if I had been given many of the answers I had hoped to hear and understand for years. I felt as though I had been set at the trailhead of a new path – the right path and I just needed to stay on it. I remember not wanting the seminar to end. I wanted to keep learning and stay in this place of hope and a sense of being washed clean. I couldn't remember what it felt like not to feel dirty and shameful all the time. But I knew it now. I wanted to linger in it.

Some genuine and authentic things happened in my heart at this event. However, as I look back, I realize that much of what felt free to me was the sense that I held in my hand, in the workbook and my notes, the direction for a changed life. And some excellent principles were taught. At the time, I didn't understand that there were also a lot of legalisms and implied promises for those who work in this system and follow the formula that they'd walk with God's blessing and overcome sinful desires. In the years since then, there have been some scandals regarding the founder of the Institute of Basic Life Principles (IBLP), including women coming forward to claim sexual abuse, harassment, and coverup.

Sadly, some famous and stout Christian leaders from that era of my life have fallen from grace, some even embracing what is popularly referred to as *deconstruction* – abandoning their faith altogether.

Of course, I didn't know any of this while sitting in and learning from Bill Gothard. It was at this seminar when the thought of following in my brother's footsteps and joining him at Bible school first occurred to me.

More than anything, I just wanted to hold on to my clean and forgiven heart. The first chance I got, I found a payphone and called home. When Mom answered the phone, I asked her to get Dad on the line too. I asked them both to forgive me for how miserable and difficult I'd been the last few months. When Mom responded, she was tearful and relieved. My Dad was also moved. To their credit, my parents were always quick and gracious to forgive me. Relieved, my heart gradually began to soften. God was working inside me, melting my hardened heart and releasing my defensive detachment, which would better allow me to make amends with my Dad.

When I returned home, I threw my *Dungeons & Dragons* game and associated paraphernalia into our burn barrel and lit it on fire. I felt this had an increasing grip on me and needed to be done. I also waited until my parents were available and asked to talk with them. I was scared but needed to keep moving forward and speak the truth. I confessed my sexual sin – the pornography and even the sexual behavior with Victor. It was swift and general. Masturbation was a word I couldn't even say at this point, so I left that unmentioned, but the rest was at least named. I wanted everything in the light – no more hiding.

The healing began with talking to my parents, but I knew Victor's parents also needed to be told. I couldn't bring myself to do it yet. I was pretty afraid of his father. There had been a couple of occasions when Vic was sporting a black eye from "running into the corner of an open cupboard door." I knew the truth, though – it was a shiner from his dad. His mother could also be somewhat intimidating, so I asked my parents to find a way of letting them know...

"And please tell them I am sorry for my part," I pleaded.

Somehow, they did it. They talked with Vic's mom and dad. Naturally, Vic was furious with me initially, but he softened in time. We were forbidden from spending time together alone.

On a Sunday morning, about a month after The Basic Youth Conflicts seminar, I saw Vic's mom in the church sanctuary, setting her things on a chair before the service started. It was early, so very few people had arrived. I made a quick decision and walked over to her.

"May I talk with you for a moment?" I asked. She was stiff and hesitated momentarily, then she motioned to a nearby side room, and we stepped in.

"I know Mom and Dad talked with you, but I want you to know from me that I am very sorry for what I did with Victor." I teared up as the emotion hit me. "I hope you can one day forgive me."

She still had her purse in her hand but quickly dropped it on a table and reached out her arms to pull me in for a hug.

"Of course, I'm upset about it, but I also know it took a lot of courage for you to talk with me... and that means a lot." She responded with firmness but also with grace. "I know this wasn't just your fault... Yes. I forgive you," she said.

What powerful words!

What was so hard to verbalize initially felt like a massive load off my heart and soul when it was finished. I didn't understand it then, but in genuine confession and repentance, our island of internal banishment and isolation transforms into a place where genuine fellowship and community can be restored or newly discovered. It's one of the many beautiful realities of the Kingdom of God.

* * *

As human beings, we have many genuine needs, not just wants. God established two core foundational needs for every person to pursue and acquire: 1) authentic belonging and 2) meaningful purpose. Even during puberty, with our emerging attractions and sexual desires, these two needs are unconsciously sought. The danger comes when we settle for intense but brief relational and sexual pleasures and miss filling either need - that we hunger for most (belonging and purpose) and the future gift of guiltless sex and committed love within the covenant relationship of marriage.

I love this relevant quote from C. S. Lewis:

If we consider the unblushing promises of reward and the staggering nature of the rewards promised in the Gospels, it would seem that our Lord finds our desires not too strong but too weak. We are half-hearted creatures, fooling about with drink and sex and ambition when infinite joy is offered us, like an ignorant child who wants to go on making mud pies in a slum because he cannot imagine what is meant by the offer of a holiday at the sea. We are far too easily pleased.

–C. S. Lewis, *The Weight of Glory*5.

My boys and I recently discussed a passage they'd read:

I am writing to you, fathers, because you know Him who has been from the beginning. **I am writing to you, young men, because you have overcome the evil one**. *I write to you, dear children, because you know the Father.*—I John 2:13-14

We mainly talked about the bold print and what that means for them today. We often minimize God's call on a young person's life or treat sexual exposure to porn or experimentation as something innocent or a rite of passage when the Scriptures are clear in both the Old and New Testaments that sexual sin leads to destruction. Of course, the effects of early exposure to sexual immorality can be overcome. These effects do not have to cripple anyone, but there is a strong tendency to pursue excitement and pleasure while getting hooked and entangled in our enemy's web of deceit. Young men (teen boys) have both the ability and the call of God to overcome the evil one – their adversary.

In this fourth stage of development (ages 12-17), where boys' bodies are flooded with testosterone and girls' bodies are awash with estrogen, new and unfamiliar attractions emerge – sexual desire and romantic curiosity. With all of this happening simultaneously (which was God's idea), it's still possible to overcome the evil one and learn to navigate the turbulent, sometimes stormy waters of our emerging sexuality.

We overcome as we submit to Jesus Christ and obey His Word. Obedience keeps us on course, avoiding pitfalls and disasters to discover His purposes for our lives. His provision of authentic community is essential here. Rather than turning to the momentary pleasure of sexual sin and resulting defilement, obedience protects and aligns with God's love and purposes - in a way that fulfills the deepest longings of our souls. We learn to delay hedonistic desires and reject momentary fixes in favor of the real deal later on. Perhaps most importantly, we learn to grow up as men of integrity rather than continually fail as unformed *adult boys* who are users and abusers.

As a young man, I was never taught to delay gratification – especially sexual gratification. I mean, I knew it was wrong. But how was it wrong? Why did it matter in any practical sense? Dad didn't have those conversations with me. The only discussion that in any way related to sex occurred when I was thirteen or fourteen. I heard the bathroom door bang as Dad jerked it open and barreled down the hallway and into the living room where I was. In his fist, he brandished a department store catalog that had been in our bathroom for months.

Dad held up the catalog and declared, "You'll never look at this again."

Shame flashed through me, and my face became hot. It wasn't my catalog, but I could only nod and mumble okay.

My sister and mother gawked at us from the kitchen. Dad must have realized that the underwear model section had become well-worn from my excess viewing, but he never clarified. As quickly as he blew into the living room, he blew back out again, and that was it. Never to be mentioned again.

Following the Basic Youth Conflicts conference, my determination to live differently lasted for a while, similar to the effects of a Promise Keepers conference, where the vast majority of guys in attendance have real breakthroughs. They feel God moving, the Holy Spirit drawing them to repent of all sinful things – including porn, adultery, sex before marriage, etc.... Most who respond to God with heartfelt conviction and tears of repentance eventually find themselves right back amid sin and familiar patterns within days or weeks of returning home.

I was no different.

As the weeks and months passed, I desperately tried to hold onto what I'd learned, especially the feeling of being clean and forgiven. However, my cravings could no longer be quelled with verses or prayer, and addiction loosened my grip on morality. I returned to my porn stash with even more enthusiasm than before.

I believe there are two primary reasons men return from an event like Basic Youth Conflict or Promise Keepers and fail to stay on their path. They went on a *mountain-top* experience. Still, they returned to their familiar and often dysfunctional environments, unprepared to acknowledge how much that environment had been crucial to their bondage to sin. Secondly, they are trying to stand alone. They returned home with no band of brothers around them. Even if they attend their church men's group, when it comes to getting down to real issues each man is facing and tempted by—his hidden fears and insecurities—most men's groups run a mile wide and an inch deep. Coming from a place of healing, where they genuinely connected to God and repented of sin, they experienced a natural high and intended to live differently from that point on. *Instead, they weakened, and like a sow [pig], after washing, returned to wallowing in the mire—II* Peter 2:22b.

If it's true that grown men who gather together don't open up and get honest with one another, how much truer is it of teenage boys? Throughout my childhood and adolescence, I had no real connection to anyone at church – certainly none of the men who may have served as mentors. So there I was, struggling to stave off temptation, juggling the craving of addiction with fleeting feelings of grace, and doing my best to abstain from sexual sin with no one to discuss it with. I had no one to lean on or edify me. At the time, I had no clue that abstinence alone wasn't the complete solution. Seeking to only abstain from sexual sin is akin to sexual anorexia, attempting to turn off sexual desire entirely. This leads to starvation and, ultimately, binging on what we are trying to avoid.

I didn't understand that what I needed wasn't the empty calories of porn, but the nourishment of Jesus, through a firm but compassionate church community willing to be vulnerable with one another. Sadly, that community is still largely non-existent in U.S. churches today. It most definitely was back then. This is the foundation of why our ministry, Love & Truth Network, exists – to help equip the Church in these vital areas of authentic relationships as an antidote to isolation, sexual sin, and identity confusion.

But back then, I had no idea what was missing from my vow of morality or why my efforts to stave off sexual sin ultimately failed over and over again. I didn't understand how broken our world was or the fallen nature of mankind, so naturally, I assumed there was something wrong with me and only me. Why was it so easy for all the other Christians to resist temptation? Maybe I wasn't trying hard enough. I had a stack of memory verses I went through daily, convinced that speaking the words out loud would inoculate my unwanted desires. But it wasn't enough – *I* wasn't enough. What was it that I was missing? What could I do to find lasting victory?

At long last, an idea that occurred at the Basic Youth Conflicts seminar reemerged and took a more concrete shape in my mind. Before, it had been easy to dismiss as unrealistic, but now the thought was back, and it kept needling me for more serious consideration and an answer. Could there be any chance for me to attend the Bible institute my brother attended? Would they let me in with only a diploma from homeschooling? My brother excelled at anything he put his mind and heart to, but I didn't see myself the same way. Instead, I believed I was a failure. I was dumb. I hated school, so why was I thinking about Bible school? I had watched my brother's faith deepen over the last few years. I wanted that, too. He had one year left, and knowing he would be there gave me the courage to apply.

To my surprise, I was accepted. I was almost seventeen and became the youngest guy on campus – slightly younger than one other freshman, but that's a story for the next chapter.

A year or two after the Basic Youth Conflicts conference, Victor and I were talking and spending time together again. He'd forgiven me for spilling the beans to our parents, and while the rules of spending time alone together were never officially rescinded, we found ourselves going for walks and bike rides again. Now that I'd been accepted to Bible school, our parents seemed to assume our past experimentation had only been a phase or something. I felt confident that was the case, too. Things had changed a lot for me. Though I still had a solid same-sex attraction, I didn't want that to rule my life. I tried to follow God. I wanted my life to have meaning.

Despite our past, one of the most encouraging things about my friendship with Victor was that we both wanted a relationship with God. By this time, when we hung out together, we'd have long conversations about faith and Bible studies. He was easy to talk to and seemed to be maturing spiritually, the same as me. Everything seemed to move in a more positive direction.

Until... it wasn't.

Maybe that's what allowed me to let my guard down. In moments of mutual weakness, our benign conversations turned toward sexual things – both of us testing the waters, so to speak, and not long after wading back into the cesspool of sexual sin. Without consideration of the consequences, Victor and I gave in to temptation again.

I did my best to cover up my sin in discouragement and failure. How could I have let it happen? All those months and more of fighting to live in a godly way were gone. All our spiritual growth felt as though it was flushed down the toilet. Alone, I cried out to God for forgiveness. But only God knew what I'd done.

Neither Victor nor I ever told anyone else what we did. And so I stuffed it down and continued with my Bible school preparations. When my first day arrived, I stepped onto campus feeling like a fake. Sick and terrified of my past, I tried to find my place at this new venue. It was supposed to be a time of enlightenment and connection, but I could dwell on nothing other than the blemish of my sexual desires somehow being discovered. Then, the entire school, as well as my family, would know what I knew. I was a fraud.

Questions for Self-Reflection / Journaling / Group Sharing

1. How has your early pornography exposure affected your view of sexuality and intimacy?

2. Have you experienced guilt or shame due to your early exposure to pornography, and if so, how have you coped (or not) with these emotions?

3. Have you ever felt like a fraud and feared exposure? Explain.

4. How has your faith or belief system impacted your understanding of sexual sin and your ability to forgive yourself for past mistakes?

5. Have you sought professional help or counseling to address any adverse impacts of early pornography exposure on your mental health and well-being? Has this been helpful?

6. How can you use your experience to help educate and guide others, especially younger generations, about the potential risks and harms of pornography use and sexual sin?

7. What steps can you take to promote healthy sexual thoughts and behavior in your marriage, healthy attitudes, or abstinence in singleness?

1 Bowlby J. New York: Basic Books; 1980. Attachment and loss: Vol. 3: Loss, sadness and depression.

2 Costello, E. J., Egger, H. L., & Angold, A. (2005). 10-Year Research Update Review: The Epidemiology of Child and Adolescent Psychiatric Disorders: I. Methods and Public Health Burden. *Journal of the American Academy of Child and Adolescent Psychiatry*, *44*(10), 972–986.

3 APA PsycNet. (n.d.-b).

4 Joyner K, Udry JR. You Don't Bring Me Anything but Down: Adolescent Romance and Depression. *Journal of Health and Social Behavior*. 2000;41:369–391

5 The Weight of Glory Quotes by *C.S. Lewis*. (n.d.).

Chapter 6

LEAVING HOME – YOUNG ADULTHOOD

I stared at the sealed envelope on my bed. It was here—the response I'd been waiting for. Weeks prior, I had applied for enrollment in the Practical Bible Institute's one-year program. My brother Dale had been enrolled for two years and loved the institute. He had grown so much in his faith and ability to communicate. He was even asked to preach at our church periodically. He'd proved himself as a model student and took the calling of God very seriously. He was excited and encouraging when I told him I also wanted to apply.

By then, I was almost seventeen and had no solid alternatives should my application be rejected. I had finished homeschooling, but my future seemed underwhelming, besides having a high school diploma. I didn't have the slightest sense of a career choice. In my family, phrases like "vision for the future" or "choosing a career path" didn't fit the daily vocabulary. Getting a job (any job) to make ends meet was not only expected but the only consideration. Before applying for Bible school, I considered finding outside work and attended several blue-collar job interviews. Still, I was quickly passed over due to my excruciating shyness and lack of trade skills. Unlike my brother, who felt an innate calling to learn more of God's Word, Bible College was little more for me than a solution to my aimlessness.

My battle with sexual sin, porn addiction, and growing same-sex attraction raged on through my teen years. I lingered inside a cycle of sin/repent, sin/repent. It was only a few months before my seventeenth birthday, but my moral deficiencies and failure to stay on the narrow path cultivated a deep sense of hopelessness. I found the words of Solomon in Proverbs 13:12 resonated deeply—so deeply that I wrote the verse out on card stock, along with multiple others, and bound them together with a metal ring for quick reference. I added new verses to my collection weekly and forced myself to review them several times a week, attempting to commit them to memory on a deeper level each time. I believed they held the answers I sought. Surely, they would begin to work inside me and transform my life.

As a result, I made some positive strides toward abstinence, but nothing changed at the pace I'd hoped it would. My desires were not disappearing. On the contrary, my temptations and urges felt immovable. While I wrestled in silence, keeping my struggles between me and God alone, I had grown to believe God despised me. In my mind, it wasn't that He couldn't help, He just didn't *want* to help me the way He helped others (or, rather, the way I assumed He did with others). Thus, I believed I was an accursed thing – *a vessel of wrath prepared for destruction.* I'd read these associated verses in Romans 9 and drew this conclusion. It made sense; a vessel of wrath is what I was created for.

* * *

I picked up the sealed letter from Practical Bible Training School and held it in my hand for a moment. I was excited by the possibility, so why was I afraid to open it? It felt strange that this envelope contained the answer to my immediate future. Finally, I tore it open, unfolded the letter, and scanned the contents ...

We are pleased to inform you that your application for the fall semester of 1982 at Practical Bible Training School has been accepted.

My heart thumped in my chest. That brief excitement faded as quickly as it had come, swallowed up by the gaping mouths of fear and uncertainty. What would it be like at Bible School? Would I be liked and accepted? What if somehow my same-sex attractions were exposed in some way? I always felt like I wore some label that outed me. Surely, people would know. I felt like a fraud and a hypocrite, but nothing else existed. I needed this opportunity.

Would God finally show up, set me free, and give me new desires if I committed to Bible School and possibly full-time service to Him? All of this was going through my head and heart. Not to mention, I had never been away from family or surrounded by people I didn't know. My secluded cocoon on our eighteen acres in the middle of forests and farmland felt like a dead-end, boring future but served as a security blanket shielding me from ridicule and rejection.

Ultimately, I overcame my fear and shame and embraced the opportunity. Indeed, God would do something beyond anything I could even ask or imagine. There was hope in this path, but nothing but gray and darkness apart from it.

The school had a dress code that required a suit jacket or sports coat and tie during all classes. I didn't own a jacket or a tie. So, as with the swimsuit that was too large and slipped to my ankles when I dove into the school pool, we would make do with a visit to the local Salvation Army for new (to me) slacks, shirts, jackets, and ties. I felt okay about my *new* clothes until the first day of class. Stepping onto campus that first day, my gaze raked over the styles and fashion of new and returning students, and I cringed so hard I almost spontaneously combusted. Straight up embarrassment in the worst way. I must have looked like a cover model for *Country Bumpkin Weekly* in my faded, mismatched, secondhand clothes.

And poor naïve me thought I looked good when I'd tried them on at home! If it wasn't for my brother already being at the school, there's no way I would have had the courage to make it through my first week.

With all I have previously shared about my childhood and youth, with the many experiences of scorn and essentially feeling pushed out of the world of men and boys, perhaps you can understand how even a tiny little Bible college could feel like culture shock.

Somehow, I wound up with a single room for my first semester. My intended roommate ended up being a no-show, and fortunately for me, this private room became my retreat when social interaction felt overwhelming – which was a good deal of the time.

On move-in day, I entered the first-floor bathroom of the men's dorm for the first time. As a young man who felt incredibly inadequate alongside other men and experienced intense same-sex attraction, I was horrified to discover the shower area was nothing more than a large open room with a series of shower heads protruding from opposing walls. This scenario gave me such stomach cramps that I carefully strategized my shower routines to avoid the rush.

On my first day of class, I rose early, determined to forego the showers and clean up at one of the sinks. To my great dismay, I hurriedly pushed through the bathroom door and found a bustling factory of morning prep—a low din of chatter and laughter, with guys wrapped in towels or robes loitering in front of gushing sinks, shaving, or brushing teeth. And in the showers? Good grief, beneath every spraying fountain of water, a naked man lathered or rinsed himself.

I felt panic rising and an intense desire to flee. I wanted to whip around and bolt back to my room. I reached for the door that had just closed behind me... but I paused. All of this emotion and decision happened in a couple of seconds. If I'd learned anything about my gender, it was that bullies could smell fear a mile away. This moment was an opportunity to be different, or at the very least, act differently. I had to take it by the reins, or else I'd fall back into the same trap I was desperate to avoid. Running away now would draw attention to myself. Anyone who'd already seen me in the doorway would notice my trepidation. I had to play it cool.

I turned quickly to the nearest urinal - in my panic, I forgot how badly I needed to use it. I took a breath and squared my shoulders, trying to look *normal* as I avoided the temptation to look back toward the showers again. Using the urinal gave me a few seconds to figure out what to do next: wash my hands and get back to my room as quickly and unnoticeably as possible. Suffice it to say, that day, rather than getting to my first class for an early start, I plopped onto my bed and hid in my room while anxiety and self-hatred at my wimpiness overwhelmed me to tears.

What is wrong with me? How many times had I asked myself that very question? I could not function in daily life with these types of limitations. I needed solutions. I needed help.

At the very least, I needed to shave, comb my hair, and brush my teeth. I waited for as long as I could before returning to the bathroom. It was mostly cleared out, allowing me to groom myself in relative privacy. I ended up being late for class on my first day, and that ritual became emblematic of each day that followed.

Other than my brother, I didn't spend time with anyone. People said hello to me in the dorm, in class, or as I walked across campus, and I'd squeak out a quiet, mousy-voiced response.

The other dynamic plaguing me at my age (almost seventeen) and with all the stress was acne. I was highly self-conscious of the fact that my face broke out a lot. I hated the way I looked. Being in an environment where most people were in their twenties and thirties, with some much older, only seemed to highlight in my mind the everyday teen struggles and my not-so-normal sexual struggles. In a word, I felt *awkward* about everything, and hiding it was nearly impossible for me.

Weeks later, I found out that a rumor had been circulating that I was stuck up and unfriendly. Imagine that! People couldn't hear me respond when they spoke to me, so they assumed I chose to ignore them. What an irony. I'm the timid, fearful one who was anything but stuck up. But that was the impression I quickly made on the small campus. I wanted to turn that around, so I worked myself up to speak to people and even performed the painful task of looking up at people who walked by instead of staring at the ground. I didn't have the benefit of the current socially acceptable posture of staring at my phone screen. I needed to push through and engage more. It felt excruciating, but it was a bit of a turn-around and the groundwork for making new friends.

Each day, at the beginning of meals in the campus dining room, a student would be randomly called on to pray and thank God for the meal. Knowing that I could be called upon at any time greatly distressed me. The idea of speaking or praying publicly was more than I could handle. The anxiety of it plagued me so harshly that I skipped meals altogether. Not only was I inhibited by stress and fear, I was now hungry all the time. But even the pangs of hunger paled compared to the horrors of possible humiliation that awaited me with public prayer. I knew I was being logically ridiculous, but it didn't matter. My brain rarely overrode my shame and fear.

In reflection, it's paradoxical that someone who craved friendship and emotional connection so deeply chose isolation repeatedly instead. Even though I had a private room, there were times when I didn't feel alone enough. Sometimes, I'd even steal away into the dorm's basement. It was a large open roomful of random items stored away and a section where some guys had set up weight benches.

But further still, another room off to one side housed a huge heating unit with a labyrinth of coils and ductwork. Sometimes, I'd tunnel through and around any obstacles until I reached the far corner. Searching, burrowing, winding down deeper into nowhere, somewhere far away from the reality I wouldn't feel comfortable in. There, I'd hug my knees to my chest and rock back and forth, back and forth, until my anxiety eased or I couldn't stand the darkness any longer.

These times of extreme withdrawal were inexplicable to me. Looking back, I believe my sense of aloneness was intensified by being around others but feeling incapable of connecting meaningfully. As bad as I felt in my loneliness, removing myself from everyone somehow hurt less. I wanted someone to see me and care enough to help. I felt lost and needed to be found.

* * *

If someone in your life is pulling away and isolating, they may not want to be alone. Instead, the pain of navigating relationships and learning how to interact in emotionally healthy ways may feel overwhelming. It's just easier to be isolated and less painful. My encouragement is to do all you can to provide reasonable support and don't go it alone. This situation could require professional support

– medical and mental health. Often, a team of family and friends can be most effective for staying in for the long haul.

* * *

Eventually, I'd push myself out of the abyss of anti-socialism. I had to make friends. I wanted friendship. And not only friendship with girls because that was always the easier route, but also the fallback. Guys were intimidating to me. Navigating how I was supposed to act around and healthily relate to my gender was always my greatest challenge. Regardless, I had to stop hiding in my room (or the basement). Life was not going to wait for me to get my act together.

Besides all that, I needed money. Besides a small grant and student loan to pay for school and books, I was broke and needed to find work. My brother had a custodial job with a local church that specifically sought Bible-school students to fill this role. They paid well for a half-day of work each week, and out of the goodness of his heart, Dale sacrificed the money he needed, sharing the work and pay with me.

I even took on an additional job at McDonald's that lasted three days after orientation and training. Social anxiety, extreme shame, and shyness were so deeply embedded in me that I was paralyzed and unable to adapt to an environment that demanded quick thinking and reflexes. Timers for fries and burgers blared in the background amid other employees' fast, methodical pace. On the other hand, I couldn't seem to learn or retain anything. I never knew what to do next. Again, I'd found another place I did not fit, and after the manager told me I wasn't working out, I shuffled the mile or so back to campus, shoulders curved forward, head down, with the weight of another confirmation that I didn't have what it takes. And again, I asked the sky, the universe, God... what was wrong with me?

* * *

I had internalized a love/hate perspective when it came to men. I was oblivious to how hyper-vigilant I was to avoid shame and rejection, particularly concerning my interactions with other men. Paradoxically, this hyper-internal readiness translated into a brain fog and mental paralysis in everyday activities. What came naturally and quickly for other guys was a conundrum for me. The *shame posture* I experienced didn't prepare me for the inevitable but instead allowed me to avoid it altogether. So, my life was significantly reduced to only those situations I deemed safe and shame-free, such as the quiet and isolated job of cleaning the church with my brother.

The love/hate dilemma I'd experienced with other guys long ago had injected uncertainty and fear into my heart. However, on the flip side, there was also envy—envy of those who could live confidently and comfortably with themselves. That concept was so foreign to me. I had no idea how to feel good about being the person/man I was.

One might wonder why I didn't find someone to open up to about all this – even my brother. The short answer is shame. I was already embarrassed about how screwed up I was, so why would I willingly expose all this to someone else?

Envy is a negative emotion as well as a sin. It leads to all kinds of unhealthy comparisons. Unlike jealousy, which is a feeling of anger or bitterness over something or someone under threat of being taken away, envy is a feeling of anger or resentment over the perception of what someone else possesses that we do not.

At the time, I had no idea how destructive envy was. I don't even know if I realized that's what I was feeling and practicing ritualistically in my head. I was my worst enemy, constantly comparing myself against other guys and always coming up short. So, through fantasy, pornography, and masturbation, envy became sexualized – a widespread practice by those who experience same-sex attraction, though largely unnoticed. Without clear recognition of the actual culprit, envy can be easily reinterpreted as what we are consciously aware of - sexual attraction.

Guys who were athletic, muscular, good-looking, and confident represented everything I couldn't see in myself. I was short, weak, afraid, uncoordinated, and anything but confident. Capable boys and men were a mystery to me, and as I would learn many years later, humans are wired to be intrigued by the mysterious.

On the other hand, girls were not at all mysterious to me. From my primary connection with Mom and my sister to the girls at church and school, girls were more readable and easier to understand. I spent all of my time in the world of girls. What interested them interested me. Their games weren't as rough or competitive as the boys, so I faced far less potential for shaming with the girls. In some ways, I felt more like one of them than a boy. As noted earlier, if I had been born in today's culture, I have zero doubt I would have been labeled transgender and pushed toward transition.

I could see plainly that I somehow had to get beyond my fear. You have to understand I prayed about these issues often, but in my spiritual immaturity and misperceptions, I felt my prayers were offered to a God who didn't like me, much less love me. I wrestled with the lie that I was a miserable disappointment to Him, and as a result, I was pretty much on my own.

Because of all the Scripture I grew up hearing and reading, I was in an odd place to believe the Bible was factual and applicable across every generation, yet I felt like a cosmic freak. I felt uniquely flawed, and somehow, the mercy and love of God that was free and lavish for everyone else didn't quite extend to me. But God was still God. He was omnipresent and omniscient. He knew me... especially all my screw-ups, sins, and failures.

Regardless of my doubts, He was still the only one who could change me. But would He? What hoops did I have to jump through to measure up and not be a disappointment? I increasingly believed (subconsciously for many years) that God was dangling a carrot in front of my face, always keeping it out of my reach. Confoundedly, I still knew life and meaning were found in Him. That kept me returning repeatedly, even though my expectations of His help and intervention dwindled. It was as if someone was continually, gradually turning down the dimmer switch of my hopes and expectations of God. Over time, many of my religious behaviors and practices were rooted in nothing more than habit and tradition.

Sadly, I was at Bible school and learning so much about God, yet none had translated into my life as an actual relationship with Him. In many ways, this caused me to split off from myself and function in a type of compartmentalized disintegration. I became a better and better Pharisee - white-washed on the outside while tarnished with shame, sin, and secret comforts on the inside (Matthew 23:25-28).

* * *

I have since come to understand that nearly every Christian lives a double life in one form or another, to a lesser or greater degree. While that is often true about porn, sexual sin, or identity confusion, compartmentalization and double-living can occur in many forms. Most essentially, it's the practice of not having anyone who fully knows you, even your spouse. Unfortunately, it's a reality that very few evangelical Christians practice the command of *confessing our sins to one another and praying for each other so that we might be healed* (James 5:16). In my youth, I believed this double-living was a problem unique to me and to others who were broken. But it isn't! All Christians struggle with sin, temptations of the flesh, etc., as we live in a broken world. Why do we hide sinfulness instead of confessing and carrying one another's burdens? We make our burdens much heavier when we hide our sins, personal struggles, and the effects of sins committed against us. No one is above or exempt from the challenges of sinfulness. Only Jesus lived a perfect life free from sin. And thanks to His sacrifice and gift of grace, we can be made clean despite our unholiness.

* * *

As I began to branch out of my dorm room and attempt to make friends, I naturally selected female companions. Women were familiar and safe. While I desperately needed companionship with other men, especially godly ones, I was frustrated by my emotional and sexual attraction to some of them. I did not know how to process it at the time.

The one upside to my social anxiety and withdrawal was that it left me with lots of time for schoolwork. My grades weren't great, but they were decent. Far better than I would have thought possible after having come out of very unstructured, undefined, and undisciplined schooling experiences. I had to do something with my time. While the friendship thing was slow, I spent time in the library, studying more than I had. It felt good to ace an exam or receive a good grade on a paper. That was a new and positive experience.

As a result, I survived my one-year Bible Certificate program and graduated. Likewise, my brother finished his pastoral tract and graduated from Bible School as co-valedictorian (sharing the honor with his best friend). For once, it seemed possible that we came from the same gene pool. All along, the opposite had seemed true. With him: clear-eyed, focused, comfortable with himself, and excellent grades, and me: fearful, undisciplined, and aimless. Throughout my childhood, I'd considered multiple times that surely the Ingraham family secret was that I'd been adopted. It was the only explanation for how I couldn't fit in with my four siblings, even if my life depended on it. The vast differences between my brother and me at Bible school made my childhood contemplation of adoption even more plausible. I listened in amazement during our commencement ceremony (my one-year certificate program and his three-year pastoral program). At the same time, he gave his flawless valedictorian speech to all in attendance—students, families, faculty, and staff. Had the tables been turned, I would have cowered in utter fear by having to speak in front of all those people. Dale did this so effortlessly and confidently. Part of me admired my brother, but part of me was resentful that his solid behavior and good choices only highlighted my screw-ups and shortcomings. Yup, I must have been adopted.

Our parents attended our graduation. Afterward, I overheard my mother tell someone how nervous she'd been for Dale to give a message to such a large group. Then, she exaggerated a facial expression of relief and relaxed body language, and her voice hitched with pride as she shared her pleasant surprise at Dale's success. It was clear to see how much she'd enjoyed the whole experience. Even Dad was beaming with adoration, too.

Initially, Dad had been against the idea of Dale going to Bible College. Dad had never valued higher education. He generally found college to be a waste of time and money. However, watching Dale's progression into ministry and becoming a pastor of his country church softened Dad's view.

I resented my Dad's lack of vision for me and the rest of his children. I felt so unformed. I wouldn't have known to use that word back then, but it was how I felt.

After the ceremony, Suzy, one of my many female friends, and I decided to get into some mischief. Suzy and I had been inseparable in recent months (when I made friends, I was loyal and usually emotionally enmeshed, too) and usually found ourselves getting into mischief. Nothing serious, but we laughed a lot, and I needed that. That graduation day, she and I decided to fill water balloons and tossed several out the window of her three-story dorm. As a large group of people passed below us, we held our breath and threw two bulging balloons over the window ledge.

Suzy peaked down just as they hit the crowd and all at once jerked back, her eyes and mouth wide open. "Oh, my God!" She hissed. "We hit the keynote speaker, J. Vernon McGee!"

Dr. J. Vernon McGee was from the longstanding and well-known *Walk Through The Bible* radio program. He was probably in his sixties and had delivered our keynote address.

Panicked and without another word, Suzy and I tore through the hall and down the stairwell to the ground floor like spooked geese. After regaining composure, we exited the building on the opposite end and nonchalantly blended in with the other students. Once we reached a secluded area, we burst out laughing. Moments like these made academic life bearable and life in general fun.

* * *

While it was more accessible and more comfortable for me to cultivate friendships with females, some situations became uncomfortable. For instance, I began to spend a lot of time with another girl, Becca, often on long walks. We'd trod along the river beside campus or down the narrow train track bridge. Sometimes, we'd even climb on the tracks and drop down to the concrete pilings in the middle of the river. This was a quiet hideaway that Becca and I had been to many times before. However, on one particular day, Becca acted oddly on the piling. She began asking me questions she hadn't asked before—personal questions— about me, my likes and dislikes, and my experiences with past girlfriends.

Though I hadn't asked and didn't want to know, Becca divulged her dating history in great detail and blathered on and on about things she liked in men. My palms started sweating, temples throbbing. Discomfort throttled me hard. Suddenly, it all made sense. Becca was flirting with me.

This kind of behavior was foreign to me, and I felt unwelcome. I wasn't sure how to respond, so I did what anyone in an awkward situation would.

"Look at the time," I stammered, glancing at my watch.

Without another word, I climbed back up to the tracks, waited for her to join me, and immediately set a brisk pace back to campus. A not-so-subtle subject change allowed me to redirect the conversation and avoid anything resembling intimacy for the rest of the evening.

This was how I dealt with unwanted advances. I even got rather adept at it. Dodging romantic opportunities were always handled the same way: with feigned ignorance. I'd pretend any suggestions of amorous interest flew right over my little bumpkin head, then redirected the conversation with a distraction. But I took no pleasure in it. Later, when I was alone, I racked my brain over what could be wrong with me. I liked these young women ... just not like *that*. They were my friends, and I enjoyed their company and didn't want to lose them, but why wasn't I attracted to them? Whenever I sensed their friendship with me shifting toward something more, I clammed up and flaked out. I had no answers, no concrete sense of the source of my discomfort. I assumed it had something to do with my same-sex attraction but was not ready to admit nor confront the fact that these attractions could be persistent and an ongoing struggle.

* * *

School was out, and summer became a blur. After graduating from the institute's one-year Bible program, and with no other real options, I enrolled for another year. I had no idea what the future held and no career direction or ambition. But deep down, I still yearned for answers and friendship; at least at school, I was starting to experience the latter. Something about the school structure also felt comforting and organized – the opposite of how I often felt internally, which was also attractive. Maybe another year would reveal God's plan for me. I had to try. I had to keep searching.

Things were easier upon my return. It was good to see casual friends and acquaintances again. I looked forward to getting back into class. It wasn't until later, during my third semester, that I developed deeper friendships. These friendships became more important to me than anything else. It was a new experience for me, and it felt good. But as always, my MO was *all in or all out*. I tended to live my life in extremes. I hadn't learned how to regulate friendships and other necessary areas of life or manage my time. As a kid, I was alone a lot. As a young adult, I was socializing regularly with a growing pool of people. There were many I liked spending time with, but I also recognized my heart gravitating toward one particular guy. Consequently, solid emotional bonds stirred, and I wanted to spend more and more time with him.

I managed to keep my emotions in check and plug away at my coursework, keeping things together enough to finish my third semester with average grades. It wasn't easy, though. As much as I tried to push Jason out of my head altogether, I was always thinking about him when he wasn't around – wondering what he was doing, fearful that he would find people he liked better than me.

I had often wished for a mentor – an adult I could open up to without fear of shame, rejection, or punishment. I trusted my brother in many ways, but I didn't expect him to know how to help me in my deepest struggles, doubts, fears, and temptations.

I also had no faith or trust in the leadership of the school. I once tried talking with the Dean of Men. The school had so many rules – most that made sense, but some that I couldn't understand. One day, I decided to ratchet up my courage, make an appointment, and ask him for clarification.

I sat in front of his desk and timidly explained why I was there. I needed him to help me understand one of the codes of conduct.

The dean looked at me quietly for a moment.

I squirmed in my seat, beginning to regret my foolishness for even approaching the topic with him. Just as I was about to apologize and leave, the dean picked up his desk phone and called the Dean of Students.

"I have a young man in my office who has a problem with the school's rules," he said. "Perhaps you might be free to join me for this conversation?"

I couldn't believe it. What was going on? I had plucked up my courage to ask for clarification and better understanding.

The office door opened a moment later, and the Dean of Students stepped in.

The Dean of Men explained my concern to the Dean of Students but did so with a projected tone I'd never used. Both men looked over me and discussed me with exaggerated long pauses.

Finally, the Dean of Students informed me that each rule had been meticulously and prayerfully put in place, and who was I to question any of them?

I was silent as I listened, my fists clenching, my cheeks flushing hot. I couldn't believe they were making such a big deal out of an honest question and proceeded to shame me.

But my only response was a nod that I understood. They dismissed me, and that was that.

For many reasons, the fourth semester proved to be a much more significant challenge than previous ones. My depression and anxiety spiked. I was only a few weeks from final exams and struggling in each of my classes. Fortunately, I could turn it around enough not to fail my classes. However, I was distracted and discouraged by a couple of key friendships. Emotional dependency quickly became an issue with my male companions. This led to frequent rumination about fearing a friendship was over or that I would ruin it somehow – which was usually a self-fulfilling prophecy.

The pain of lost friendships and my mismanaged emotions bled into and occupied every area of my attention. With only a few exceptions, I hadn't been able to experience healthy, regular male connections and friendships for most of my life. When it finally presented itself, I was incapable of emotional self-regulation. I wound up smothering my friends, spending too much time with them, and silently seeking too much support and exclusivity in friendship. These situations impacted me much more deeply than they should have, especially my schoolwork. I had a terrible time concentrating on anything.

My parents had just returned to the area. They'd been wintering at a simple Christian retirement village in Florida. Having sold our local home, they returned to upstate New York and moved into a tiny travel trailer they ended up parking at a forest campground more than an hour away. When they drove up to campus for a visit, I was in the thick of it—deep in an overwhelmed state. A couple of guy friends were pulling away from me, and I didn't know how to handle that. I was eaten up with questions about what I did wrong and trying to figure out ways of fixing it. But all my attempts only made them want more space from me, spiraling me into greater anxiety. I needed relief from the hurt and confusion. The intensity felt unbearable... of course, my young mind and heart exaggerated and amplified all of these feelings, but I didn't understand that then. No young mind does.

In retrospect, I can see that time in my life was a growing pain—one of those many experiences we all need to learn from and push through to the other side. We give ourselves a more significant advantage when we can do so while being aware of God's help and grace. During my parents' visit, my Mom tuned in to the emotional roller coaster I was on. She reminded me that finals were right around the corner and it would be a shame for me to lose a whole semester of credits. As any loving mother would have, she hated to see me hurting. Mom suggested I focus on my schoolwork and bring up my grades as a distraction from my problems and that once the semester was over, I could spend the summer figuring out my drama.

On the other hand, Dad couldn't have cared less about me staying at school. He didn't like seeing me upset. Again, he had no use for higher education, even Bible College. He had softened on that because of my brother's success, but it was an easy posture to fall back to when he saw I was not doing well.

For Dad, being a Christian, living a decent moral life, getting married, having a family, and finding a simple job that paid basic bills each month were all he cared about. Those are good things, but beyond that, he had no other aspiration for any of his children.

Questions for Self-Reflection / Journaling / Group Sharing

1. Has there ever been a time when you have given up or wanted to give up on Christianity? If so, explain.

2. Have you ever been disappointed or angry with God? If so, explain.

3. What were some of your struggles launching from high school into college? If you grew up in a Christian home, was your faith challenged in college?

4. What unhealthy behaviors have you relied on to cope with disappointments, doubts, or challenges?

5. Have you ever received professional or pastoral counseling? If so, did you find it to be helpful? If so, how?

Chapter 7

OUT OF THE FRYING PAN

To Mom's frustration, Dad told me I could get my stuff and leave with them immediately if I wanted to. I couldn't believe it! Just like that, the pressure lifted. The gloom and doom of lingering in angst and heartache for another three weeks vanished. So, despite my mother's anger with Dad and disappointment with the whole situation, I hurried to my room and packed my things.

Two people I had grown to highly mistrust and dislike, the Dean of Students and the Dean of Men, were both unavailable. To me, they were smug and condescending, caring far more about exacting punishment for rules that were bent or broken than ever caring about the heart or motives of students. Back then, and often even now, it seems that Christian teachers, professors, and academics were far more concerned with the information students could retain for a test than impacting a heart for a deeper spiritual life or engaging in spiritual formation.

Even though I was nervous, part of me wanted to tell one of them that I was leaving. They couldn't do anything about it, and I wouldn't have to endure their stares. I settled for going to the admin office and telling the director I was withdrawing from classes and leaving. He was greatly disappointed, but after a few questions, he could see that I wouldn't be deterred, no matter how sensible his encouragement was to stay at least and finish the semester. He was a nice man. I had some dealings with him concerning payments and a grant. He had always been kind, but I wasn't interested in listening to good sense. I just wanted to get out of there.

I tossed my things into Mom and Dad's car, and we drove back to their lush green campground in the middle of nowhere.

Out of the frying pan and into the fire became an apt proverb for my new home in the forest. Indeed, all the pressure was off, but now there was no pressure, just ... nothing. No people, no friends. There were no cell phones or internet back then (thank God, in retrospect). There was no way to reach anyone without using the one payphone outside the little camp office or driving thirty miles, which only happened when my parents needed to buy weekly groceries. Pathetically enough, grocery shopping was the highlight of each week that I didn't dare miss.

"Man, if anyone knows how to screw up their life, it's you!" I scolded myself.

If I had only dug in and worked hard during my last few weeks of school, I could have passed all my classes and been in a different position to figure out my summer. I was an 18-year-old guy stuck in the middle of nowhere, living with my mom and dad in their tiny camper.

My dad had pitched a screen room outside the camper where they spent a lot of time reading, playing cards, and passing time outside in the breeze, protected from the myriad of biting bugs. It was peaceful for them. It was agonizingly quiet and devoid of people and all activity for me. I had grown up isolated. Not because I wanted it but because I was so fearful and believed the labels and rejection from many peers. That prison was finally broken open for me, especially in my third and fourth semesters, and I didn't want to return to that emptiness again.

* * *

After weeks of listless boredom, I headed for the nearest town, about thirty minutes away, and began a job search. A janitorial company hired me. Dad was thrilled. I was not. Still, I was allowed to use their only car to drive myself to and from work, but that was the only thing I could do without specific permission. I stopped at a run-down liquor and convenience store one evening after work.

There were magazines in plastic wrappers near the front of the store. No one else besides the older male cashier was in the store. I looked around for a snack but was drawn to the magazines. These weren't just Playboys; these were much more hardcore. I found a small section of gay porn and quickly grabbed the first thing that caught my eye – embarrassed to linger longer with the cashier watching me. I paid and left.

When I returned to the camper, Mom and Dad were asleep by this time. I unrolled my sleeping bag in the tent and stayed there all night. I eventually fell asleep, but not before using my flashlight to scour through every magazine page. I had one small lockable suitcase to put the magazine in for safekeeping.

I felt like crap in the morning. I hated going back to porn, but I was also bored and ready for any distraction or interruption to the dullness. That's when I also got the idea that as a healthy way of connecting meaningfully with a solid Christian friend, maybe my parents would let me use their car to visit him back at Bible College.

Mark, one of the Bible study leaders back at the Institute, had stayed in touch with me, writing occasional letters and chatting when we could coordinate a payphone call from the little camp office. We couldn't stay on a call for more than a few minutes as we had to dump in change frequently.

Mark and his fiancé stayed on campus and worked over the summer, and he invited me to come up for a visit on Friday. Knowing this was a good connection, my parents let me borrow their car overnight. I was anxious for some social time with a solid Christian brother, and I longed for wholesome conversation and prayer with someone other than my parents—God bless them.

I had never opened up to Mark (or anyone else at school) about my porn struggle or my same-sex attraction, and those secrets remained buried deep inside me. I had no intention of divulging them to him on this visit. But regardless of what he didn't know about me, I needed the fellowship and encouragement, and my excitement along the drive to see him reminded me how long I had been without any meaningful human interaction.

Mark had always been kind and gracious toward me. However, that didn't quell my self-consciousness around him. He was a gym rat and jock, and I was about the furthest thing possible from that. Somehow, though, we'd clicked. Early in our friendship, I recognized that he was way ahead of me spiritually. He was a mentor, but he didn't treat me like a project or as if I was inferior to him. As a result, I'd grown to trust him fully.

On campus, Mark met me at the main door of the men's dorm. He hugged me, and we walked back into the familiar space and down the hall.

"Hey, toss your stuff in my room, and let's get something to eat." He grinned.

I smiled back, fully relaxing now that I was here and anticipating a fun time of fellowship. "Sounds good!"

"I want to hear all that's been going on with you since you left."

"Ah, yeah, not much to tell." I snorted. "I've been bored out of my mind. Absolutely nothing to do in the middle of nowhere."

Mark opened his door, and I dropped my bag on the extra twin bed.

"I did get a job," I continued. "Just a janitorial thing, but it gives me some money and gets me out."

We left for dinner. It felt good to be back and have someone to talk to who was interested in what was happening with me. It was great catching up with Mark. Our various conversations that afternoon were exactly what I missed most about school. That night, I stayed in his room and used the extra bed since all the rooms were set up for double occupancy. Neither of us could go to sleep right away—it seemed we had so much to talk about! Into the late hours, we discussed God and speculated over His plans. What was He calling us into? What lay ahead? Of course, marriage was right around the corner for Mark, and it was clear that he was ready for it. I could tell from how his voice softened and lifted when he spoke of his fiancé.

Our late-night chat broke open something in me. I didn't want to stay in hiding with everyone forever. What emerged out of our fellowship was the sweet fruit of trust. And man, did I need to trust someone! Not only that, but I needed someone to share my struggles with. I needed to confess the temptations I wrestled with, especially the recent porn purchase and use, and I desperately needed my spirit to be strengthened.

But I was also afraid. Afraid that if I told him everything about the porn and same-sex attraction, Mark would ask me to leave his room.

But at that moment, lying on the dorm bed, staring up at the ceiling, I also realized something else ... I wasn't giving Mark the credit he was due. I was projecting my insecurities onto him. In my apprehensiveness and shame, I'd neglected to see the opportunity God had provided for me to communicate and confess—to reach out and be seen and heard. Mark had been a positive influence in my life, always inquiring with genuine interest. His questions that night sliced right through the barriers I'd erected around my heart. He wanted to know my innermost truths.

So why shouldn't I tell him everything?

And to be honest, I was tired. So tired. Exhausted from the labor of burying and hiding my darkest secrets, worn down from and attempting to carry the burden on my own. Mark could only know how to pray for and encourage me if he knew all of me – my whole struggle. I took the risk and shared the significant issues and struggles – without getting too much in the weeds and not wanting to make Mark feel weird by over-sharing.

Mark listened attentively and patiently and, at times, asked for clarification.

"I'm so sorry for what you experienced as a kid by the neighborhood boys." He empathized. "That had to be confusing and terrible. Did you ever tell your parents about it?"

"Yeah," I responded. "I told my mom. She told my Dad and later told me I couldn't play with those boys again, but that was it. They didn't know what else I might need to process that experience and find healing."

I don't know if I had ever felt so heard before. I wasn't rushed. My lifelong, intense fear of rejection felt like it was thawing, and a part of it was melting away by what I was experiencing in this time of confession and sharing. I had no idea how powerful and healing just speaking the truth out loud with a trustworthy person could be.

We started talking shortly after the sun had set, and now it was several hours later. I had shifted from a rather curled up, self-protective posture on my bed – anticipating possible rejection, to now resting stretched out on my back with my hands behind my head – looking out the window into the darkness, aware of twinkling stars in the night sky. I felt a burden lifted. And I knew we'd be praying soon.

Mark hadn't immediately changed the subject or deflected in some way. I'd opened up and made myself vulnerable, and he'd just ... accepted it.

"Mind if I ask you more about your struggle?" Mark asked. "I want to understand it better."

"Sure," I answered, my head buzzing with new energy.

The room was dark, save for the dim starlight peeping in through the window, and maybe that made it easier to open up. Mark asked some general questions, which I answered, and then even more inquiries came. Soon, the questions shifted from inquiry of my general struggles to something else, something of a more personal nature. The energy I'd felt moments before transitioned to an unsteady heartbeat. There I was—eager to release the sin I'd carried and reconcile with God and my fellow brothers in Christ and myself, while Mark seemed to be after something more.

It seemed apparent that he wanted the details I wasn't comfortable disclosing. I wasn't sure how far to go or how to stop the conversation at all. I'd opened up—I'd trusted! Now I felt a precarious sense of being out on a limb, with only

Mark to help me, but now I was wondering if he would help or saw the limb off and watch me fall. My heart had opened more than it had in a long time, but I felt it fading back into a closed and protective position.

The next thing I knew, Mark sat up, and his bed creaked. A second later, his standing silhouette blocked the moonlight through the window. He took off his shirt and shorts and climbed onto my bed.

"It's okay," he said. "No one has to know."

I didn't know what to say in response to that.

Prayer and encouragement were not what Mark had in mind any longer. I never anticipated this scenario: my friend, a mentor—a soon-to-be-married Christian leader, a jock—taking sexual advantage of a struggling brother.

My sudden and intense sensations of betrayal, confusion, and disappointment fizzled as sexual desire ignited. This is where I'll shut the door on this scene.

Suffice it to say, it didn't proceed well or end well. So much for ministry and mentoring.

The following day, I slowly awoke to a groggy and gross sense of what had happened. Mark was dressed and piddling about at his desk. He couldn't wait to get me out of his room. He was short with me, abrupt and cold, and his every movement implied I should get going. Shame overcame me like scalding hot water. How could I have allowed that to happen? I wanted to ask for his forgiveness. I wanted to talk about what happened.

"Do you want to talk about it?" I asked sheepishly. "Where do we go from here?"

Mark shrugged dismissively, detaching himself completely. "We don't go anywhere."

I grabbed my toiletries and went to the bathroom. The lights were off, and it was empty. Quite a difference from my first experience in that room. I flipped the lights on and went to the nearest sink, staring at my face and eyes as I drew closer to the mirror. I felt dead inside. I leaned my forehead against the mirror.

"You stupid moron," I whispered to my reflection. "What the hell is wrong with you?"

Dejected, I cleaned up and went back to Mark's room.

As soon as I walked in, he began listing off all the stuff he needed to get done that day. He returned to his door and opened it, asking if I needed help carrying anything to my car. It was apparent I didn't. I only had one backpack. This was a nice way of ushering me out of his room. We walked down the hall toward the main door. I stepped outside and turned around.

"Goodbye," he said, almost cheerfully, as if nothing had happened.

Quickly, Mark swung the metal door shut and locked it behind him. Dumbfounded, I stood there with my backpack, staring at the door.

What a mess. My guts twisted and ached. I thought I felt rotten before – staying with my parents, bored, listless, returning to porn. Nope, this was a new low. Again, I pondered how I could be such a screw-up.

I drove home that morning numb and joyless amidst the failure and shame. I was also carrying a burden again, more burden than before, the burden of a complicated new messy bond. What was I supposed to do with that? How did Mark and I move on from this? Instead of helping me through my sexual behavior and sin, he'd initiated me back into it.

* * *

I don't recall whether it was days or weeks later, but my Mom and I were outside in the screen room, washing our clothes with an old-fashioned washboard and rinsing in a tub of water. For larger loads, we would stop at a laundromat in town when we went for groceries, but when there wasn't much, we washed everything in this manner and hung the clothes on a taut line stretched between two trees behind the camper.

My Dad was also outside, working down the driveway by the road with a shovel – repairing deep ruts in the gravel base that had formed overnight under heavy rains and water runoff. I had been distraught, especially since the encounter with Mark. I was trying to keep it all in and act like everything was fine, but I was angry and snapping at my parents, withdrawing to be alone, turning to porn for escape, and feeling more miserable. It was on this day that I couldn't take it anymore. I saw Dad working down the driveway with his back to us. He was hard of hearing, so I knew Mom and I were essentially alone. I was rinsing and wringing out a pair of shorts.

"I think I'm gay," I blurted.

My mom abruptly stopped scrubbing a wet, soapy shirt against the washboard. "What did you say?"

She knew she heard me.

"I think I'm gay," I repeated.

"I've been so afraid you'd say that one of these days," she said with a tremor in her voice. She clenched her teeth, close to panic mode. "Did your father hear you?"

"Of course not. He can't hear anything," I was about to say as I glanced down the driveway at him.

But he was no longer working on the gravel repair. Instead, he stood in the driveway, leaning on his shovel, looking directly at me.

My heart pounded. I grabbed the clean laundry and ducked out of there to the clothesline– anything to avoid what might have just happened.

Nothing further was said about this for the rest of the day. A couple of days later, just before heading to work, I asked if my Mom had talked with Dad about it. She said she had. He hadn't said much. He never spoke to me or followed up about it. It became that thing I said once, and that's where it stayed.

Still, breeching the subject to Mom and knowing Dad was aware stoked a healthy fear inside me. Along with it came the desire to rid myself of porn, as well as the tyranny of past failures. I repented of them and acknowledged them as sins – even the recent ones. Later, I burned the porn magazine and started applying myself to take my sexual thoughts and temptations captive.

The apostle Paul warns us in I Corinthians 6:18, "*Flee [sexual] immorality. Every other sin that a man commits is outside the body, but the immoral man sins against his own body.*" Just two verses earlier, Paul warns us in verse 16: "*Or do you not know that the one who joins himself to a prostitute is one body with her?*"

Paul uses prostitution to make clear that even in the most transactional (I'll give you sex for money) and least loving scenario, the sexual union was designed to join two bodies into one—just as God designed for covenantal marriage. It is clear from these verses that there is no way a sexual relationship was meant to be a casual, no-consequence experience. God's purpose and design for us is that our sexual relationships and encounters are for forming one flesh and knitting together two people into one – within the commitment of covenantal marriage between one man and one woman. Could it be any surprise that, whether we feel them intensely (as I did) or are jaded and detached, our sexual experiences have the power to impact us in incredibly damaging ways?

By all appearances, Mark ended up continuing with life as if nothing happened. Just as he had said, no one else would know. For him, nothing changed. But I did wonder how that worked exactly. How did a Christian leader coax a vulnerable person to trust him, misuse an opportunity for ministry and prayer, only to take sexual advantage, and then go on with life with no apparent angst or remorse?

We all know this happens. Tragically, this kind of stuff makes its way into the news. It's clickbait on the internet and engulfs like wildfire on social media. We're shocked as we read and watch the double lives and sexual compromise unfold in prominent Christian leaders like Ravi Zacharias, Bill Hybels, and Ted Haggard, to name a few.

Over the last twenty years, I have personally known a few Christian leaders who began so well and stayed faithful for years. Still, they also began living double lives somewhere along the line, and relational compromise unfolds. Sexual sin eventually shipwrecks their lives, marriages, ministries, and many relationships around them.

As a leader, what Mark did to me in my condition of vulnerability and confusion was terrible, which doesn't in any way remove my responsibility for my own volition to sin. What he did afterward by throwing me out of the dorm and not re-engaging with me or asking for forgiveness was terrible. He had been a leader and an encouragement to me spiritually. Now, that was not only gone but marred and shattered.

However, I don't think Mark ever intended for a sexual encounter to happen between us. He was looking forward to a fun time of fellowship and support. While grooming does happen tragically, even by far too many in spiritual authority and Christian leadership roles, I don't believe that was the situation with Mark. I think he had been genuine up to that point. Perhaps there were some areas of sexual sin that he wasn't dealing with from his past or in his current life, but I believe the sin that he initiated and that I responded to was spontaneous, not planned, or groomed.

I write all this now with the wonderful blessing of healing and greater objectivity. I didn't understand any of this at the time. I was in pain over an important lost friendship, the feeling of being used and thrown away, and the part I played in all of it. I'm reminded of Paul's admonition to the Galatian believers in Galatians 6:1: *Brethren, even if anyone is caught in any trespass, you who are spiritual, restore such a one in a spirit of gentleness; each one looking to yourself so that you too will not be tempted.*

Life was already so complicated. I'd been carrying around the guilt from my terrible emotion-based decision of dropping out of Bible school. I was dissatisfied with my janitorial position. And now, I had to juggle the shame and regret of a tainted friendship and feeling used. Where did I go from here? I was floundering and lost. I needed something more out of my life, and I needed it fast. Where else could I go but to the Lord?

After intense soul-searching and prayer, I gathered the courage to reapply to the Bible Institute. I highly doubted they would take me back, but if so, that would be a sign that God was in it. With renewed vigor, I applied and waited to hear back. Maybe my time away was what I'd needed to collect myself. Maybe things would be different now that I could see how wrong I was to quit. I had fully repented of my return to porn and my part in sinning with Mark. I felt like I was beginning to envision a more straightforward path for my future. I wasn't sure they'd take me back, but after a few weeks of waiting, my acceptance letter came.

I was going back to school.

* * *

Summer eventually ended, and the first day of school arrived. It felt good to get back to school. Unlike last time, when I felt like a fish out of water, this time, the painful social awkwardness was nearly non-existent (at least outwardly). Knowing how the campus was laid out, what to expect from my surroundings, and seeing some friends from school all settled over my shoulders like a familiar blanket. Finally, aside from the Mark incident, my anxiety primarily lifted.

Upon arrival, I learned Mark was still in his spiritual leadership role. Coincidentally, as I moved boxes into my new room for the semester, our eyes met in the men's dorm hallway. Mark quickly averted his and headed in the other direction. What happened between us was a couple of months ago—plenty of time for me to marinate on how he'd treated me. I was still ticked. He was supposed to be a spiritual leader; instead, he'd taken advantage. Now, he was still in a prominent leadership role on campus. That annoyed me.

My only solution in moving forward with my life was to ignore Mark and press on with what I needed to do, and for the rest of the semester, I did just that. He was in a position of authority over the dorm, but I didn't pay any attention to him. I didn't try to embarrass him or make it obvious, but I wouldn't play the game. As far as I was concerned at the time, he was a fraud as a Christian leader.

One day, a few weeks after the start of the semester, a new, awkward, geeky freshman I had become acquainted with was hanging out in my room and talking with me. I understood Jim's struggle to fit in and get started at school on the right foot. I wanted to help him acclimate as much as I could. Mark stopped by the room to remind us of curfew.

"Whatever," I said, brushing aside his authority altogether.

"Where's Kenny?" he asked of my roommate.

I only shrugged.

Mark pulled the door closed behind him.

I wasn't trying to disrespect him intentionally, but I had difficulty ignoring my irritation.

My new friend was shocked. "I can't believe you just talked to him like that. And he didn't get after you about it? Wow. I see him with other guys, and he sure doesn't get pushed around."

I shrugged again.

"I think he's afraid of you," my friend said.

Well, *that* was a brand-new thought. That idea had never entered my mind until that moment. But it made sense. I had something on him. Mark knew that. Not that I would've exposed him, but Mark didn't know that.

But the semester continued, and other than Mark, it started pretty well. Some of my old friends (girls, of course) seemed excited to have me return. There were even a few guys who welcomed me back. They encouraged me to sign up for choral auditions as a baritone, and to my surprise and delight, I made the cut. Chorus practice became a highlight of my Bible school experience.

Within a couple of weeks, I made a new friend, too. Richard was a freshman—athletic, strong, and confident. He was also on the singing team. I didn't know why he wanted to spend time with me, but he seemed content enough to. We started a regular study routine that benefited us both. One of the reasons I liked him was because he thought I was a lot smarter than he was. That was a first for me. But he might have been right. I often helped him prep for exams and research papers.

But in keeping with my usual MO, I soon developed a strong emotional dependency on Richard—these growing and intense feelings of emotional need felt automatic. I didn't want them, but invariably, I was swallowed up and overwhelmed by obsessive thoughts about our friendship. It wasn't a sexual thing, mind you, but there was a very unhealthy level of need on my part, which I now understand as relational idolatry and emotional dependency. As I'd done with Victor, I began to zero in on Richard with tunnel vision, wanting an exclusive friendship. The more time we spent together, the less time I cared to spend with anyone else, and the more jealous I'd become when he spent time with someone else.

Of course, I tried to hide how I felt, but my poker face was laughable. My feelings were always on my sleeve. I thought of our friendship as a David-and-Jonathan-like relationship, but that was way off base from reality. David and Jonathan were always about blessing and releasing the other into God's complete purposes and plans. Each gave to the other. But with Richard, I became grasping and jealous. My behavior was centered around *my* unmet needs and *my* wants. But at the time, those glaring differences were unclear to me, so I used the Bible to justify a very unhealthy way of relating to another guy.

As is almost always the case, in the beginning, emotionally dependent relationships *feel* amazing. But they always fail. One person gets sick of the clingy, life-sucking friend. The dependent one notices them pulling away, which prompts him to cling more tightly. It's a tried-and-true recipe for ruin. This can also be true of dating relationships and even some marriages. Even Christian ones. Emotional dependency is never healthy and never sustainable. Initially, it feels good. Until it doesn't, and then it's miserable.

After a few months, Richard instinctively pulled away and set some necessary boundaries between himself and me. I'm embarrassed to say that there were times when I sat on the floor just inside my room, behind the closed door (when my roommate wasn't around), and listened to the sound of Richard's boots on his way down the hall to his room. I'd wait until I was sure it was him, give it a few moments for him to get settled, then knock on his door, cool and slick. I had just happened to be in the area and thought I'd stop by to see how his day was going. These drop-in visits were becoming less welcome and wanted, but I didn't know how to stop pursuing a solution to losing him altogether... which only pushed him away more solidly.

With Richard, as with all my companionships, I had a way of tuning out the world in favor of spending time with them. At the time, I had no idea this was called emotional dependency. As a result of my choices and out-of-control emotions, my grades began to slip again. It wasn't just Richard either, although he was the first for that semester. I managed to find myself caught up in a couple of unhealthy guy relationships. I say relationships because even though I thought of them as friendships at the time, I now know they weren't. They were more like serial associations, monogamous and emotionally unhealthy relationships masquerading as great friendships, and they were pulling me down. I'd never graduate or find my way when all my energies went into keeping my latest *friendship* intact. Something had to give.

* * *

An important note: this is the stuff of which a relatively new movement - so-called "spiritual friendships" are made: intense need, emotional dependency, and relational idolatry. Many advocates of celibate gay Christianity (also referred to as Side-B) believe these enmeshed relationships are more than just healthy. They think they are admirable. Many in this movement advocate for lifelong same-sex commitments – essentially marriage without sex.

First, what are the chances that those who experience strong same-sex attraction and intense emotional need *will be able* to refrain from sex? Powerful romantic emotion naturally leads to a deepening desire for sexual expression and connection. Secondly, even if two men or two women (or even a claimed celibate polyamorous group of several people – yes, that's the next thing) can somehow refrain from sex, this kind of emotional neediness and pursuit is idolatrous. This kind of passion directed toward someone of the same sex leads them away from godly living and is far from an expression of an accurate biblical worldview.

Once Richard and I had our inevitable final falling out, I descended into a dark pit again. I was like a drowning person flailing in deep water and about to go under. If anyone came to my rescue, my black hole of emotional need would also drown them. I was too dangerous, too risky. Like a succubus, I'd drain the vibrant life out of whoever got close to me until they had no choice but to escape. I was completely blind to this utterly destructive pattern. In my mind, there was always something wrong with the other person. Yes, I was too trusting, loyal, and committed to my friends... When, in fact, none of that was true. My need was devouring and insatiable. No one could sustain my brokenness for long. And so I would try harder without understanding that I was the problem, and the pattern repeated itself. My unhealthy and disjointed methods of relating were all I knew.

One of my brothers had lived in San Francisco with his girlfriend for many years. Sometimes, when I was desperate, I'd call him, and he'd talk me off the ledge. He cared about me, but he didn't care a thing about Christianity. Instead, the heavy-handed, legalistic Christianity he'd grown up with had propelled him in the opposite direction. He wanted me to be happy, no matter where that pursuit took me. He hated and rejected morality as defined in the Bible. He invited me to move out where he was and check out San Francisco.

"It's an incredible city," he'd say. "You'd love it here. Come and stay with us as long as you need."

Once again, I was in a season of such inner turmoil that I felt overwhelmed. With several broken friendships and complete disinterest in my classes and grades, all I could process, or rather, all I was stuck in, was the pain I felt at the moment. Making wise and reasonable decisions for tomorrow or next week, let alone my general future, were the furthest thoughts from my mind. Male friendships had become like crack cocaine to me. I didn't know how to live or function when they fell apart, and I couldn't get my needs met any longer. So, I would try to find another *seller* (another male friend) who could supply the fix of a sense of security and worth I craved.

So one day, under all this emotional angst and not exactly in my right mind, I called my brother from the dorm payphone and asked when I could move to San Francisco to be with him. He was excited, not believing I would ever even fly out for a visit, much less move there. I had never been on a plane before. And the thought of leaving the small town I was used to and flying out to a massive city like San Francisco alone had once seemed impossible. I could never gather enough courage to face those unknown fears, or so I once thought.

Once again, I stopped by the school office and dropped out. This time, I also went to speak to my choral conductor. He said I was making a big mistake. But at the time, I didn't care if it was a mistake, and I felt like I just had to get away.

Questions for Self-Reflection / Journaling / Group Sharing

1. Did you ever develop patterns of quitting or escaping challenging or complex situations? If so, explain. How has that impacted your life – in the past/in the present?

2. Or, have you developed an achieve-at-any-cost mindset? If so, explain. How has that impacted your life – in the past/in the present?

3. Have you experienced disappointment or even abuse in some way – verbal, spiritual, or sexual by someone in spiritual authority? How did that impact you?

5. Have you worked/prayed through those experiences with a counselor or mentor?

6. How might that experience still be affecting your life and relationships today?

Chapter 8

THREE STRIKES, YOU'RE OUT

I was eighteen and boarding my first flight from Syracuse, New York, to San Francisco, California, on what seemed to me to be a huge plane. I flew more than five hours across the country but was finally on my way to see my brother. I found my seat toward the back of the plane. Once airborne, I realized I was sitting close enough to the smoking section - in the very back (it was allowed then) that I had to breathe secondhand smoke all the way.

When I arrived at the San Francisco Airport, I must have looked like an idiot as my eyes nearly popped out of my head. The size of the airport - the bustle and pace were wild. An overwhelming sense of trepidation rattled up my spine. That, and the throbbing in my head and clogged ears from our descent, made me second-guess my impetuousness. How was I to know what to do? How would I find my brother in these crowds of people moving in every direction?

I wandered around in total discomfort, my ears muffled and ringing when I finally heard my name announced over the loudspeaker. I picked up the nearest information phone and later found my brother's girlfriend, Rebecca, and headed home, wherever that was.

Home was a rented Victorian-style house in the Mission District of San Francisco. I sure knew how to pick the extremes. The last time I quit the Bible Institute, I moved to the middle of nowhere with no one around. I was in one of the country's biggest and most bustling cities this time.

I was up early the day after arriving, reading my Bible and praying. My uncertainty and fearful sense of once again stepping out of the frying pan and into the fire, but on a scale and magnitude I had never before achieved, seemed to stir a religious revival. *God help me!*

Around lunchtime, my brother stumbled into the kitchen and asked if I wanted breakfast. There was no food in the house. He went out and returned with two bean burritos. I had never seen a burrito before and wasn't crazy about the beans, but something was better than nothing.

It's hard to describe my San Francisco experience. The home my brother, Rebecca, and another friend rented together felt incredibly scary. I was given an empty bedroom to use - little more than a sleeping bag on the floor and a door without a lock. I moved the sleeping bag into a corner of the room away from the door and unzipped my suitcase beside it. This was now my dresser with all the clothes I had brought. Music blasted every hour of the day. Drug use was as routine as morning coffee. My brother, his girlfriend, and other friends habitually stayed up for days partying, then crashing hard for at least a couple of days.

Somehow, they planned their binges around their nighttime data entry positions in a high-rise downtown office building. I went with them several times to get out of the house and see some of the city. I felt safe with them as they knew their way around and were comfortable walking the streets and riding BART – Bay Area Rapid Transit - to get wherever they wanted in the city.

It was during some of these outings to and from work, as well as occasions back at the house, that I felt a little interrogated by my hosts about why I was still reading my Bible and listening to Christian music and why I hadn't put that aside and joined them in their partying.

"All the rules of Christianity hold you back," Rebecca had said to me on more than one occasion. She was typically kind to me but also clearly irritated that I stayed aloof from them when they and their friends were partying.

Rebecca and my brother would give anyone struggling the shirt off their back, but their drug use and way of life were foreign and frightening to me. Once, in the middle of the night, I was awakened by a loud banging on the front door. Terrified, I desperately tried to wake someone up, but they were all passed out and unresponsive. I hurried quietly down the stairs to the front door.

"San Francisco P.D.!" someone called out.

I peered through the small window in the door to see four police officers standing outside – one about to pound on the door again. My mouth turned dry like leather. I felt shaky and unsteady but quickly twisted the locks and opened the door.

Upon seeing me, they gave their official introduction and said the name of my brother and his girlfriend, asking if they lived there.

I stepped aside and made room for them to walk by. Three went up the stairs while the only female officer momentarily questioned me at the door before we joined the others.

They were in my brother's bedroom, loudly calling their names, shining their flashlights in their faces, and walking about the room. I noticed an ashtray on the floor with some mostly smoked joints and a small bag of pot beside it. I thought for sure they were going to be arrested and dragged off. Then what was I going to do in a house their druggie friends had open access to? My sense of being unsafe and vulnerable intensified. Finally, they both groaned and yelled out at being disturbed but eventually stirred enough to answer some questions.

It didn't last long. The police ignored the pot and didn't explore for anything else. They seemed satisfied with whatever they learned from my brother and Rebecca and filed down the stairs to the door. I followed behind to lock up again. I felt embarrassed and frightened by all that had happened and the reasonable assumption of guilt by association.

The female cop was the last to walk out the door. She turned for a brief moment and looked at me directly. "Be careful."

Her tone was professional but caring.

I was relieved she knew enough that I wasn't a part of all this. Still, I was there. How long would it be before I was influenced into the same life?

The next day, I used my key to the front door while the rest of the house was comatose. I decided to explore a little and find a newspaper to review the help wanted section. Something had to change. I couldn't stay in that house any longer.

I had only been outside the house with my brother Bob and Rebecca. I was a little overwhelmed and fearful to be alone amid the bustle and shops, but I tried my best not to let it show. Instead of just buying a paper and running back to the house, I decided to walk and explore the area for a while. I had a simple map of my surroundings but did not reference it too often. I slipped it inside the newspaper so it looked like I was reading it rather than checking my directions.

My exploration turned out to last for hours. All the while, my anxiety about the unknown and unfamiliar surroundings faded the longer I was out.

When I returned, the house was still quiet, but I knew they would have to be up some time that night for work.

Eventually, I heard Bob shuffle down the hall and into the bathroom. When he emerged and walked into the kitchen, wearing a robe that looked like it should have been on Rebecca, I was sitting at the small kitchen table scouring through the help wanted ads. I had circled a few to consider and possibly call about.

"Good morning," I said in mock cheerfulness, guessing it wasn't feeling good to him by the looks of his scraggly hair. "Did you even glance in the mirror?"

"Shut up," he snapped.

"Do you need a comb? I think I have an extra."

"Shut up!" Bob repeated, scratching his head and trying to pull his fingers through the knots. "How you doing?"

"Oh, you mean after last night's neighborhood police department showed up at the door? I had to answer it because you were passed out. Good! So good!"

Bob looked in the fridge and stared at the empty white interior, hoping someone had wandered to the store between drug binges to stock it with delicious food. He closed the door and glanced at the closed cupboards.

"There's nothing in the pantry either," I said, returning to my folded paper and the ads section.

Bob pulled a chair beside me, reached into his robe, and pulled out several crystals.

"Nice." I returned to the paper.

"They're more than nice. Watch what I can do with these."

Bob held them in his left hand and extended his right index finger over them. Without touching the crystals, he gently moved his finger over their surface as if stroking a delicate butterfly, yet without contact.

"Look!" he said. "Do you see them changing? Watch the surface."

Of course, nothing was happening, except maybe in my brother's mind. The drugs weren't out of his system yet.

"When are you guys leaving for work." I needed to change the subject.

"In a few hours, probably." My brother's tone was mildly disgruntled at my dismissal of his crystal power. "What are you doing there, anyway?" He motioned to my newspaper.

"Help wanted ads," I said.

"Really? What are you going to do?"

"I don't know yet."

"Is it because of what happened last night?"

"It's because of everything – the drugs, the crashes, the..."

Footsteps sounded down the hall—Rebecca making her way to the bathroom.

"Never mind," I said. "Thank you for giving me a place to stay while I'm here."

I took the paper to my room and circled the ads I wanted to call about. Now that they were up and moving about, I felt more comfortable using a payphone down the block than their landline. I called on a few live-in childcare positions. The live-in part was incredibly appealing. One family from Walnut Creek wanted to meet me. I managed to take BART and a bus to a drop-off where the husband picked me up. They interviewed me and hired me on the spot.

I was homesick after two weeks of cleaning bathrooms and babysitting two children. Nothing would alleviate the gnawing sensation in my gut. What was I doing there? I wasn't accomplishing anything. Tears became so common by then that I knew I had no choice but to give my notice to the family and resign. I used all my money to purchase a one-way plane ticket home.

San Francisco had not been the adventure I'd hoped for. Nor had my time with Bob and Rebecca been the family/community experience and guiding mentorship I so badly craved. I'd been so terrified of my surroundings in that big, unfamiliar city that I lived like a saint. I'd never prayed more in my life. It could've been the rock bottom that propelled my spirit toward a more severe approach to godliness. But whatever it was, it didn't last long.

On the flight back, I sat beside Andy, an amiable and talkative guy. At some point during our flight, I realized he wasn't just being friendly. He was flirting with me. It turned out that he didn't live far from me. Though we parted ways, he gave me his address and phone number after we deplaned. I wrote him a letter immediately, and a week or so later, I received a lengthy response. We exchanged several letters and phone calls and made plans to meet. I borrowed a car to visit him.

Andy and I got along well, picking up and building on our written and phone communication. He got us both drinks, and we chatted casually before the conversation turned flirtatious. He took my hand, pulled me off the couch, and led me back to his bedroom. After some time, another man slipped into the room and the bed. A jolt of panic shot through me. What was happening? Who was this?

Unbeknownst to me, Andy already had a partner. Theirs was considered an open relationship. I'd never thought of such a thing before. My sense of romantic and sexual relationships had always assumed monogamy. I have since realized and learned that most long-term relationships between two men are *open*, meaning either person is free to have sex with someone else, or they practice bringing a third or fourth person into their sexual relationship.

Andy and his partner both assured me that this encounter was all okay and normal for gay partners. For quite a while, I felt awkward and shameful about being with two guys. I knew being with any guy sexually was a sin in God's eyes, but this seemed even more so to me. I started to get out of bed to leave. Andy caught my wrist when he realized what I was about to do. He and his partner spoke kind and flattering words about how much they wanted me to stay. They assured me they wouldn't do anything I was uncomfortable with.

Too late. I already felt massively uncomfortable.

But I hesitated, and in my hesitation, sexual temptation reignited. I stayed.

On my drive home, my feelings of lust and desire shifted to feelings of disgust with myself. I hoped to connect with Andy on a deeper emotional level with how our letters and phone communication had been. I fully suspected we'd wind up in bed together, but the whole thing had played out in my mind as much more attached to a sense of emotional connection. Instead, as I drove home feeling dirty and used, my naïveté gave way to the realization that this was a pre-planned and practiced scenario for these two men – one that I had blindly stepped into and, without much resistance, decided to participate in.

What I didn't understand as I drove was that this experience would further desensitize my soul and mind. Knowing I had engaged in this act willfully, I felt filthy and like I couldn't ask for God's forgiveness. I was unworthy of it and detached from the conviction over time. I dug a deep grave, shoved the experience down, and buried it alive rather than taking it to the Cross for forgiveness and cleansing. I was learning to detach and split off from myself and the awful feelings of shame and internal conflict. In the short term, this felt useful for numbing the pain. In the long term, this coping leads to great spiritual battles, emotional turmoil, and even mental health challenges. Not a good solution.

* * *

So, you won't believe this... but seriously, I can't make this stuff up. Upon my return home from California, I once again decided to solicit the Bible Institute to allow me back. This would be attempt number three for me. The school accepted my application for some unknown reason (perhaps nothing more profound than low enrollment numbers), and I returned. I admit, this time was a little weird. The second go-round was nice. I had come back to what was familiar and easy to settle into. People make mistakes and sometimes need a do-over, so there is no shame. But a third time?

"Exactly how many times are we going to do this?" I thought to myself.

It felt like I was living in the movie *Groundhog Day*, only it hadn't been written or filmed yet. And even if it had, the school forbade students from going to movie theaters, regardless of the film's rating.

Come to think of it, maybe that was the situation that prompted me to ask the Dean of Students for clarity the prior semester, where he called in the Dean of Men to chastise me for having the gall to question any of the school's rules. A few other students and I disobeyed that movie theater rule (which made the whole going-to-movie experience much more exciting). We broke that rule exactly once, and it certainly wasn't anything racy or lewd—perhaps *Star Wars* or *The Last Starfighter* or something like that. But wouldn't you know it – a student saw us coming out of the theater and reported us the next day. We all got hauled into the office for reprimand and punishment. *Be sure your sins will find you out*—Numbers 32:23 seemed applicable here.

But in round number three, I did feel stuck. I didn't feel like I knew how to improve my life. I was going around in circles. Was I ever going to graduate? How long would it take me to get through a three-year Bible Institute? I began as the youngest student on campus and could have graduated as the youngest in my class, but that fun fact no longer sets me apart. What was currently most unique about me was my third return and attempt at school. I don't know if that had ever been done, but it certainly was not a record of achievement.

Same-sex attraction was nearly always a dominant feeling. Nothing had changed there despite how much I prayed and asked for help. I knew the school's position on homosexuality, and I agreed with it as it was biblical. The issue wasn't their position but rather the general tone and complete lack of help from the staff (and almost all Orthodox churches).

I'm reminded of a conversation about the church's position on LGBTQ+ with a dear Anglican pastor and friend who once raised the question to me: "Garry, if we say that God has clearly said something is sin, then how can we in the church not offer meaningful support for those who want to turn away from that sin to follow and obey God?"

Excellent question, but one that I doubt was ever asked in the church when I was a young person struggling with these desires that I never wanted and wished I didn't have. Being a member of a church or a student at Bible College or Seminary who believes and speaks to the truth about God's law and created intent for marriage, sex, and identity while at the same time finding no hope or support is incredibly frustrating and demoralizing. Other than to repeat the condemnation of homosexuality, there was never a mention of hope.

I'll spare you most of the details of this college stint. It was a wash/rinse/repeat of the last two times. But one of the critical things that was different this time was the school required me to see someone for counseling. Pastor Grant was a counselor-in-training – a pastor getting his counseling license and needed to fulfill his licensure hours. The fact that I was forced to meet with him greatly irritated me. But I was somewhat comforted that my friend Suzy (the girl I'd thrown water balloons with) was also mandated to see him.

In the beginning, Suzy and I made a game of it and compared notes after each session to see how outlandish we could be, with Pastor Grant being none the wiser. This felt like good fun and a barrel of laughs for both of us.

But truth be told, Pastor Grant was a pretty nice guy. After several sessions, I grew to kind of like him. So, I stopped with the charade and started mainly providing truthful answers. Weeks later, we still weren't getting anywhere helpful, and I certainly wasn't going to offer the whole truth to him. I didn't trust that these sessions were confidential. I was sure he was reporting back to the Dean of Students.

But one day, I entered the office Pastor Grant was using for one of our sessions, sat across the desk from him as usual, and waited while he surveyed me thoughtfully. I could see the wheels of his mind turning as if he were debating what to say or ask. This was different behavior for him. I was starting to feel nervous.

A moment later, he spoke deliberately, "You know, Garry, I've been coming to this campus for quite a while. I've had the opportunity to observe students from this office window, and I've noticed you several times. I've been struck by how sad and miserable you seem whenever you're alone. It got me thinking about what might have happened to you to cause such despair?" He paused, frowning.

My cheeks flushed hot. I didn't like where this was going.

"Have you ever been sexually abused?" Pastor Grant asked outright.

A punch to the gut.

Oh my God! Oh my God! I screamed in my head. There was nowhere to run, no way to escape the vulnerability, the helplessness ...

Frazzled, I scrambled for what to say. I wanted to lie and assure him I was perfectly normal, but my hesitation was so apparent he'd never buy it. Pastor Grant watched me, waiting for an answer.

Then, all at once, from some unknown place inside, a deep belly laugh erupted from my mouth. I could not contain it at all—unbridled, uncontrollable laughter. I doubled over in my seat, practically convulsing in hysterics. I couldn't catch my breath. My reaction was so bizarre, and I was horrified by it, but I couldn't make it stop. The more I tried to compose myself, the more I laughed. And the sight of Pastor Grant's bewildered face made me erupt again.

Finally, my horrible fit of laughter subsided. Nothing remained but uncomfortable silence. I was completely disarmed.

Pastor Grant reassured me that our conversations were confidential. As much as I wanted to believe that, I didn't. I was sure the deans would look for information. That made me feel anxious. But maybe Pastor Grant would be true to his word and not pass along confidential information. I wanted someone safe to know me. I wanted someone who knew me to provide solid advice and biblical wisdom.

I saw an opening with a Christian leader for the first time, and I took it. He had just asked a direct question and completely neutralized my defenses. He named the painful and shameful memories I carried from early childhood. He did it with concern and genuine kindness. Even if I wasn't 100 percent sure I could trust him, I felt like I needed to try. I went on to share the whole truth and admitted to the sexual abuse and early porn exposure and my struggles with porn, though I didn't say it was same-sex.

That burden of secrecy was so familiar that I wasn't typically aware of how much it weighed me down until I felt someone was sharing it with me. That's what opening up and talking honestly with Pastor Grant accomplished for me. I no longer felt alone in the experience and abuse. That simple fact brought relief. Unfortunately, I don't think he had much training on these matters. He was so well-intended but not equipped to help.

I don't remember how long it was after this meeting or if there was any connection, but later, I sank into a severe depression. There were many mornings when I didn't get out of bed. I had a roommate this semester, and he voiced his concerns that I'd been missing so many classes.

Looking back, I can identify my pattern of sinking into depression. I'd be fine when keeping up with my classes, but once I slipped and fell behind, a debilitating depression fell over me. It didn't matter that I could logically see a way forward by doubling down and catching up—once the mountain felt too high, taking even one step toward it overwhelmed me. It triggered depression every time.

Every morning seemed like a huge challenge. Depression was the most intense as I was waking up, and more often than not, I gave in to the temptation to roll over and stay in bed – for as long as possible.

On one of these mornings, I slept longer than intended and realized I was missing my first class – again. I dragged myself out of bed late and went to clean up. In my robe, I strolled to the front of the building and stared out the large window there. The main hall, women's dorms, and classrooms were across from me. All at once, two men caught my eye as they strode across the parking lot toward my building. One of them was the Dean of Students. They looked like the FBI in their long trench coats and purposeful expressions.

Panic straddled my shoulders. Jolted awake, I bolted to my room and put on my clothes. My pulse raced. I just knew they were coming for me. I needed an escape, even if it meant jumping out my bottom floor window once I threw on my clothes and shoes.

But before I could tie my laces, footsteps pounded down the hallway and stopped at my door.

KNOCK, KNOCK, KNOCK.

I was already opening the window when my roommate, still in bed, sprang up at the sound of the knuckles on the door. I should've climbed out the window, but instead, I froze.

The door opened, and the same men stepped into my room.

"Get cleaned up and get to class," they told my roommate. He was a good student and rarely overslept. "We're here for him."

My roommate grabbed his clothes and went to the bathroom to clean up. There was nowhere to run.

Someone had reported me talking about suicide the night before. This caught me off guard, and I almost laughed. At last, I realized that a stupid joke between me and another friend had been overheard and misunderstood. I tried to explain this, but the Dean of Students interrupted me.

"It doesn't matter," he said. "We've also checked your class attendance and grades. You're doing terribly. Pack your things. We've called your brother, and he's coming to pick you up. You're being expelled."

With that, they turned and exited my room, their trench coats flapping out behind them. They clomped down the hall and disappeared. Stunned, I plopped down on my desk chair, my mind a blur of thoughts and emotions.

Not long after, my brother Dale arrived. He was furious. Understandably so. I had squandered three opportunities to make something of myself.

We packed my stuff in Dale's car, an all too familiar activity by now, while anger raged inside me. How could I have let it come to this? I cursed myself, my circumstances, and the Institute. And where was God? Where was the Church? Where was my providence, my deliverance? Bitterness rose from my stomach so harshly I could taste it. I fed on the bile of my hatred and anger and realized something immediately.

I was done. Done with all of it – God, Christianity, and especially the church.

Questions for Self-Reflection / Journaling / Group Sharing

1. Have you ever been in a situation where you had to figure it out on your own and didn't feel like you had the tools to know where to begin?

2. How did that feel to you?

3. What was the outcome?

4. Did you grow through the experience?

5. Are there secrets you've been holding that you don't want anyone else to know?

6. What are those secrets?

7. Are you willing to find someone to share them with now?

8. Have you considered counseling or a support group to help you process unhealed issues? What are your options for support?

9. Have you ever felt like you've struck out and disqualified yourself from God's grace or His plans and purposes for your life?

10. Have you recovered from that sense of loss? How?

11. Might you need to revisit that for more profound healing and to rediscover God's plans for you?

Chapter 9

LURED IN

I shoved all my worldly possessions into the trunk of my brother Dale's car and flopped into the passenger seat. He sped away from the Institute while I stared out the window, seething. Over the years, I learned to internalize most of my emotions, especially the dark stuff. But on this day in particular, I sat and stewed in silence over the raw hatred I felt toward God, His Church, and the Christian college that had just kicked me out.

I couldn't do anything right, least of all function as a Christian. On the other hand, Dale was the only one of our five siblings who hadn't given our Mom and Dad a painstaking ride. As a young boy, Dale gave his life to Jesus while watching an evangelistic Billy Graham crusade on TV. As long as I'd known him, Dale had always had a genuine heart to pursue the Lord, eager to please Him and live in service to Him. He even gave our sister one of his kidneys. When I was around ten, my sister had total kidney failure at age sixteen. She wound up on dialysis and a kidney transplant donor waitlist. Dale saved her life by donating one of his. At the time of my writing this book, our sister is still alive and active, thanks to him.

That's a tall order to live up to and one of the many thoughts that ran through my mind as I left Bible school for a third time. This time, though, it wasn't by choice. The decision had been made for me. Another failure was not what I needed. I was nineteen—I should've excelled and grown into a bright future. Massive failures were something that should have spread out over a lifetime.

After settling into my brother's basement, I had to find a way to get through the daily motions of life. To do so, I relied on negative emotions for fuel. Anger, bitterness, and self-pity became food to get through the day. Dale expected me to attend church because he knew I needed exposure to God's truths, and that's what we were accustomed to. I didn't want to attend his church. I went with my aunt, but inwardly, I was just going through the motions.

However, there was one positive aspect of my life, and that was my counseling appointments. Pastor Grant had agreed to keep meeting with me. Once a week, I drove more than thirty minutes to see him. In one of our sessions, I opened up about what had happened to me (and what I had done) over the previous summer between Mark and I. Even with Pastor Grant's usual poker-faced composure, I could see slight indications in the furrow of his brow and slightly widening eyes, showing that he was upset and angry at the way Mark had taken advantage of me.

It was brutal and shameful to confess this, but at the same time, I felt relief in finally bringing the secret into the light. I needed help processing my feelings about this – the loss of a friendship and mentor and the violation of someone I trusted. And then, of course, there was how Mark treated me afterward. I was a mess inside, and I knew it.

Before telling Pastor Grant about Mark, I clarified again that what I shared with him was confidential. He assured me that it would be, save for the exceptions of a crime in planning or intent to harm oneself or others. Afterward, however, he asked if he could share my confession with the Dean of Students.

"No!" I said bluntly. "This isn't something I'm ready for others to know about. Not yet".

"I think this is something the school leadership needs to know about," said Pastor Grant. "What he did to you was wrong on many levels, and he's still in a leadership role."

"You're right, I know, but I need more time. I'll do it myself," I said. "Let's talk about it again next week. I'll try to be ready to share this myself after next week's meeting."

I didn't want this information to come from anyone else but me. It didn't seem right to have someone else talking about it on my behalf. I wanted to believe Pastor Grant meant it when he said what I shared was confidential. I needed a week or two to prepare what I'd say and how I'd say it.

However, by our next meeting, Pastor Grant began with an apology. He had felt compelled to talk with the Dean of Students when he was at the campus. He told him what I had shared in confidence.

"What the hell!" I was stunned. I couldn't believe it. Pastor Grant had taken away my opportunity to do what I wanted and *needed* to do. My trust in him diminished that day.

Looking back, I can see how this pastor, new to counseling, didn't know how to help me. A few weeks later, he said this verbatim during our session.

"Garry, I feel like I've taken you as far as possible. I don't have expertise in sexual addiction or homosexuality, but I believe you have the tools you need, if you apply them, to continue going in a good direction."

He said he had taken me as far as he could, and that was that. Another trusted mentor released me back into the wilds, albeit with a few more tools than before, though I didn't know what those were. He didn't make a referral or provide any other support suggestions.

I just sat there, not knowing what to do or say next. It was awkward. Should I go ahead and leave? Just as I was about to stand, Pastor Grant offered a prayer. I guess that was the closure.

I walked to my car, feeling... blank. I didn't know what to think. I guess I felt dropped, entirely without resources. Pastor Grant didn't know how to help me. That was true. And the betrayal of his commitment set me back toward him as well. But he had become a connection. Meeting with him was a consistent commitment that felt like an anchor point. Now that was gone, with no warning or way of preparing myself. He could have reached out for other sources of support for me, but he never mentioned even attempting that.

It's hard to explain the internal and emotional agony of opening up to others about what I was going through. While I needed it more than anything, I was treading waves of shame, guilt, and hurt, and my instinct was to bury them. This would prevent others from dealing with them and allow them to see what I had let happen. So, for these instances when I built up the courage and did the hard work of opening up and sharing, only to be dismissed, ignored, or expelled for lack of solutions, it salted the wounds more deeply.

* * *

After completing numerous applications and interviews for everything from fast food to bag boy, I found a job at a local men's specialty store in a nearby mall. I had no real work experience, but at only fifteen hours a week, the manager was willing to give me a chance. Even after attending Bible College, I remained painfully shy and sheltered from essential social interaction. I didn't know how to relate to customers, making this job a formidable challenge. On my very first and quiet day of work, after our lone customer left the store without a purchase, my manager yelled at me from the back of the store, "Garry, you have to actually talk to the customers!"

It didn't happen immediately, but I learned to stop folding clothing long enough to approach customers. Once I got the hang of it, I could loosen up and dabble in small talk, eventually leading to sales.

Even though things got better at the men's clothing store, I needed another part-time job to supplement my income. Coincidentally, I received a call back from a small insurance office I had interviewed for weeks prior for part-time administrative work. The man I spoke with, who was also the boss, asked me to come in for a second interview, which I was excited about because surely it meant he thought I was a good fit for the job. I thought the interview went well. He even shared a little about his wife and kids. I was hopeful.

That evening, I received a phone call.

"Is this Garry?" the caller asked.

I recognized his voice. Instantly, I was excited.

"I wanted to offer you the office job we discussed today."

"Thank you so much!" I replied with a fist pump in the air. "When can I start?"

"There's just one other important thing I must discuss with you." The tone of the man's voice changed and seemed odd. "I've met with you twice now, and I get the sense you and I could have more than a boss/employee relationship. What do you say?"

What? I was dumbfounded!

He went on to explain that although he was a married man with kids, he was not only interviewing for the role of administrative support but also a discreet sexual partner. My jaw nearly hit the bed I was now sitting on. My pulse began to race. He explained that his wife and kids could never know about the relationship but that as his special someone, I would also be a part of his family.

I quickly declined and hung up without another word. This was not what I was looking for, and it made me feel dirty and gross. Here, I thought that perhaps I'd be wanted for a legit job, and instead, he propositioned me. Even weeks afterward, the memory of this strange guy's offer nagged me. I had to wonder, what was it about me that could lead a total stranger and potential boss to think I'd be interested in such a twisted arrangement?

Growing up, I remember feeling marked, in some inexplicable way, the feeling of being different and not fitting in. I was often labeled by other guys as *fag*, *queer*, or *sissy*. That proposition brought back a familiar sense of being marked. These labels and experiences can tremendously define how we feel about ourselves. We can agree and label ourselves with the things being said about us - because if others see something about me, maybe it's true.

On the flip side – I later experienced the power of godly affirmation and Kingdom-like vision for me and my life through Christ-followers calling out what they saw to be true in me based on the certainty of God's Word. I especially needed to hear these truths from other men. They saw what was true when I couldn't see it. They saw what was true even when they couldn't see it in me in the natural, but they called it out because God gave them a vision for who I was – His son, a man made in His image, His workmanship. But God was still awaiting my surrender, agreement, and cooperation with all He had for me. He wouldn't force me. He wanted my *yes*. Like a master sculptor, Jesus could see the image He ached to reveal underneath the complex, formless, and even disfigured and marred exterior I was trapped within.

Proverbs 18:21: *Life and death are in the power of the tongue.* Why do we as Christians – why do we as Christian men – allow the world and chaos to speak more compellingly, frequently, and loudly than we do to one another? We are nearly silent in building one another up. We can play a profound role in a person discovering who they really are and who they can truly become.

Why are we so stingy and bashful of securing our brothers, sisters, and children around us in the good and glory of who God made them to be – who they truly are? Our powerful words of grace, clarity, and vision for another who cannot see anything good about themselves – empowered by the author of life, are the carefully delivered chisels skillfully placed by the sculptor that begin to reveal the masterpiece beneath. Our words are powerful. Let's use them to rescue lives and set prisoners free.

* * *

I was still attending church regularly, as expected by my brother, and within the six months since I'd been booted from college, I met a girl there who I liked. This was the first time I was so strongly both physically and emotionally attracted to the opposite sex. This was a new feeling. I liked it but felt awkward knowing how to express it toward and with a woman. Sharon and I became rather serious pretty fast, and in a way, it was a relief. Finally!

I had been trying to live as I thought I should. Maybe this person was the one? She loved Jesus... and I knew I was supposed to love Him... maybe I even did... maybe not. My sense of God and my relationship with Him was very complicated. I would describe myself as highly conflicted toward Him – *I hate you, don't leave me.* Discovering this relationship with Sharon also gave me a softer heart toward God, at least temporarily.

Maybe, with Sharon by my side, I could ignore the past and turn the final page on my life's last few miserable chapters. My family adored her, too. There were just so many things to like and love about her.

As Sharon and I attended the young adult group one evening, I overheard two guys talking about a gay bar downtown. Their tone was derogatory and mocking, but that's not what interested me. It was the first time I'd ever heard of a gay bar in my area, and curiosity jolted me like a flash of lightning. I thought those were only in New York City or San Francisco, not rural upstate NY.

Right there during group time, with Sharon in the other room, my head spun. Memories, images, and sensations returned to me all at once, and I didn't know what to make of it. But I knew one thing for sure — I wanted to find that bar. It was ridiculous on so many levels. I'd never even had an alcoholic drink before, much less been inside a bar. I got a rush of adrenaline on the spot and came up with an excuse to leave early. Sharon and I had been dating for several months but had driven separately. I should have recognized my intense selfishness in leaving her to seek out the gay bar. In my fascination and intrigue, I gave minimal regard to the fact that a sweet young woman loved me.

But that isn't what went through my mind as I drove to the middle of town. Much of the local nightlife thrived there, but I didn't know one bar from another. Mind you, this was a time before the Internet, Google, or GPS. Gay bars weren't usually listed in the phone book in a way that indicated their gayness. I had no way to determine where this place could be, and even then, how would I know it when I saw it? LGBTQ+ flags weren't waiving out front back then. But where there is a will, there is a way, and I was on a hunt to find the local gay community. At this point, it wasn't about looking for sex or lusting. The drive I felt inside compelled me to find others like me.

I can't tell you how many nights I drove into that same town, parked in a different spot, and combed the storefronts for this bar (no doubt I would have hit my daily

10,000 steps if I'd been wearing a tracker back then) all the while attending church regularly and acting like everything was fine. Finally, one night around midnight, I found it. I was pretty sure, anyway. Across the street from the adult bookstore and an old movie theater was a small venue under a neon sign and busting at the seams with people. Loud music and dancing spilled out onto the sidewalk and street. Baffled, I sat on a bench and watched, working up the nerve to make my way up there and mingle in. Ultimately, I couldn't do it, at least not right away. Fear of the unknown prevented me from doing what I wanted.

In retrospect, it was more than that. The Apostle Paul writes about a seared conscience in I Timothy 4:2 and a defiled conscience in I Corinthians 8:7. I knew what I wanted to do, and I was about to sin. I had no business searching out this place, let alone lingering around it.

I'm also reminded of Solomon's words in Proverbs 7:6-27:

'For at the window of my house I looked out through my lattice, And I saw among the naive, And discerned among the youths a young man lacking sense, passing through the street near her corner; and he takes the way to her house, in the twilight, in the evening, in the middle of the night and the darkness. And behold, a woman comes to meet him, dressed as a harlot and cunning of heart. She is boisterous and rebellious, her feet do not remain at home; She is now in the streets, now in the squares, and lurks by every corner. So she seizes him and kisses him, and with a brazen face, she says to him: 'I was due to offer peace offerings; today, I have paid my vows. Therefore, I have come out to meet you, to seek your presence earnestly, and I have found you. I have spread my couch with coverings, with colored linens of Egypt. I have sprinkled my bed with myrrh, aloes, and cinnamon. Come, let's drink our fill of love until morning; let's delight ourselves with caresses. For my husband is not at home; he has gone on a long journey. He has taken a bag of money with him. At the full moon, he will come home.' With her many persuasions, she entices him; with her flattering lips, she seduces him. Suddenly, he follows her as an ox goes to the slaughter, or, as one walks in fetters to the discipline of a fool, until an arrow pierces through his liver; as a bird hurries to the snare, so, he does not know that it will cost him his life. Now, therefore, my sons, listen to me, and pay attention to the words of my mouth. Do not let your heart turn aside to her ways, do not stray into her paths. For many are the victims she has cast down, and numerous are all her slain. Her house is the way to Sheol, descending to the chambers of death.'

Solomon (or any other observer) could have been looking down at me through the blinds of one of the apartments or office windows across the street, watching the scene outside the bar unfold. They might have wondered what I was doing if they had noticed me. Why was I lingering near the bar but not going in? Why did I seem nervous, drawn, and repelled simultaneously?

If they were regular observers, they might have spotted the same young man returning night after night to linger outside the bar but not go in. If they were as astute as Solomon was (although with all his wisdom, his life ended in great folly), they might have intuited what was happening with me: my conscience was being seared. Freeing me to a place where I would trample it underfoot to make my way into the bar, finally mingling with the people I was so curious about.

My girlfriend knew something was wrong, but I avoided her, spending all my extra time outside work and other commitments near the bar. Somewhere in all of this, I began smoking. Where my life had once been characterized and dominated by the outer appearance of *a good Christian guy,* I was shifting toward embracing a different image. I stopped attending church, although I didn't say anything to my brother or aunt.

Living a double life wasn't foreign to me. It came naturally as a double-minded, church-going kid and young man. I have mentioned it before, but it bears repeating because this is one of the most common and broken ways Christians unconsciously live. We wear our *sinless* Christian mask to church and around Christian friends, then set it aside when we cave to temptations of the flesh. Perhaps our Christian masks are the ones we wear most frequently, but we have several others that hide our vulnerabilities and sins of self-medication.

Why do humans feel we must cover up the truth of our pain, loneliness, emptiness, and boredom? We're good at distracting ourselves from proper remedies. We're experts at consoling ourselves with food, alcohol, porn, or sex. We use social media or binge entertainment to fill our empty places or ease the gnawing edge of our sadness. All the while, Jesus has already offered His yoke, which is easy and light (Matthew 11:30). He wants to carry our burdens. Yet, we often resort to unhealthy, sinful ways to cope.

Denying self, honoring God, selflessly giving what is best for others, and fulfilling our commitments are all biblical ideas and mandates that used to be highly regarded by nearly everyone. Today, however, living *our truth*, pursuing what makes us happy, discovering who we are, and foregoing commitment to any person or group who doesn't help us live *our best life* now are all ways society (even some so-called Christian congregations) blesses its followers, condoning modern-day false religions as good and just.

That's where I was and where society told me I should be: full of self. I covered myself with a veneer of Christianity, armed myself with enough biblical knowledge to keep up appearances, and lived the lie that I was an authentic Christian. I even fooled myself sometimes.

In retrospect, however, having lived in and formerly identified with the LGBTQ+ community, I can honestly say that I wish Christians and the efforts of the Church could be as available, warm, and open as the LGBTQ+ community. There is so much that's broken within those who identify as LGBTQ+, but so often, they are far more relational and available and are waiting with open arms. In my experience, they are more available and accessible than many churches and card-carrying Christians.

In modern Christianity, relationships are thin, and people aren't willing to give their time toward deep and authentic relational connections. Yet that's what we were all made for! The nuclear family has become the dominant focus in most churches, and while the family is essential, it often leaves hurting, lonely singles feeling like they're on the fringe of the church. We're busy people, and we allow the cares of this life to choke out the most important things that truly matter.

On the other hand, when the masks come off, and we get to see the person behind the image, we often find high levels of selfishness and narcissism. I hear about it through stories of heartbreak from moms and dads, wives, husbands, kids, and other loved ones who express the pain they feel when a family member succumbs to living their *true self* as a member of the LGBTQ+ community. It's difficult to watch those whom we desperately love fall for the lies that society pushes. Instead of soul searching, many hop on board with flagrant self-centeredness. Life is now about *them*—that's what they tell their family and friends—and if you can't support and celebrate their new *true* self, you'll be punished for it or cut out of their life altogether.

* * *

During all these dramatic decisions and changes in my life, I avoided my brother and his wife as much as possible. He had been serving a church nearby as a pastor for a few years, and by this point, they were parents of one child. Their hands were full with ministry and family, so it wasn't difficult to slip by them and retreat to my basement bedroom.

As I began venturing into the downtown nightlife, returning to my brother's house in the wee hours of the morning became routine. On one particular occasion, I slipped in to find my brother sleeping on the pull-out couch in the living room. That was odd, but I just wanted to get to the door that led to the basement. I tiptoed across the floor, around the pull-out, and toward the basement door. I'd started smoking by then and reeked of cigarettes—all the more reason to get to the basement.

I reached out and grasped the doorknob.

"I feel like we're losing you." My brother's voice was quiet but steady.

I paused for a moment; my heart softened a bit. I perched myself on the arm of the couch. "Why are you sleeping out here?"

"I picked up a bug." He rolled over, coughed, and groaned. "I'm running a fever."

I wanted someone to see what I was doing and my destructive descent. To say something to me, to offer a lifeline. But people aren't mind-readers. I also know I seemed closed and committed in the direction I was going. No one would have thought I was open to their input.

He asked what had been going on with me, but it was clear he was in no shape for a counseling session. I told him we could talk when he was feeling better. As rotten as he felt, he didn't fuss about it. We said goodnight to each other, and I retreated downstairs to be greeted by their German Shepherd, who usually slept with me in the basement.

I was exhausted. I'd been staying out until 1 or 2AM for many nights, but as I lay in bed before drifting off to sleep, I reflected on Dale's words: *I feel like we're losing you.* How transparent I must've been, despite my best efforts to wear the Christian mask. I wonder how many other Christians can say the same thing about certain times in their lives. I had indeed been pulling away for a while – really, since Bible school. At the beginning of my shift away from God (or at least the appearance of knowing and walking with Him), I had never dreamed that I would sink so low. I'd allowed myself to pursue self-gratification and, therefore, fall ever more deeply into a pit of self-pity, which made rejecting Him easier and easier.

After that night, I wondered if my brother might inquire about what I was doing and where I was going. But life was busy, and I was out of the house far more than I was around. I had two part-time jobs with a wide-ranging work schedule. It would have been hard to track me down, even with me crashing in his basement. At the beginning of this hedonistic exploration of boundaries, a part of me wanted someone to notice my downward spiral. I didn't know how to stop.

What was once early curiosity peeking over the cliffside quickly and easily became a step too close to the edge. The edge was rocky and precarious, and I could not catch my footing. Before I knew it, I'd tumbled over, and from there, it was straight down. The thing is, this can and does happen to many Christians at one time or another. Once we get too deep or aware of our sin, we tend to hide, just like Adam and Eve hid in the garden. Sin makes us ashamed. Guilt tastes sour. By that point, the last thing I wanted was any input or connection with Christians.

That scenario with my brother reminded me of curfew at Bible College. We weren't allowed to leave the dorms, and certainly not campus, after 9PM unless we had a job that required it or special permission to do so. I often felt empty and lonely at school – my grades were usually a struggle because my interest in studying waned, and I was usually in a friendship issue of one kind or another. I had trouble sleeping at night, so I would sneak off campus and wander through the neighborhood or the large cemetery down the street.

After months of sneaking off campus, in the thick of my depression and invisibility, I started marking the official campus sheet whenever I left. I even wrote in the late departures of 11PM or after, leaving my return time blank. Instead of sneaking around, I got to where I'd slam the heavy steel door as hard as I could and let it *bang* closed behind me. Ironically, even as legalistic and rigid as the school officials and RA's were, no one ever noticed what I was doing or that I was gone.

Now, in hindsight, I understand that my cry for help was also an impossible expectation. In my boyish heart and fantasy, I inadvertently put the responsibility for my spiritual and emotional well-being on everyone but myself – especially key people like my brother, pastors, and other influential spiritual leaders.

That said, could some fellow Christ-followers have seen where I was emotionally and spiritually and reached out? Of course! That's part of why I'm writing my life story today – to offer some insight for Christian leaders and followers on what to look for and how to engage with someone hurting and making self-destructive choices. But people on both sides of the situation (those struggling and those whom God has called to help them) must have realistic expectations and healthy boundaries. I was undoubtedly not owning my role in that. Not even close.

Unrecognized by me then, self-pity had seeped in and rooted itself in my life. It became a *compadre* of sorts, always comforting me, always justifying my actions, while alternately highlighting the hurtful or dismissive behavior of others. Oh, how *they* mistreated me —misunderstanding and mishandling me. I was a victim, and in my head and heart, I silently built cases against them, making me a collector of injustices.

I experienced enough bullying and shaming in school and church as a child that I constantly anticipated negative encounters. I had been a victim, but now I was trapped in a victimhood mindset. I desperately needed to give that negativity to God. But no one encouraged me to find my worth in Him who had created me – to embrace His life-changing, life-freeing grace.

Concrete events of abuse, bullying, and shaming from my past mingled with my jaded perceptions of what *could* happen. Often, we function more through the lens of perception than reality, and it wasn't until many years later that I sensed the Lord clearly and firmly revealing to me, "You are far more judgmental against others than anyone is toward you."

I was shocked when I *heard* this warning coming from a place within. That couldn't possibly be right. *I* was the one who had been poorly treated. *I* was the one who was rejected. *I* was the one who... sized others up instantly and presumed to know them and what they thought of me. I was the one who learned to reject others before they could reject me... huh?

When the Holy Spirit provided this insight, it was the first time I sensed God revealing the truth to me in a way that captured my immediate and total attention. God, in His firm mercy, showed me the ugliness of my own heart toward so many others. It was the start of my spiritual maturity and part of the humility God required of me to see what He wanted to show me. More of that later.

* * *

A double-minded man [is] unstable in all his ways. James 1:8.

Night after night, I returned to my perch on the bench outside the bar downtown. Even with the broad lack of acceptance of homosexuality back in the 1980s, it was a popular bar and dance club. One night, out of the blue, some guy joined me on the bench, his back toward the bar. We started chatting, nothing serious, when I noticed someone coming down the sidewalk. A bolt of fear and shame shot through me. Had he seen me? It looked like he found some buddies in the crowd. Maybe he wouldn't notice me.

I tried to focus on my conversation with the stranger, but the familiar face moved closer and closer. It couldn't be who I thought it was. It just couldn't.

But it was. And yes, clearly, he saw me. He was not only someone I went to church with but Sharon's younger brother. He came right up behind the bench and glared at me. His buddies looked confused and uncomfortable in the crowd they were walking through. I pushed back a rough, awkward swallow, grasping for what to say ... but my acquaintance never said a word, just stepped back over with his buddies and strolled on, fists shoved into his jean pockets and brow furrowed.

I could only imagine how angry he must've been for his sister, but even worse, as a brother in Christ at the same church, he must have been crushed to find me hanging out in front of the local gay bar.

The bar was about to close. It was almost 2AM. My lingering outside was ridiculous. I finally mustered up the nerve, and without giving it another thought, I jumped off the bench and was through the door in a few strides.

I convinced the bouncer to let me in despite closing time to buy cigarettes.

The crowd had thinned out, which made me more comfortable. I needed a feel for the venue. Would it feel like home? Or would it be weird? Would I be embarrassed?

I approached the bar, and the bartender smiled and gave me a friendly once-over. "Sorry honey, I already did the last call. No more drinks tonight."

"Could I just buy a pack of cigarettes?" I asked.

"Sure. Which brand?"

I told him and pulled out some cash as he rang up the sale. "You're super cute, you know that?" He said and flashed another smile. "I don't think I've ever seen you in here before. Are you new to the area?"

"This is my first time here," I said, grabbing my cigarettes and smiling back as I turned for the door.

"We're open again tomorrow night," he called. "I'll be working. Why don't you come back and stay awhile?"

And just like that ... contact: *initiated.*

I'd broken the barrier. I'd set myself at ease. That friendly bartender (who later became a good friend) was all it took. I showed up again early the next afternoon.

Suffice it to say, this was the end of my relationship with Sharon. I felt like I had finally found my people, and it eclipsed everything else in my life. Nothing else mattered to me. I didn't care about how these decisions impacted anyone else. I was blinded by my selfishness and the euphoria of it all.

Sharon reached out and asked to meet. I didn't want to, but I knew I owed her an explanation for my disappearance and dropping our relationship with zero communication. I was a total ass.

We met at a park we had often walked in. A lot of our conversation is a blur now, but I recall many tears and pleading on Sharon's part. Not just because of our relationship but far more because she knew I was shipwrecking my faith.

"Where is God at for you in all of this?" she implored.

"I don't care where God is!" I retorted. "Where was He when I wanted His help for years? He was nowhere to be found. I'm done fighting these feelings."

I stopped a moment and looked at Sharon. "I am genuinely sorry I've hurt you. I know I'm a schmuck for the way I handled all this. But I can't go back. I don't want to go back! Not to church, not to God, none of it. I'm sorry."

That was it. That was the last time I saw Sharon.

It's hard to describe where I was emotionally and mentally by this point. In a way, I had let go of everything holding me back to embrace this new life entirely. I had finally found *my people.* My past life didn't fit into that, and I didn't want any part. I knew it broke Sharon's heart. But *my* heart, on the other hand, soared with meaning for this new life, community, and identity. Life finally made sense. What else could top that?

I was suddenly popular. Gay men liked me and wanted to spend time with me, not always for sex. There were genuine friendships that developed. Their doors were always open. They delighted in seeing me walk into the bar or their home. Huge hugs, kisses on the cheek, and endless laughter were common characteristics of my introduction and foray into the LGBTQ+ world, as was alcohol. A lot of alcohol.

There was a temporary euphoria in cutting ties with my nearly lifelong struggle. Finally, accepting it and rejecting God's path felt liberating... until this bright, primrose path led to places I never dreamt I'd go, to things I never imagined I'd do, and then into darkness and death. I was fooled for quite a while, but then, for several years, I felt powerless to break out of it, even if I wanted to.

Many months into my new community and identity, I discovered countless other hallmarks of homosexuality that weren't at first apparent nor as flattering as all the peace and love talk. There were all kinds of drug use and dependency, a revolving door of one-night stands, open relationships, multiple sexual partners, depression, anxiety, domestic violence, hopelessness, aging out of the hot young crowd, and thus relegated to the status of a *troll* - older men who sat together at one end of the bar, hoping a young, virile guy would get drunk enough to go home with one of them.

Little did I know then how destructive my foolish and godless decisions would be later.

* * *

Working retail in the local mall - the men's clothing store - grew on me, and I learned to excel in customer conversations. Quite the feat for the once shy and introverted young man that I was. I gained a good understanding of the store and our product and found that I enjoyed displaying, promoting, and selling our merchandise. They promoted me to "Third Key," which meant I could supervise and open and close the store.

I was still working two jobs. However, when I wasn't working, I was at the bar - day or night. What transformed into a dance floor in the evening was used as a hangout space with comfortable couches and chairs during the afternoon, always with light ambient music in the background. Before long, I started dating Daniel, a guy who worked at the bar. He was a part-time bouncer. He asked me to move in with him within a couple of weeks.

Darkness is repelled by light. I didn't want to be around any of my Christian family. Of course, I internalized that their lack of understanding and compassion repelled me from them. But in hindsight, it was good old-fashioned sin and crappy feelings that resulted from giving in to sin. So, I parted ways with my brother, said goodbye to his German Shepherd, and moved out of his basement to live with my boyfriend.

This relationship with Daniel was about so much more than sex. It was about feeling like we were making a home together and being there for each other. At the time, it felt more natural than being with a woman and trying to meet her needs. I always felt a deep deficit, even fear, when meeting a woman's needs. Platonically, I deeply understood women, but that's where the understanding began and ended. I always felt like an empty pit of nothingness in a romantic relationship with a woman. I felt as if I still needed a father or a masculine rescuer. I knew she needed and desired something from me, but I had nothing to give. The well was empty. So, I usually ran at a woman's first hint of romantic interest.

A guy on the other hand? It felt like he had something I needed. It felt like another guy could pour *into* me rather than my perception that a woman needed something *from* me. Even today, it isn't easy to explain all this as clearly as I would like. I was utterly clueless about the dynamics and reasons for my conflicted emotions and attractions back then.

I now understand that Daniel and I were two hurting young men. I was nineteen, and he was ten years older. The gaps and chasms we felt in our masculine souls were filled in through the masculinity of the other, at least temporarily.

I did maintain communication with my parents during this time but avoided anything that wasn't casual chit-chat. They lived in New York during the summer and in the Christian retirement village in Florida during the winter. That made it easy for me to keep them in the dark about my new lifestyle. When we did talk, I went along with whatever was said about church or God and fostered the illusion that I was living with a friend to be closer to work. Of course, my mother knew more than she was letting on. News like this kind of debauchery traveled like a virus throughout families and small-town churches in what was more euphemistically called "prayer chains."

Okay, okay, undoubtedly, there have been good things to come of church prayer chains, but back then, they seemed to serve a dual purpose. These telephone prayer huddles could have given Twitter a run for its money in disseminating information. The classic definition of gossip is when someone who is neither part of the problem nor part of the solution inserts themselves into the dialogue about someone else's business and life. Growing up in church, I saw the church prayer chain's good, bad, and ugly. Often, there could be too much side speculation over the more scintillating topics and far less time devoted to actual prayer. This shows how even the godliest people still come from a fallen world and are just as susceptible to breaking Jesus' commandments as anyone else.

Satan has used gossip as a destructive force within the Church. Gossip shatters trust and prevents men, women, and young people from seeking and receiving the help we all need. But that's a topic for another chapter and another book... and yes, it's in the works.

A few weeks after moving in with Daniel, I received a letter from my favorite aunt. She had always been an emotional and spiritual rock in my life and a ton of fun, too. Daniel was at his day job, and I had just poured a cup of coffee in our little apartment kitchen when I opened her letter. I don't know what I was expecting, but I was unprepared. I read the first few lines, and then, all at once, I buckled over like someone had punched me in the gut. I leaned against the kitchen wall for support and slowly slid down until I plopped onto the floor. I can't recall all the details of that letter, but I will never forget a few key points: how awful my aunt felt for my parents because I was such a shameful son, how ashamed she was of me, and how ashamed God must be. On top of it all, she flat-out told me that I'd lost my salvation. The letter went on for a couple of pages where she called out my behavior for leaving the church and Sharon.

My aunt was right about many things she said, but I had to wonder what result she had hoped to elicit with one hand-grenade sentence after another. If she intended to garner some thoughtful reaction or remorse on my part, she had failed miserably. It certainly didn't stir up repentance or a desire to reach out to her for help or advice. There was a lesson in that moment that changed how I believe people of faith should support one another. It's part of why I wanted to tell my story. As a church, we always have room to grow in edifying and guiding our brothers and sisters in Christ. Throughout the ages, shaming one another for sin has never changed hearts and minds for long—not where it matters.

That isn't to say that sin shouldn't be called out properly for the sake of the one practicing sin and the community. It also isn't to say that church discipline doesn't have a proper and healthy place in the Body of Christ because it does. But first, we appeal and work to expose, in love, the damage that's being done in the life of the one living contrary to God's design.

All that letter did for me that day was put me on the defensive, make me angry, and force up a wall around my heart. However, I was emboldened to call my aunt, and when she answered, I exploded. I told her she didn't know who I was, how long I'd struggled with these issues, or how long I'd prayed for God to help. She had no idea how hard I had fought against the pull within. She tried to calm me down, but there was nothing else to say.

It was a very long time before we spoke again.

In retrospect, as a mature adult, I can see that, at the time, my aunt did not know how to respond to the direction I was going in. I'd always known her to be a sweet, wonderful woman who loved Jesus, people, and me. But she knew I was on a path that led away from God and toward destruction. In her defense, that letter was her acting out of fear, worry, hurt, and yes, even shame. Like many Christians in the mid-80s, she had no idea how to navigate the challenges of loving a prodigal son without affirming his sin. Stern words alone were not the solution. That said, there is a difference between too harsh a reprimand that repels our loved ones and guidance so loose that it turns into tolerance and support of sinful behavior.

When I came to a place of genuine repentance and surrender to God, it was easy and natural for my aunt and I to repair our relationship. She's still my favorite aunt.

The truth is, I felt a strong sense of conviction over my new lifestyle and had zero doubt that it was wrong. But part of me didn't care. I was still angry with the Church and God for His lack of help or care. Or rather, my perception of that. Still, another part of me couldn't find moral goodness in many of my decisions. I was lying, deceiving my parents, and living a lie to myself.

That's why I perpetually distracted myself. Work, boyfriend time, all-nighters at the bar, brief stints of sleep, and then up the next day to do it all over again. I didn't have time to think or feel. Quiet, reflective moments and time alone only made me uncomfortable, even miserable. My conscience lingered on the periphery, waiting to offer those flash warnings of right and wrong or danger. I wanted nothing to do with inner urges of correction, which is the moral law God has written on our hearts and consciences.

As you may expect, I began to consider the possibility that perhaps the traditional Christian view of homosexuality had been wrongly interpreted. How could something that felt so hardwired, so deeply woven into my identity, so *right*, possibly be so wrong? Daniel solidified my sexual orientation. For starters, he was kind. He was also crazy about me, which was a new experience. No one had ever been crazy about me before.

He was my first long-term, live-in, gay relationship, and I believed he was the path to my authentic self and true happiness. Without reservation, by this time, I fully embraced the gay label. There was no longer any doubt in my mind that I was gay. For me, being with a man worked. It aligned with all of my attractions and desires – not only sexually but emotionally. When I was with Daniel, whether it was making dinner, talking about our future, or watching a movie on the couch, any vestiges of reservation were swallowed up in the sense of finally belonging to someone who loved me and wanted me.

For the first time in my life, accepting all that I felt and finally giving full release to my attractions wasn't so much like coming out of the closet as it was being released from prison. I was finally free, and I was never going back.

I began searching the Bible for the missing pieces. Surely, crucial parts had been misinterpreted and misunderstood. But to my great disappointment, I couldn't find the loophole. As much as I scoured the Scriptures, I could find no ambiguous language in any of the six most referred-to passages that dealt with homosexuality. The closest argument I could knit together was with the fact that the Old Testament prohibitions in Leviticus also had bans around sowing seeds of different types in the same row or sewing together a garment made of other materials. But that wasn't satisfying for long because I also understood a significant difference between God's ceremonial law (which could be required for a time and season) and God's moral law (established from the beginning and never wavering).

Frustratingly, I found my conviction in God's moral law only further reinforced by the truth I had tried to dance around. As much as I wanted another possibility or alternative interpretation (even a flimsy one would do!), there just wasn't one. Three Old Testament and three New Testament passages condemn homosexual practice unambiguously:

•Genesis 19

• Leviticus 18:22

• Leviticus 20:13

• Romans 1:26-27

• I Corinthians 6:9-11

• I Timothy 1:10

In addition, there is also the glaring fact that nowhere in Scripture can even a single positive reference to homosexual practice be found. It was right there before me—all the answers I needed and God's moral law in my heart (as much I had stifled it) telling me what I needed to recognize. Yet, in my free will, I chose to wait it out and adopt the mindset that I need not draw hard, fast conclusions so quickly. After all, it isn't good to rush to judgment, right?

Despite this, however, I longed to feel like a good person. I wanted to believe that there was still some spirituality that existed within. I found ways to validate myself because the need for validation never wanes, especially when we live unfulfilled spiritual lives. For the next couple of years, I approached Christianity like a buffet from which I could pick and choose. Whatever teaching or biblical concept I didn't like, I rejected it. I happily put anything that tasted good or gave me instant gratification about myself onto my plate.

Today, I am incredibly grateful that pro-gay theology hadn't yet been popularized when I was wrestling with what I believed to be true. I have read the books and watched several videos that have revised the Bible according to fleshly desires and justification of sin. Now, I can clearly see the house of cards this false teaching is built on, but back then – when I desperately wanted to find a way to live in sin and still feel okay with God – it would have easily been a deception to fall for. Jesus referred to such false doctrines as building your house on a foundation of sand rather than a firm foundation of truth. Matthew 7:24-2.

Questions for Self-Reflection / Journaling / Group Sharing

1. Has a Christian leader ever violated your trust? If so, how?

2. What has the impact of that been? Have you ever genuinely forgiven him/her?

3. Do you experience mistrust of leaders/Christians?

4. Do you need help in moving forward and beginning to trust again? If so, what are your options for support? Will you take action?

5. Have you ever used a bad attitude or behavior as a cry for help? Pause and pray - really consider this question. If so, how?

6. What would you have wanted someone to say or do to help you? Are you willing to seek help now?

7. Have you ever rejected what you knew was true to justify what you wanted? If so, how?

8. What kind of impact have those decisions had on your life and relationships?

Chapter 10

UNSTABLE &
DOUBLE-MINDED

My deception and double living concerning my identity put a band-aid on my spiritual affliction for a while. On the one hand, I wasn't fooling myself. On the other hand, I invested too much in my justifications, as if they were permissible to God. These justifications allowed me to put on blinders, close my ears, and soothingly ignore what I knew deep down to be true.

While deep in our sin, how many of us fall into this diabolical trap?

Well into my season of reimagining righteousness in the way that best fit my lifestyle, I learned that Dallas Holm, a Christian performing artist, was on tour. He was one of my favorite singers and musicians, and when I mentioned it to Daniel, he was happy to see him with me. The night of the concert, while packed like sardines in the venue's colossal foyer and waiting for the doors to open, a distinct chuckle rang out amidst the clatter, chatter, and laughter of the sea of people. Goosebumps prickled my flesh. It was a laugh that brought back long-buried memories. I turned toward the sound and, at that exact moment, with a slight break in the crowd, met eyes with Martha on the far side of the foyer.

I had known this woman from my Christian school experience, and later, she and her husband joined the church my family and I went to. They had always seemed like genuine Christians – real people with real issues, but they were doing their best to walk with Jesus. I'd been drawn to both of them. In retrospect, what was different was they didn't window-dress everything. They openly shared more of their struggles than nearly anyone I'd known in the Church up to that point. That forever endeared my heart to them. In truth, I don't know that they were even close to being genuinely vulnerable. Still, it was refreshing to see some explicit representations of honesty and hear about personal struggles with sin.

Martha's face lit up, and she wiggled through the crowd to deliver a huge hug. My stomach tightened as I introduced her to Daniel. I didn't know what she had heard about me if anything at all. Did she know I'd embraced a gay identity? Or that I was living that life with the man before her? If she did, she did not acknowledge it. As typical of her character, her face radiated joy, and not for a second did she make either Daniel or I feel unclean or unwelcome. I also didn't mistake her love for affirmation of how I lived my life.

In these situations in the past – around many other Christians who were far less gracious, I often felt dehumanized and looked down upon. I have heard this same complaint from others in the LGBTQ+ community regarding the Church and the experience of many Christians – real or perceived.

Let me share a quick story to give you a very different example than the one Martha embodied. Daniel and I were browsing in an antique shop in Ithaca, New York, and decided to head for some other shops. We turned to exit but bumped right into a relative of mine, a pastor.

I was so caught off guard that I exclaimed, "My gosh, Tim! What are you doing here? How are you?!"

Tim glanced between me and my partner. He didn't sneer, nor did he put on a friendly smile. "I'm well."

He shifted from one foot to the other, seemingly uncomfortable with such intimate and close proximity with a real sinner.

Here we go, I thought. Tim's gaze turned into a glare, which left no disguise at his disgust.

If I had noticed him earlier, I may have anticipated his disdain and prepared myself. Nothing can truly prepare you for the brutality of face-to-face judgment from those dead-set on inflicting it.

Stoic-like, Tim waved and made a wide berth around us as he continued shopping.

I didn't bother introducing Tim to Daniel that day.

Back to the concert - when the doors opened and everyone started pouring in, Martha hugged Daniel and me and hurried back to her companions so they didn't get separated in the crowd.

The performance and preaching were excellent and compelling. Ultimately, Dallas Holm shared the gospel and gave an altar call. Daniel didn't hesitate to go forward.

My jaw dropped.

Shock mixed with joy and adrenaline raced through my brain. This possibility had crossed my mind, but I didn't have much faith that it would happen – that Daniel would give his life to Jesus!? I had shared with Daniel what I believed to be true biblically, about salvation, and even about our relationship, but I also acknowledged that I wasn't living it. This moment was all so weird because while I was happy for him, I was living a compromised life. My head and heart were a jumble of thoughts and emotions.

I snatched up our jackets and followed him to the stage. Within minutes, Daniel stood in front of the prayer counselors, palms turned up in an open posture. *Where had he learned to do that?* I couldn't make out every word, but there he was, along with many others, praying to repent of sin and receive Jesus as Lord and Savior.

Okay, great, I thought, but now what?

Daniel had given his life to Christ. But what did that mean about us? What did that mean for our future together? Did it change anything?

Being in a long-term, monogamous relationship with Daniel created a new conflict. Not only had the novelty of our commitment to each other faded, but now, with Daniel's turn to faith, how did romance fit into the equation? What did *love* look like in this dynamic? Was I genuinely loving him by staying his partner, and did God bless it? Or was my temptation of the flesh leading him away from God and toward destruction?

I hated all these thoughts. Why couldn't it be simple?

But actually, it's always been simple. The Word of God is abundantly clear on sexual sin and homosexuality. It becomes complicated when we ignore God's laws or try to tweak them to our liking.

But simple doesn't mean easy. There was no easy button here. Truth had become razor-sharp at every turn. I had already begun to feel a deep sense of conviction and failure whenever we were sexual. Daniel hated to see me overcome with grief and guilt. He wasn't sure how we should continue our relationship and intimacy either. He believed in Jesus for salvation, but he wasn't sure about the inerrancy or authority of the Scriptures. If our being together was wrong, he was willing to stay committed to one another without sex. Our solution would be to live in a gay-Christian partnership but without sex.

But... That didn't seem exactly right either. How could we add something to our identity in Christ – a label that, if we were to act on, would be a sin? It left us in a strange and unbiblical place. So, for a time, we remained just two guys who loved each other and exclusively honored our monogamy. We settled on life as a committed married couple without the ceremony and intimacy.

Of course, all of that sounded good in one sense, but neither of us could resist fleshly temptation when it came down to it. Daniel demonstrated more strength than I did, but desire is an itch that craves scratching, and eventually, we'd give in again. Each time we slipped, those familiar feelings of regret and anger resurfaced and filled me with shame.

Soon, it became apparent that my attempt at a celibate life with my partner would never work. I also concluded that same-sex intimacy was forbidden and outside of God's design, as was how we lived together. Even if Daniel and I were successful in our celibacy, biblical marriage is about so much more than sex between a man and a woman. It was, and is, about making a home and a family together – being one flesh together, raising children in the complementary nature of God's design. He created man and woman to correspond to each other uniquely, meeting very different needs of one another and, more importantly, of children. Two men or two women can never fit in the same way. At the most rudimentary level, biblical marriage requires covenantal commitment, with the sameness of our humanity and the diversity of our radically different sexes mingling to reflect God's intention and design. It is only then that couples flourish. I had to conclude that celibate gay-Christian identity and attempts at such a partnership are contrary to God's design and will.

Truth became abundantly clear: Daniel and I were playing house and playing with fire.

After a year of living together, I moved out, much to our mutual sadness. Conflicted, yes, but also fully assured that God had called us both to surrender not only our sexual relationship but the disintegrated identity we had embraced as gay men. Part of what propelled me forward (and I believe a significant amount of my regret over sexual sin) was knowing I was getting in the way of Daniel's relationship with God. I had been a Christian longer than him and had knowledge he did not yet possess. I knew I didn't want to be a stumbling block. I cared too much about him for that. This was a few months before my twenty-first birthday.

* * *

My parents were still wintering in a small cottage they rented at the Christian retirement village in Florida, but they were tired of it. Throughout our phone conversations, they seemed to sense an opportunity for my brother and me to move closer. They scraped some money together for a down-payment and bought a piece of heavily wooded land back home in New York. It was across the road from a river, very close to where we grew up. It was an incredibly peaceful and scenic location, with a dairy farm just up the road from us. They relocated their camper onto the property, which became a homebase while designing and constructing a small house.

This setup was about forty minutes away from Daniel's apartment, and it became my retreat in more ways than one. I was getting my life together and reconnecting with my parents on a more mature level. I even helped my dad build his house. Despite Dad's relational challenges, he was a genius at making anything and doing so frugally. This allowed me to learn from him.

As Dad was retired, the house project was well underway by the time I arrived to live with them and help out. I was still working retail and driving back and forth, so life stayed busy. We didn't have air guns for nailing. We used hammers and nails. Each night, I woke up with my right arm throbbing and cramping. Mom would rub salve into my arm, bringing enough relief for me to fall asleep until morning and start again. And so, the cycle continued until one day, by summer's end, we could move in.

To my Mom and Dad's delight and answered prayers, my brother Bob, their other prodigal son, his girlfriend (now wife), and another couple they were close with in California relocated to be near them. They rented a small property with a trailer just down the road from us. For a while, it seemed everything my parents longed for might become a reality. More than anything, they longed to see their two wayward sons come to genuine faith.

But appearances are often not reality.

Mom and Dad were thrilled when I told them that Daniel had given his life to Christ. They were even more delighted when I decided to move out and live with them. Daniel started driving down to our church every Sunday. My parents accepted him and treated him like a part of our family, so he began spending a lot of time with us. With some space and boundaries, this allowed Daniel and I to redefine our friendship. There were challenges, however, because Daniel and I had so much fondness for one another. That meant we had to be deliberately careful not to fall into the same old patterns as before.

I wish I could tell you my struggles and failures with sexual sin and identity confusion dissolved. I wish I could confirm that from this point forward in my life, I remained faithful and resisted the temptation of the flesh by taking up my cross daily to follow Jesus (Luke 9:23).

But I wouldn't be telling you the whole story if I did that. The truth is, God had provided me with an exit ramp from my life of emptiness, sin, and destruction. Maybe it didn't come until years later, but looking back at this season of my life now, I can see the work I was doing to try and make better choices, even when it was hard. It was the start of my practice to put God before other things. These acts of obedience allowed me to see my error and how empty I felt inside, even though I was in a loving, monogamous relationship.

The consequences of sin during my relationship with Daniel had been grating on my soul, and the weight of sin was exhausting. At the time, I couldn't fully understand it. I only knew something wasn't right, so I believed I was strong enough to resist it. But as I look back, I see where I went wrong. While the Holy Spirit guided me toward genuine repentance and surrender, I drowned out His whispers with the voice of my vanity. Instead of surrendering my whole self to the God who loved me and paid my debts of sin, I foolishly tried to claim and maintain control of my life. This was my Achilles' heel, blocking me from grace and limiting my efforts to be supplied from my religious fervor and power. No wonder making better choices seemed unsustainable.

The words of Isaiah 57:10 offer an apt description of my early life experience. The prophet describes how the people of God had become compromised by partaking in the sinful, idolatrous patterns of the nations around them. He says that they were growing weary in their search and "*the length of [their] road*," but they found renewed strength within themselves to keep going their own way, under their own fleshly striving and power, rather than turning in whole-hearted repentance back to God. That was me as I grasped and struggled to find my way and meet my needs.

* * *

Now that I was living with my parents, I started looking for a closer job. My shyness and overt insecurities were essentially a thing of the past. I also had some decent work experience and solid references, so it wasn't long before I landed a good job.

I quickly became a respected and valued team member at the new, larger retail clothing store. My hours increased, and I made new friends. Christine, one of the managers, and I clicked right away and started spending a lot of time together. She had several gay friends and fully supported it. She assumed I was gay also and often probed me for answers as to why I didn't embrace my apparent sexual orientation. Her opinions of God differed significantly from mine in that she took the more palatable approach of God's existence as some nice guy in the sky who wants everyone to be happy.

Christine had a friend who owned a popular, upscale nightclub. She often worked there on weekends, and after some convincing, she roped me in as a coat-check. My first night was so profitable, on tips alone, that I couldn't believe it. So, how could I resist that kind of supplemental income? I continued my job there, but soon, as you may expect, it wasn't only the money that got a hold of me. I was smack dab in the middle of a party environment, with free drinks and late nights, and this sent me on a downward spiral once again. Whatever relationship I had been pursuing with God was stowed away as an inconvenience and, therefore, ignored.

My new friends often talked about gay nightclubs in the area, especially the dance club, and it didn't take long for them to coax me into going with them. Instantly, I was hooked again. The flesh is weak, and when we set ourselves up with scenarios that place us in direct contact with temptation, more often than not, we fail.

The lies came next. I told my parents I was working the coat check at the other club late at night, so they didn't know where I was until 3AM. To myself, I mused that this just made it easier on all of us—shielding the truth from my parents and saving myself from judgment.

I don't remember how it all happened, but the manager of the gay dance club took a liking to me and offered me a bartender position. It took a month of working slow weeknights to get proficient enough for the bustling weekends. A good-looking guy sat in my section on my first Saturday night and flirted until closing. He returned later that week on a quieter night, and Matthew and I hit it off.

Before long, we were dating and sexually active. Once again, I became captivated and wrapped up in a new relationship. I did what I always did in these situations:

I compartmentalized, closing my Christian file cabinet drawer and living out of my gay identity drawer. I lived a double life.

I'm reminded of how many times friends of mine who have had full-blown drug and alcohol addiction thought they had learned their lesson and finally hit bottom, staying clean for a while – maybe for months, seemingly with great promise. But something or someone would come along and derail them. I was living a similar pattern.

Of course, one of the most significant weaknesses in my life, and a pattern I see played out in the Church repeatedly, is having nearly zero relational accountability. They might have a men's or women's group or a small group, but rarely is anyone sharing the deep wounds of their hearts or their deepest struggles with sin or addictive patterns. The same was true for me. Without true walking partners who know us fully, we will fail.

About a month later, it became clear that something was bothering Matthew, and he broke up with me right at the same bar where we'd met. My heart dropped. I didn't understand. He made a few other excuses about why we weren't working out and disappeared. I finished my shift fighting back tears, trying to distract myself from my broken heart with other customers.

Once again, I was sore with the aches and pains of rejection. It wasn't unfamiliar territory for me, but that didn't make it hurt any less. The fear of being alone and the rotten feeling of being dirty and used overwhelmed me. Ironically, I knew that my relationship with Matthew had divided me from my parents and God, and I hated that. But rather than repent and get my heart right with God again, I fell victim to the negativity weighing me down—the shame, regret, sinfulness—and chose to console myself with even more sin, rebounding from one guy to another.

I even reached a place where I no longer wanted a long-term relationship. It was much easier and much less risky emotionally to seek nothing more than casual sex. A mutual lack of commitment sets low expectations. No need to hurt afterward. But that notion was a lie, a deception. I did hurt. I was seriously damaging my soul, which I didn't understand then. A slow degradation of wear and tear that put me farther and farther away from God and dulled my sense of right and wrong.

Months passed, and at some point, during a conversation with Daniel, I told him what was going on. We made plans to share an apartment, and within a few weeks, we found a house to rent.

Of course, this meant I had to come clean to my parents. I finally admitted what I was doing and where I was working. They were, in a word, crushed. My mom wept right in front of me.

The shame and regret I felt at that moment was too much to bear. Denial, and maybe even a little anger, took over. I hardened my heart, moved forward with my plans, and Daniel and I moved in together as friends, not boyfriends.

Chaos reigned once again. My flesh was firmly in the driver's seat now. Anything that offered even momentary decadence drew my attention. I was particularly vulnerable to good-looking guys who pursued me and made me feel wanted or valuable. But that feeling was always short-lived.

* * *

Tuesday nights at the bar were dead. I was working alone, making small talk with a couple of regulars at the far end of the bar when a blonde woman sat down at the other end. She was probably around thirty, with shoulder-length hair, bright eyes, and someone I'd never seen at my bar.

I approached her. "Hi there. How's your night going?"

"Good, good." She smiled and ordered a simple soda.

It was unusual for someone not to order alcohol, but I got her a drink and offered her some small talk, which somehow led to her sharing deeper stuff from her life. Cliché, though it may be, people tend to open up to their bartenders. She put me at ease, and I shared a little about my background.

Between refills at the service bar and maintaining my other customers, I talked about all topics with this mysterious woman for over an hour – even faith and Christianity. I even shared a bit of my journey of faith with her.

Abruptly, but not unkindly, my new friend looked me square in the eyes and asked, "What are you doing here?"

It was more rhetorical than a demand for a response, but her tone had an almost urgent ache.

Then she said something I could never forget. "You don't belong here."

At the same time, a new customer walked in and sat down, and I had to greet him. My mind whirled as I mixed his drink. What a bold thing for this woman to declare. She didn't even know me ...

Yet she was spot on.

Cordially, I chatted briefly with the new customer, but inside, I couldn't wait to return to my other conversation. I didn't even know this precocious woman's name. I turned to head back and ask her, but she was gone. The space where she'd sat was empty.

My head buzzed with new energy. How bizarre. What had just happened? A stark sensation washed over me, and I shivered. A keen awareness told me God had orchestrated that encounter.

However, rather than respond in repentance and obedience, I tucked away the experience and moved forward on the path I'd chosen to follow despite its superficiality. I was blinded by instant gratification, living for the moment and desperate to have my emotional needs met immediately. I gave little regard to the future or where my trajectory would ultimately take me. Suppose I had been honest with myself and considered where I'd be in five or ten years. That alone may have been a catalyst for profound change. But that contemplation would have been far too sensible for where I was at in life.

I preferred the scales over my eyes. That's what partying is all about—dulling the pain and emptiness with momentary distractions. Then, trying in vain to string all those disjointed experiences together into something meaningful, moving from one broken relationship to the next, using one to repair the emotional crash of the last (and anything else prior).

Sounds exhausting? It was. Remember Isaiah 57:10? No matter how tired, used, hungover, or dirty my soul felt, I fell back into the same cycle of going nowhere the next day.

I often say nothing mimics or counterfeits the authentic, healthy emotional intimacy God designed us to flourish in, like sexual immorality. Satan, the world system, and our flesh deceive us into believing that a live-in, committed relationship or causal sex with anyone and everyone we desire will serve and fulfill us. Eventually, though, that novelty wears off. What's left is the empty but incessant craving for momentary distraction from pain—the numbness that drugs, alcohol, sex, etc., offer. We become addicts in an uphill battle between desire and resistance that eats away at us, weakens us, and renders us helpless. All that's left are junkies needing a fix. Our hopes, dreams, and good intentions are replaced with a vicious cycle of unfulfilled godlessness.

* * *

One late night at the club, when I felt particularly lonely and unfulfilled, one of my customers stayed back after closing, and we hooked up. This was someone I hadn't known for more than thirty minutes. It was a perfect example of how my drug of choice, AKA sex, had become habitual and meaningless. While there were other one-night stands, this one distinctly stands out because I recall a profound sense of wretchedness in my heart. Before we had even been intimate, I just wanted to get it over with. Alone together in my apartment, I focused on a tiny sliver of light that had filtered into my bedroom from a street lamp. It held my attention during my encounter with this guy, and once the deed was over, he got up, dressed, and disappeared. It was a new low point for me, and that's saying something. No doubt my soul recognized it. I rolled over and crashed for a few hours, just before my alarm blared and demanded I start a new day of meaningless motions. I dragged myself out of bed and set off for my retail day job - wash/rinse/repeat.

When I wasn't working the bar, I was often at the club anyway – drinking, hanging with fun people, numbing my secret pain with a party atmosphere. One night, Paul, an attractive guy I had known from the bar scene, joined our group, and he and I got chatty. He went on and on about how much he loved Virginia Beach and wanted to get back there, but that he was without a car. He had lots of friends there, and the beaches were amazing. There also seemed to be a welcoming and plentiful gay culture, and his stories, combined with too much alcohol, prompted my spur-of-the-moment decision...

"When do you want to go?" I asked.

Paul looked at me in astonishment. "Don't tease me about it."

"Seriously," I said. "When? If there's somewhere I can stay, we can leave tomorrow."

After hearty assurances on his part and another round of drinks to celebrate, we left to pack and get some sleep.

My car had just been repaired after requiring some costly transmission work. Thankfully, it was running well enough now, so when morning rolled around, I picked up Paul and his belongings, and we were on the road to Virginia Beach.

Remember, quitting and moving on to something else was my MO, even when that something was far worse than the present circumstances.

After eight hours on the road, we arrived in Virginia to anything but beach weather. Dark cold, with wind whipping all around us, we pulled into a driveway with ice crunching beneath the tires. I rolled to a stop, and BOOM!

Something fell off the bottom of my car. Paul and I grabbed a bag of clothes each and trudged to the door to meet his friends, who he'd assured me were excitedly waiting for him. So why was the house dark? Paul knocked. We waited. Finally, a guy answered the door, but there wasn't excitement on his face. More like shock, quickly shifting to apparent irritation and anger.

And there it was, clear as day: everything Paul had told me had been lies. We weren't arriving in Virginia Beach to meet up with a happy LGBTQ+ family waiting to welcome us. It was a total setup. We'd just arrived unannounced on the doorstep of an ex Paul had lied to and stolen from on his way out of town, which was the last time he had been there.

"What do you want?" Richard asked, brow furrowed, jaw stiff. "You can't stay here."

"Well, um, it's so good to see you, too." Paul giggled nervously as he was about to add some nonsense he'd undoubtedly been rehearsing in his head for the past eight hours.

I couldn't believe it. There I was, eight hours from home, with my car broken down and no money to fix it, freezing in the biting wind, and now with no place to stay. I could only assume that Paul had somehow believed he'd be able to manipulate his way in once we arrived.

But Richard wasn't buying it. He looked over Paul's shoulder at me. "How'd you get roped into this? Did he tell you how wonderful it would be once you arrived?" Without waiting for an answer, he looked back at Paul. "Where'd you drag him in from?"

"Um, I lived in upstate New York," Paul answered. "Garry drove us here today, but his car just broke down by your house." He vaguely gestured toward my car.

Richard glanced back at me. "I'm sorry you got messed up with him."

"My thoughts exactly," I responded.

Richard stepped to the side of the door frame. "I'm not heartless enough to leave you out in the cold. You can both sleep here tonight." He turned back to Paul. "But just tonight."

I was so grateful to escape the cold that I didn't care. Richard showed us to a guest room where we would have to share a bed.

"Um, I don't want to put you out any more than we already have," I said, "but do you mind if I sleep on your couch tonight?"

That one request moved me up a notch or two in Richard's estimation.

"Not at all," he said. Then he addressed Paul. "So, you led him down here with lies?"

Paul opened his mouth to defend himself, but Richard raised a hand as if to say, *Don't bother. I already know the answer.*

Later, after getting ready for bed, I stepped into the guest room where Paul was. He did not look ready for bed at all. On the contrary, he had changed into clubbing clothes. He insisted he couldn't wait to visit some friends and that he'd return later. I couldn't believe it.

Richard could, though—he wasn't the least bit surprised.

"Don't bring anyone else back here!" he called as Paul closed the front door behind him. He looked at me, his head shaking. "What a mess."

"I'm so sorry for all this," I offered. "I had no idea that—"

"It's not your fault," Richard interrupted. "I know exactly how he is."

At the time, I was so ticked at Paul. I couldn't believe he lied and manipulated me into such a dangerous situation, eight hours away from my home. But, of course, in hindsight, I was the same as he was. I had lied to my parents and lied to others. I had behaved like an absolute scumbag to Sharon. The list goes on and on. It's ridiculous how we can act morally superior and ignore the beam in our eye own while pointing out the splintering sin in someone else's.

Sidenote: This kind of hypocrisy reminds me of a time much later in life when I was doing street ministry and handing out bags of food to people experiencing homelessness in Houston, Texas. One day, while talking with a heroin addict I'd gotten to know, I mentioned one of the guys around the corner to whom I'd just delivered some sandwiches.

The guy made a face at me that showcased his rotten teeth and barked, "Don't you know he's a crack addict?!"

It took me a moment to process. That moment was a rude awakening. The pot had just called the kettle black, and I realized I was also a pot. I'd been doing the same thing toward Paul that this addict had just done toward another addict.

Inside Richard's home, he warmed up some leftovers and made some hot tea, and the unexpected night turned into a pleasant evening of getting to know each other. But the long day finally got the best of me, and I went to bed on the couch and crashed hard. I only woke up briefly when Paul waltzed in obliviously that early morning.

When I woke up the following day, Richard had already gone to work but left me a key and a note that I was welcome to return. I was stuck between a rock and a hard place. I might have considered driving back home that day, but I couldn't because my car had broken down, and I had no money to repair it. I was so thankful Richard was being kind toward me. It was a huge relief.

I figured I might as well make the most of being in my situation, which I couldn't change immediately. So, I searched for work by scanning the newspaper for possibilities while Paul slept in until the early afternoon.

I ended up with an interview that same day, but other than phone work, I didn't quite know what I was applying for. As much as I hated telemarketers, I hoped it might be that rather than bill collection or a sex-talk line. I showed up to a room full of other potential candidates for a company with many positions to fill. It turned out to be a telemarketing job. It would do for the time being, so I accepted a position.

For the next few weeks, I walked to work. I called people when they were trying to relax or eat dinner and repeated my script countless times over the phone for four-hour stints. I became good at it, consistently having higher sales than anyone else. My boss was also a decent guy. He would call the group and tell them what they needed to change to increase their close rates.

After which he would say to me. "Everything I said to everyone else, ignore it. Just keep doing what you're doing."

I never thought I'd be good at telemarketing, much less enjoy it. But I liked my boss's encouragement.

Richard allowed Paul and me to stay with him temporarily as long as we pulled our weight with chores, which I gratefully did since I had yet to be paid. Paul, however, did nothing but sleep when he was home. Little more than a grifter, he survived by using others—for everything from meals to partying to a place to lay his head. I learned that he'd managed to sleep his way into even the most luxurious residences, both upscale hotels and affluent homes.

This could have been so much worse. Thank God nothing happened between us.

One afternoon, when Paul and I were both at Richard's at the same time (since it was too early for Paul to be clubbing), Richard informed Paul that he had overstayed his welcome. He gave Paul a deadline for removing himself and his belongings by the next day.

It didn't surprise me, and I didn't feel bad for Paul after witnessing his behavior, but my pulse accelerated. What did this mean for me? I had no car and nowhere to go. I had only worked a few days by then and hadn't been paid yet.

Richard turned to me then and said, "Garry, you can stay as long as you like."

Whew, what a relief.

Paul didn't put up a fight or even attempt to manipulate, as he'd been lining up something for himself anyway, so that day was the last I ever saw of him.

Good riddance!

With Paul out of the house and things quieting down, Richard began to treat me differently. He had always been gracious, treating me better than I deserved, considering how we met, but something now felt a little different. It wasn't so overt that it felt like a response was necessary, so I just treated him as a friend. I liked Richard and was grateful for him taking me in. He was nice-looking, but I didn't feel strongly attracted to him. Maybe that would change.

A week or so later, as we were winding down and getting ready to turn in, Richard asked if I would sleep in his bed rather than the guest room. So much for subtlety.

I agreed, unsure of what else to do. But I was afraid it would change our friendship too quickly, and I wasn't ready for that—how could I be? Nothing was stable then, and I had little to offer emotionally or financially. Afterward, I told Richard it couldn't happen again. I didn't want that to be what our friendship was about.

He agreed. And he apologized for being so forward in asking me.

Several days later, when I returned from work, Richard approached me sheepishly, and I could tell he had something on his mind.

"I'm so sorry to tell you this," he said, "but a couple of weeks ago, I had sex with another guy."

"Um, okay." I rubbed my chin, studying his remorseful expression. I wasn't sure why he was confessing this since we weren't a couple – I didn't know him at that point anyway.

Richard's lips puckered to one side as if the words he wanted to say were stuck inside his mouth, and he needed to dislodge them. "Well, he ... he gave me crabs."

"Crabs?" I asked. "What're you talking about? Like crabs at the beach?" I was baffled.

Richard blinked a few times and quirked an eyebrow. He couldn't believe I'd never heard of the non-seafood version of crabs before. "No, it's an STD. They're like lice, only in your pubic region."

"That's disgusting!" I exclaimed. "I don't have those! How would I know if I did?" The idea of lice or anything like lice – anywhere on my body – felt so gross and dirty.

"You'd be itchy... down there," Richard said.

I paused for a moment. I hadn't been aware of anything unusual. "I don't feel anything itchy now."

"Well, just in case." Richard held up a small white and red bottle. "This is the stuff you can use to eliminate them."

"Oh, okay, great." I nodded. "But I don't have them."

The next day at work was my first sensation and confirmation that I did indeed need to find and use whatever it was in that little white and red bottle.

When the realization hit, I was furious—not at Richard, but that this happened to me. At the same time, it was also a slap in my face that the way I was living had consequences. This was mild compared to many other possibilities. For a while, it cast a pall over everything I had been doing and how I lived.

Crabs and STDs aren't a gay thing or an LGBTQ+ thing. They are a sexual promiscuity thing – gay, straight – whatever. When we won't do sex and marriage God's way, the consequences are immense. Whether an STD is ever contracted or not, casual sex, friends with benefits, or anything outside of God's design for sexual expression does damage to the people involved. It damages our soul – whether we realize it immediately or years later. Sexual sin damages the human person, especially within a lifestyle of promiscuity, regardless of sexual preference.

"What do I do?" I asked Richard, feeling filthy and grimy.

Richard explained the instructions.

I went to the bathroom and immediately used the solution, but it took several rounds of treatment to eliminate the gross little parasites.

* * *

After six or seven weeks, I had enough money to fix my car. Up to this point, Christine and I had kept in touch. Initially, she was furious I'd disappeared without notice, especially after learning from mutual friends that I'd taken off with Paul. She was sure I was headed into a mess, but after I called her from Virginia, I apologized, and we discussed it. We stayed in close touch, and she was glad later when Paul was no longer in the picture. She even came down for a visit and got a hotel in the area with enough space for me.

It was great to see her again. It reminded me of all the friends I'd left back home. I realized how much I missed my parents, too. Suffice it to say, it wasn't long before I announced my plans to move back. Christine was thrilled. It turned out that had always been part of her plan to visit. She had only purchased a one-way fare to Virginia, hoping to drive back with me. So, I said my heartfelt thank you and goodbye to Richard, then Christine and I hit the road the following day.

Thus was the detour of Virginia Beach in my life. I learned a lot. More street-smarts than anything else, thanks to Paul. Truthfully, it could have been much, much worse. But even in my rebellion and ignorance, God commissioned His angels to watch over me, although I wouldn't see that until years later through the lens of hindsight.

I moved back in with my parents. I know I took them for granted far too often. They were always there for me, though never settling for or accepting a lifestyle of sin for me. They couldn't make my decisions for me, but they could pray, speak the truth, and love me. They were so grateful to have me back, even though my practice of sin and instability was hurting my mother's health. Things with my brother were also a challenge she had to manage. My brother's and my compounded foolishness and rebellion had stirred up a cauldron of grief in my mother's heart. Anxiety bubbled up inside her, becoming harder and harder to manage.

I found a new job in the fashion jewelry industry, which required regional coverage across New York State. Up to this point in my life, this was the best-paying job I had ever landed, and things seemed to be getting back on track, financially at least. I met another guy through a couple I was friends with, and soon, we were in a monogamous relationship that lasted about a year. By that year's end, our companionship was little more than turbulent. He cheated on me with one of my close friends, and everything in our relationship unraveled. I couldn't sleep, and for weeks I barely ate. This violation of our relationship was a massive deal to me, and then to have one of my long-time friends initiate it felt like a more extensive loss than my boyfriend.

As my chapter title indicates, this period of my life was a long season of extreme unpredictability and double-mindedness. With each week that passed, I felt like I lost my way a little more down the dark, thorny paths of godlessness, in which my heart became ever more blind and hardened with denial of my sin.

New job opportunities seemed to be the only bright spot in my life. Christine had become a regional director for a specialty clothing store and offered me a store manager opportunity in her territory. It sounded like a fun challenge, so I relocated to Pennsylvania and helped her open a new store. Not long afterward, I was asked to move and open another store, and then another, etc... I became the go-to guy for renovating and opening new stores. I trained in Wilkes Barre and moved to Hazelton, York, and Long Beach Island, New Jersey.

This meant I was moving around a lot, which was not a great solution for instability but great for distraction. As you may expect, I became even more lonely with each relocation. I would go back home to New York to visit whenever I could get away, and my parents were the one stable relationship in my life I could rely on. But my heart was elsewhere, and whatever city I was in, I searched out the gay bars in the area. They became my frequent haunts for socialization and hookups.

The crabs experience was only a temporary deterrent to my sin. Once the loneliness and emptiness spiked, nothing else mattered. I returned to my addiction while my spiritual life was in the toilet and had been since my last year-long relationship. Every time God rescued me from my sin and mess, I just seemed to wind up back there again. I was sick of abusing His grace. I wasn't going to straddle the fence any longer. I was all in or all out... or at least that sounded good then.

My role as store manager was one of the most fulfilling parts of my life. I hired everyone who worked at my stores. This allowed me to know and value each person. I was eager to see them grow and excel personally and at work, and I poured into their lives. I loved that ... except no one was pouring into mine. Of course, my choices and rebellion had cut me off from all that could have been offered if I'd been deeply connected to a church, but as they say, hindsight is always 20/20.

Christine and I remained very close. She oversaw nine stores and was actively involved with each, but she spent more time with mine. I began to feel a growing love for her, which was neither romantic nor sexual. Still, I wanted to spend more time with her. We'd often joke about getting married someday if neither of us had met anyone in ten years. Even though we joked, there was some comfort in knowing the future didn't have to be one where I was alone.

On one occasion, following a night of drinking and partying with friends back home, I stayed at her apartment. We had slept in the same bed many times before, always platonically, but we were both open to exploring something more that night. We joked about marriage, but could that even be possible? And could we have a sexual relationship without romantic attraction? Or...was it even romantic attraction that we felt?

Somehow, one thing led to another, and that night it happened. We had sex.

The next day was awkward. But we were determined not to let this drive us apart. Nor did we want to rush into anything. My proclivity was still exclusively toward men, so how would this heterosexual thing work?

I went back to work in Hazelton, which allowed Christine and I to do our own thing while we figured out what we were feeling. Christine was making regional rounds a month later and stopped at my store. We discussed some new merchandise display ideas in the backroom when she blurted, "I'm pregnant."

My brain fogged over—the moment was surreal. Then, a long moment of silence.

"Wait, what?" I asked, gaze widening.

Christine looked up at me from the office chair. "I'm pregnant."

"Is it Philip's?" I asked.

Philip was a guy she'd had a decade-long affair with and the source of numerous abortions Christine had had. She'd confided in me months ago that abortion had been a form of birth control for her.

Her expression was just short of, "Duh, stupid."

And then it registered. My heart missed a beat, and my throat tightened. "Oh, my God!"

The backroom door opened, and a coworker popped her head in. "Is it okay if I go to lunch now?"

No. No, it wasn't okay at all. Nothing was okay. How was I supposed to watch the storefront for her at a time like this so she could go to break? My world was splitting into pieces.

I forced a smile at my coworker. "Uh, sure, no problem...just... uh, just give me a couple of minutes, okay?"

"I already scheduled the abortion," Christine said once she'd left. "But I wanted to let you know first." Her gaze fell to the desk.

"No, wait," I implored. "Don't do that yet. Let's think this through."

Later that night, Christine came over to my tiny studio apartment. I knew I wouldn't be in the area long, so it was just enough space to get by before moving to another town.

Together, we discussed everything—the possibility of keeping the baby and getting married, the possibility of adoption ... and the tragedy of another abortion. I didn't want her to abort our child. How could I abandon a baby I helped to create? I had so many conflicting beliefs. I knew my lifestyle was wrong, and abortion was killing a baby – no matter how small. I didn't want to add one more massive sin to the ever-growing heap.

Christine, however, was non-committal one way or the other. She agreed to think on it a while longer and left the following day to continue her route until she had visited all the stores in her territory. When she arrived home, she called me in tears. She'd suffered a miscarriage.

I was immediately concerned for her and how she was emotionally and physically. I was also sad about the baby. But given our circumstances and the type of person I was, what kind of father would I be anyway? I took consolation in the fact that a choice we had consciously made didn't end the baby's life.

Truthfully, though, the more I thought about it, the more I wondered if the loss had been an actual miscarriage or if it had just been easier for Christine to claim it was.

* * *

Oddly, the answer to that question revealed itself fifteen years later. By then, a relatively new friend and I shared stories one afternoon. I'd met Linda at church through mutual friends. She told me how God had intervened and rescued her from her downward spiral toward destruction.

I'd told her about my relationship with Christine (without mentioning any names) and how I hadn't seen or heard from her in years after the pregnancy and miscarriage.

Suddenly, Linda held up her hands, palms facing me, and said, "Wait, stop...," pausing as if she was having a profound experience.

I laughed out loud; she was acting so ridiculous. For a moment, I even thought I'd overshared and worried I'd offended her.

"Was your friend's name Christine?" Linda asked, her tone incredulous.

My jaw dropped. Then I laughed again. What were the odds these two women knew each other?

It turned out that the two had met and became close friends after I'd moved to Florida and then Texas, losing touch with Christine. They were best friends for several years.

"Did Christine tell you how many abortions she'd had?" Linda asked.

"Six," I answered, my voice hitching.

"Add a few more to that number," Linda replied. "And the only reason I'm bringing that up is because she had many abortions and told me that outright, but she never mentioned a miscarriage."

My heart plunged into my stomach. Even after all those years, it hurt knowing that Christine had purposely taken our baby's life. Maybe ignorance was better than learning my child's fate.

* * *

A few months passed, and Christine asked if I would relocate to York, Pennsylvania, to open a new store. I had been planning on it. At the same time, my parents decided to sell their house and return to spending extended months in Florida again. It forced me to find my place, and since they were getting rid of everything, I took all the furniture for the place I would be renting in York. I wasn't doing the tiny efficiency room again.

The truth was my mom's worry and anxiety weren't getting better. She needed distance from my brother and me and the heartache we were inadvertently causing her. She still had a daughter who loved the Lord and their other son who had been a pastor for years, but even their obedience and faithfulness could not make up for the turmoil she felt over my brother and me.

My sister and brother-in-law helped me move into my new place. While I enjoyed having my own space again, it didn't take long before I felt the familiar gnaw of loneliness. I should have gotten a dog. That could have saved me a ton of heartache and foolish decisions.

But there it was. That awful, anchored, and pungent feeling was rooting into my soul. I had to distract myself, numb myself from the grinding pain however I could ... the quickest, most superficial way I knew how...

Thus began my hunt for gay bars in the vicinity.

Alcohol became more and more of an everyday means to numb my pain and negative feelings. Jack Daniels became my drink of choice. I bought their large 750ml bottles and displayed them on a shelf like trophies.

One evening after work, like nearly every other night, I intended to go out somewhere — anywhere, but for reasons I can't remember, my plans fell through, and I ended up staying home. By this point in my life, my cooking skills had blossomed. I preferred cooking for others, but on this night, I made myself marinated chicken breast, roasted potatoes, and other vegetables. If I had to be alone, I could at least treat myself to something nice and hope it would distract me from my emptiness. I popped in a movie and set up my tray with my freshly cooked dinner.

About ten minutes into my meal and movie, I had a sudden epiphany... I was okay. I was better than okay. I felt *good*. I was genuinely enjoying the moment. I point this out because, as trivial and insignificant as it may seem, this moment was a pivotal shift in the right direction for me. It had a profound effect that became a life-changing event. I sincerely wanted never to need anyone again. The pendulum swung too far in the opposite direction.

Up until that point, I had always needed someone else in my life, romantically or sexually, for me to feel okay. But that night, I didn't need those things. I realized I didn't need them at all. The needle that controlled the trajectory of my life wasn't just bumped off course temporarily, it was spun in a different bearing. I now recognized the strength of being alone and being content. I realized how wonderful it would be not to need someone else to make me feel okay. To be okay and content with just me would be freedom indeed. Maybe there was a difference between being lonely and being alone after all.

This began a whole new way of living. I still went out, but not as much. I was no longer compelled or driven by loneliness like I had been for years. My risky sexual behaviors diminished – not entirely, but significantly. By then, it was clear that I had been more driven by loneliness than lust. How I wanted to utterly detach from neediness.

Months later, my job asked me again to relocate, but this time, it was to open a summer store on Long Beach Island, New Jersey. But this wasn't just another move. It was much bigger than that ... a radical encounter blindsided me. I'll explain in the next chapter.

Questions for Self-Reflection / Journaling / Group Sharing

1. Have you experienced God sending a messenger to you in your life of sin?

2. Recount that experience/s

3. How might you better prepare to be a messenger of God for someone else?

4. Including both love and truth is essential as we approach a prodigal. Does your approach lean more toward mercy or sharp rebuke?

5. How might you build up what's lacking?

6. How have you been unhealthily emotionally dependent? Is this an area you still need and are willing to grow in? Explain.

7. Have you struggled with sexual sin or addiction? In what ways?

9. Is this still an area you need support in?

10. What are your options for support?

Chapter 11

GOD'S WAR

1 988, I set up and managed a seasonal store on Long Beach Island, New Jersey, for the summer. Much of the island was divided down the middle by a single main street running north and south from point to point, with shops, hotels, and houses, all practically on top of the other, on the east and west sides. My company rented me a small cottage that was part of a larger bed & breakfast between the beach and the mall where my new summer store would be located until Labor Day. Shoppers frequented this store, mainly for a break from the midday sun and throughout the day - on the hunt for bargain clothing, of which we had plenty.

I was responsible for keeping this store open and payroll expenses low, but Christine often came down to help with the store. Our friend Mike frequently tagged along as well. I'd been working nearly every day for a month and needed some time off, so Christine and Mike stepped in and took my place to allow me to get a break and a long weekend.

I set out home, eager to see my parents, who were back in upstate New York over the summer, but mainly anxious to meet up with old friends I could party with. Before leaving the beach, I'd reached out to several of them to see about getting together ... but everyone I called was swamped with work or school, was out of town, or had other commitments.

Uncanny, really. How could all those people be tied up at the same time? It wouldn't hold me back, though. I plowed onward, sure I'd have plenty of friends to hang with from the club I used to bartend at.

Due to working and living in various places between central New Jersey, Pennsylvania, and upstate New York, I had several friends to stop in and visit along the way. As I drove home, I made quick detours to see different ones, but oddly, not one was home. I also stopped by some of my old stores that were still open. Yet all the people I most wanted to see weren't there.

Nothing turned out how I'd hoped, so I switched gears and drove home to see Mom and Dad at their camper. It was good to be with them. They updated me on everything they had been up to in Florida and told me about some of the people I knew there at the retirement village. Every year, elderly friends pass away. It seemed to be a constant cycle. I filled them in on my busyness with work and how I'd been opening new stores but steered clear of anything more intimate or personal than that. They were especially interested in my latest job opening a summer store. The island sounded fascinating, but neither could have handled the crowds and chaos. Mom asked if I had found a good church. Of course, I hadn't even attempted that.

"I just moved again," I reminded her. "Finding a church when I'm constantly moving is hard."

"Oh yes, that's true." She nodded and replied in understanding.

Of course, that wasn't the real reason, but it seemed the best answer to give my mom.

After some time, they began to yawn, and I could see they were tired. It was time for them to go to bed and for me to get to the bars. As I told them goodnight and started for the door, their brows furrowed, and their faces fell with long, defeated looks of disappointment. They didn't want me to go. But they remained silent, treating me like the adult I was despite the heart weariness weighing them down.

* * *

The night turned out to be a bust. I didn't run into anyone I'd hoped to see. I ended up returning to my parents to sleep off my boredom. The next day was a repeat. And I'd taken off work for this? Nothing was coming together.

Then a thought occurred.... Could this be God interfering with my party plans? I put the notion aside. How silly. But it wouldn't stay buried—the idea kept coming up, and when I gave a little more consideration to the reality that the only people available to me on this particular weekend were my parents, I knew it was true. A revelation too big to ignore. God had to be behind this.

I spent the next morning with my parents and left for New Jersey a day early. When I passed through an area of Pennsylvania, memories of my time there came back to me—the local music store, my former clothing store. I wanted to see them, so I drove there.

I stopped in both stores and said hello to familiar staff, but I perused the selections while at the music store. I needed something new to listen to. Maybe Madonna had something new out. While seeking out the pop albums, I passed a tiny section labeled *Christian*. If I'd have blinked, I'd have missed it. What compelled me to thumb through that particular genre eluded me. My heart was fuming at God for ruining my plans with old friends.

Back at Bible school, Amy Grant and Sandi Patty were two of my favorite artists. However, our school viewed both singers as too worldly, especially Amy Grant. But I'd always liked their music. Amy Grant had crossed over to secular radio and pop charts by then, becoming a big deal. She and Sandi Patty had new music out on CD, and for whatever reason, I found myself purchasing them at the checkout counter. It didn't make sense. I was angry with God, after all. I wanted nothing to do with the church. Yet there I was, buying Christian CDs.

In my car, I unwrapped the cellophane and pushed one of the discs into my player, backing out of my spot and navigating to the interstate again. The new music washed over me as I sped along the freeway. As I barreled past, I almost overlooked the *Welcome to New Jersey* sign. It wasn't just the melody or the particular singing style that drew me in. That was an initial appeal, but as the miles flew by, the lyrics were weaving their way inside my heart and soul with such delicate intricacy that my self-guarded walls couldn't prevent their entry and began to crumble. Each new song and verse became a trove of rich truth and insight. I found myself listening intently to each one. Something was happening within .... words, truth, and spirit were melding inside me. I knew I wanted something so much more than my life had become. These songs stirred a longing and connected me to hope. It was fragile at first, but it was there.

My cheeks were dampened with tears. My heart squeezed. More and more lyrics sank deeper into me—a place tarnished with sin. Recalling this memory, only snatches of lyrics play in my mind, but it was enough to find the whole song by Sandi Patti.

In Heaven's Eyes

A fervent prayer rose to heaven

A fragile soul is losing ground

Sorting through the earthly babel

Heaven heard the sound

This was a life of no distinction

No successes, only tries

Yet, gazing down on this unlovely one

There was love in heaven's eyes

The orphaned child, the wayward father

The homeless traveler in the rain

When life goes by, and no one bothers.

Heaven feels the pain

Looking down, God sees each heartache

Knows each sorrow, hears each cry

And looking up, we'll see compassion's fire

Ablaze in heaven's eyes

In heaven's eyes, there are no losers

In heaven's eyes, no hopeless cause

Only people like you with feelings like me

Amazed by the grace we can find

* * *

In heaven's eyes, there are no losers. In heaven's eyes no hopeless cause...

That was it!

So many of these songs had gently, imperceptibly softened my heart and began to shatter my defenses, justifications, and excuses.

I was no longer tearing up; I was full-on sobbing. I lurched forward in my seat. Suddenly, heaves of self-hatred, shame, and fear gushed up from my core. All this time, I believed God didn't love me, that He'd never loved me. How had I believed that lie?

I had to get off the road quickly—I could barely see where I was going.

I pulled off on a wide-open stretch of pavement on the shoulder and turned off the car. Here, I could let it all out, and I could release the hold I had on myself. Maybe I could peel the scales from my eyes.

In no time, the front of my shirt was drenched in tears and snot. I bawled like I never had before. An aching desire emerged inside my heart to exclaim and confess it all. I needed to speak up, speak out, and expose my heart of repentance to God ... but what should I say? There was so much to say. There was so much shame.

God makes all things new.

With my soul no longer smothered in lies, sin, and self-deception, my ugly sin and rebellion revealed itself. My haughty and defiant judgments against God were unveiled. All the declarations I'd made and held against Him for so long were laid out on the surface. I could hide from them no longer. I could hide from Truth no longer. For so long, I'd hated Him, mistrusted Him ... all because He'd allowed things to harm me because He hadn't answered my repeated prayers for change the way I'd wanted Him to. Because He hadn't taken away my same-sex attraction as I thought I'd needed. He didn't give me the way that would've been easiest for me.

My hands gripped the steering wheel for support. Face to face with myself, I needed something to steady me while I stared into the bottomless pit of my rebellion. It was jarring, crippling, and scary as hell ...

* * *

But I wasn't alone in this. I knew now more than ever that *God was with me.* In His severe mercy, the Holy Spirit revealed what I needed to see in myself. All at once, I felt a sudden kinship with Job, not in his genuine suffering, but in his careless words about God—how his inconsiderate statements about God and His character had missed the entire point. God had spoken to Job directly afterward, and Job's response was to raise his hand to his mouth, horrified. How could he have spoken such rash things about his God? That's how I was feeling. I was keenly aware of my dumb, dull, and bold statements against Him.

In that sense alone, I would align myself with Job—a man who endured loss far beyond anything I ever had. Unlike Job, most of my pain and loss directly resulted from my sin.

I was vaguely aware that cars and trucks flew past me on the highway, their engines rumbling and whirring, but I paid them no mind. Only one thing, one Person, mattered at that moment: Jesus. Finally, emotion gave way to actual words, and I tried to speak them out loud, but not one syllable would emerge without sobs.

It wasn't just about the words; I know that now. The profound meaning behind them crippled me into speechlessness and tears. How does one give voice to the wailing of their soul?

At last, breathless and tear-strewn, my heart calmed, and I cried out to my Lord and Savior.

"Jesus, I am so sorry for my sin. I've made a total wreck of my life. I don't even know if You want what's left of me, but if You do, You can have it!"

With each word, my heart surrendered even more. Not a trivial kind of surrender or one of total defeat. No, this surrender was a resounding, heartfelt call to Him to take me as I am.

Finally, it became crystal clear that this was the missing ingredient. All this time, all these years, I had been craving salvation, memorizing all the neat, organized verses from my Romans Road salvation process (and many more) without any genuine surrender. Here, I needed God's grace to yield, but I had a role to play in that yielding, yet I had ignored it, essentially demanding God's salvation when I hadn't entirely given myself over to Him.

But this intense revelation and urgent, divine epiphany left nothing to be disguised. The time was ripe for the taking, and I would not let it slip through my fingers again. Now, I relented. My heart pulsed and squeezed. Immense joy swaddled my soul, leaving a residue of sweetness I had never known. This was peace. This was a surrender from the heart.

"Take control, Jesus," I whispered. This, for the One who had given his life for mine.

So simple, yet so complex and essential at the same time. That can only come from our magnificent Creator and the One who moved heaven and earth to make a way where we could not.

I realized that I'd always been my worst enemy in those moments. All along, God had wanted to give me the fullness of joy and true pleasures without regret. The words of Psalms 16:11 blinked to life:

You will make known to me the path of life; In Your presence is fullness of joy; In Your right hand, there are pleasures forever.

At last, I was home. At last, I now understood that I belonged to Him.

I don't know how long I sat on the roadside, but I was in no hurry to leave. This was holy ground. My heart and soul were united for the first time, restored by the blood of the Lamb. My spirit was made alive. No longer was I just a kid who'd grown up in a Christian home. I was a new creation—a temple of the Holy Spirit.

Everything had changed. Instantly, I was born again and adopted by my heavenly Father because of His Son.

Yes, I still had flesh to contend with, but I was a new man within. Transformed. *That* is what the power of Christ does for us. I was lost, but now I was found; blind, but now with sight. *That* is His amazing grace.

My flesh, though weak, would bow before the authority of Christ Jesus.

* * *

I still had another day off when I returned to the beach cottage. This was indeed a gift. God had intervened and interrupted my hedonistic plans, and I was overjoyed. My coworkers, Christine and Mike, were surprised to see me back a whole day early.

"I'm sorry things didn't work out," Christine said with a sympathetic frown.

"No, it's okay." I beamed. "This is perfect."

"It is!" Christine's voice hitched an octave. "There's this new club down on the island. We should all go! Let's close the store and go out afterward!"

Screech and halt. Wait, what?

I wasn't the same person as when I'd left. How would I explain this to them? How would I explain that I had zero desire to go out drinking or anywhere near a bar or dance floor?

I gave Christine a little smile. "You guys go ahead. I think I'll walk on the beach after work, probably go to bed early."

Christine's jaw dropped. Her gaze found me from over the top of her sunglasses. "Uhhh, what's wrong with you?"

Mike was rehanging and straightening clothes on the other side of the store but also paying attention to the exchange. He side-eyed me from over the swimsuit rack.

I stepped back toward the exit, ready to move on. "Nothing, nothing. I'm terrific."

"I don't believe you," Christine called. "Let's talk later."

I waved her off, chuckling, greeting other shopkeepers along the walkway.

It was a crazy feeling. I felt free. I felt emancipated from the tyranny of my old self and the cravings of my flesh. It felt like I was truly beginning life for the first time – and I was.

At the plaza's main entrance, seagulls dotted the sky and perched along the light posts and pavement, squawking. Even they seemed to be cheering me on as I stepped off the pavement and onto the powdery beach sand. I walked past our little cottage for another half block to the beach and ocean beyond.

The water was chilly on my toes and feet. I turned northward, wading ankle and calf deep in the rolling tide, and walked with God, my footprints pressing into the shore for a few seconds before washing away again. I thought of the *Footprints* poem I had read and seen countless times before. It had always seemed like an encouraging reflection on God's faithfulness, but it also seemed to me that it was for everyone else, not me... until now.

I talked out loud. No one could hear me in the noise of the waves as I poured out my heart with thanksgiving and gratitude in a way that made me both wince and gleam. All these years when I'd thought He was ignoring me, He hadn't been. He'd fought for me all along. As the old hymn says, *I was amazed by His grace for one so unworthy.*

For a long while, I talked and walked with God, and by the time I arrived back at the summer rental, Mike and Christine were getting ready for their night out.

Christine was in the tiny bathroom off the kitchen, door open. She was at the sink, her hair done up and brushing her teeth while mumbling something and glancing at me.

I couldn't understand a word. "*What?*"

She spoke louder through the foamy toothpaste in her mouth and lips, waving her hands as if I could read her form of sign language instead.

"That isn't helping," I called as I turned and walked into our shared living room/bedroom.

Grunting, Christine returned to the sink and rinsed her mouth.

I planted myself on one of the three twin mattresses that lined the walls of the tiny bedroom/living room. Leaning toward the nightstand, I pulled out my Bible and thumbed through the New Testament, wondering where to start reading. I knew I now had fresh eyes and was anxious to read familiar passages – in many ways for the first time. I was anxious to experience what I had been missing.

It had been a long time. Too long.

Christine emerged from the bathroom and stepped into our common room, brushing out her hair. "You should change your mind and come with us." She grinned. "Don't stay here by yourself."

I almost felt bad for her at that moment because I knew she couldn't feel what I felt or understand what I understood—until she was ready. "Thank you," I said, "but I'm good. *Really.*"

Mike laughed from the kitchen.

Christine noticed my Bible and glowered at it. "What are you doing?"

I gave her a shrug. "It's my Bible."

"I can see that. Why?"

Christine did go to church fairly regularly. But it was a church that was more of a social gathering, not a Bible-believing/preaching church. Christianity had no real impact on her. She was nice, but faith did not inform how she lived, and the idea of a relationship with God was a foreign concept.

I knew this seemed weird to her. I understood. It wasn't that long ago that I had rushed off to Virginia Beach on a whim. She was likely wondering what kind of cult I had started mingling with. One that encourages you to read your Bible.

"Because I want to read it." I smiled.

"Don't give me that look," she said.

"What look?"

"That innocent-looking smile!"

I just laughed. Mike laughed from the kitchen.

"Hey!" Christine shot back at him over her shoulder.

So much of this open banter was just how we loved each other. She was really into me as her best friend, and I felt the same way about her – it was more than friendship in a way, but whatever it was, I knew she felt threatened by what she was seeing in me after just part of a day.

I didn't feel defensive. I knew what was going on. I knew she would need spiritual eyes to see what I was seeing and experiencing. And there would be plenty of time for those conversations.

"Go," I told her kindly. "Have a good time. I've got plenty of leftovers here. Go!"

Christine headed for the front door. "Alright, you don't have to throw us out."

Mike followed her, the door slamming behind them.

My shoulders instantly relaxed, and I settled into the mattress.

As evening hours expanded into the night, so grew my ravenous appetite for the Word. I couldn't read enough Scripture. This consumption was unlike anything I'd experienced before —committing words to memory or skimming over laborious passages. The text had come alive. The Holy Spirit was weaving a tapestry of faith, hope, and love into my heart, and I was invigorated.

After an hour or two, I took another stroll along the beach. The stars twinkled overhead, competing for attention with the waxing moon, reflecting off the surging waters and surf. Many sky-gazers enjoyed the salty night air, but I didn't want to talk with anyone. Only God.

Pleasantly tuckered and fulfilled, I retired earlier than usual and slept hard until my cottage mates arrived home with a stir. I pretended to be asleep so Christine wouldn't start talking to me, and they would at least make some pretense of being a little quieter so as not to wake me. It wasn't long before I managed to fall back asleep, but around 2AM, I was wide awake again. I'd always been a heavy sleeper, so this was new—this energy inside filled me with anticipation and excitement, and I wanted to explore it on a deeper level.

Christine and Mike were softly snoring on their twin mattresses. Quietly, I snuck out and set my bare feet to sand again, walking and talking with Jesus. High in the starlit sky, the moon cast shimmers on the gentle waves. The beach was empty, but my heart was whole. I don't know if words can describe the peaceful contentment I experienced that night—the idyllic scene, the sounds of serenity, the once elusive connection with Him that now felt so solid and firm.

This was the difference between being born again versus following a set of rules, between walking in the newness of life versus the rituals of something called Christianity. Imagine it, I thought! This new life in Christ had always been before me and available, yet beyond my capacity to grasp due to a lack of surrender. How many others couldn't see the forest for the trees?

My heart itched, and my soul yearned to show them.

How many others, like me, treated God as if He were nothing more than a cosmic genie, hoping they'd rub the lamp correctly and get their wishes?

Something new was dawning on me—a fresh awareness and crisp perspective. There was work to be done, and I wanted to work in service to Him who had saved me. Both for myself and for the sake of others. I shuffled my feet along the silky sand that night and pondered where to start.

* * *

"You're possessed," Christine stated flatly, her gaze concerned.

We sat at our tiny kitchen table in the beachside cottage, just the two of us. I responded with a roll of my eyes and an outburst of laughter.

"I'm not joking." Christine narrowed her eyes. "I'm concerned about you. You're not the same."

About a week passed since I surrendered and accepted genuine life in Jesus. I'd found a church nearby and attended the Sunday prior. I liked it. The preaching was great, the people friendly, and they had what appeared to be a very active young adult ministry. Still, this new lifestyle and awakening were as foreign to Christine as burkas and hijabs.

I had to laugh again.

"Garry, you're like reading your Bible all the time," she continued. "I wake up at night, and you're not in bed. What are you doing? You never go out with us anymore. What's gotten into you?"

"None of that means I'm possessed," I said, amused.

Oh, the irony. The idea that being filled with the Holy Spirit and coming into genuine faith could be interpreted by my best friend as demonic possession said everything. She couldn't feel the scales over her eyes. I explained what happened to me on my drive back from New York, but she didn't get it.

"I've been wanting to tell you," I explained. "I've even been trying to tell you. It's not like I'm hiding anything. Something important happened to me, and it's all new... but ... I know how you are."

"What's that supposed to mean?" she asked with a little jerk of her neck.

Despite my assumptions, I owed her the benefit of the doubt. Once again, I began recounting the details of my trip back home – my original intentions, finding inspirational music, and finally, God's intervention on the highway.

Christine listened more closely to my explanation. Instead of a joy-filled expression, though, her face fell with concern. "I'm not so sure this is a good thing."

She had been raised in a religious home that supported church attendance but not reading the Bible. Spending time in prayer wasn't commonplace unless you were in a tight pinch and needed something. As a result, Christine had not experienced any natural fellowship with God. Those were practices that saints, pastors, or priests did, not regular people. My explanations and behavior seemed extreme to her and made her uncomfortable. I knew with Christine, it would be more about showing her than telling her. I wanted her to get it - even to experience this new life with me, but I couldn't push her.

Ultimately, she convinced herself this was just some weird phase I was going through. She often treated me as though this phase would pass any day.

It didn't.

The church in New Jersey was one of the most vibrant I had ever been a part of. I quickly felt at home and began growing in this community. I plugged in and bonded with the pastor and his family. They had one son around my age, another older, and another younger. I spent a lot of time with them and the young adult group.

There were many guys and gals in the young adult and college ministry. It was easier for me to feel like more of a part of the larger church on Sunday mornings than the group for young adults. They seemed like the cool kids. They seemed self-assured and confident, whereas I was used to not fitting in anywhere except the LGBTQ+ community. I wanted to be a part of them, but growing up, I always felt like I stuck out like a sore thumb in most of my peer groups.

One of my biggest struggles was feeling as though I didn't seem like much of a real man. I was fresh out of the LGBTQ+ world and had embraced a gay identity. I accepted and adopted mannerisms, gestures, and even voice inflection with a feminine tone more than masculinity. I wasn't flamboyant, but the markers were there.

In this new life in Christ, that fact always bugged me. I wanted those things to change quickly, but they didn't. At this point, many characteristics were just unconscious ways of being. Still, I felt like they were markers that clued in everybody to my former life and identity as a gay man. I had turned away from that life (and many other sins) to follow Jesus, but still contended with an outer shell that seemed to follow me everywhere – announcing my past to anyone paying even a little attention. That was a challenge to battle through when I often wanted to run away and hide in isolation. I only anticipated rejection and embarrassment among the Christian groups if I continued to hang out with them.

As a Christian, I was now determined to work through my fears and apprehensions. I needed Christian friends, and this was worth fighting for. One evening, the young adults were invited to someone's beach house for fun and fellowship. I was looking forward to the evening. Just after start time, I arrived to find people were paired off into tows or threes on various decks, yard chairs, or rooms. Others showed up after me, but they already knew one another well and quickly slipped into the conversations.

Self-consciousness began to kick in. Everyone there was caught up in conversations already, and I felt a growing sense of being out of place. It was that familiar feeling of the lunchroom as a kid, standing awkwardly, holding my food tray and trying to figure out who might be willing to let me sit with them. The feeling grew intense, and I suddenly wanted to leave. I didn't want to be obvious about it – the gathering had just started, and I felt like an idiot going so soon, but I had to get out of there.

I slipped out of the living room and into the kitchen for a drink. Several women were talking in one corner around the tiny kitchen table. I lingered at the sink and drank my water, eyeing the opposite kitchen entry from where I had entered. This way led closer to the exit. There was also a deck in this direction, off to one side, where people congregated and talked. I moved in that direction, but rather than going out on the deck, I slipped out the door and made a beeline to my car. I was so angry at how I was feeling, unwanted and invisible, so I cranked up my music and took off down the island's main drag back toward the safety and isolation of my little cottage. However, only a few miles down the road, I felt a clear and keen sense of disobedience and of returning to familiar ways of feeling and coping. I sensed God telling me to turn my car around and go back. Almost immediately, I yielded. I didn't want to, but He was clear. So, I chose to humble myself and return. I didn't know what I would say if anyone saw me leave and then saw me return just minutes later.

Thankfully, I didn't feel the need to explain myself. No one questioned me or mentioned it. Everything proceeded as it had been. I just slipped back in. Except this time, almost immediately, someone engaged me in conversation and questions – they were friendly and wanted to get to know me. Before long, a buddy of theirs walked up and joined in. That's how the rest of the night went. Lots of laughs and talking. A couple of guys brought their guitars, and before long, we were all singing worship songs long into the evening.

"Hey," someone said. "Let's go to the beach and swim in the waves together!"

It was a bright, full-moon-lit night. The night was perfect. Since it was a beach town, we all grabbed towels from the house or extras people carried in their cars. So off we went. The waves were strong and pretty high that night. Regardless, we all ran into the ocean. Everyone grabbed the hands of those beside them as the waves crashed against us. Over and over again, we stood against the water as the waves crashed against us. We all tried to keep ahold of the hands that we held before the waves knocked us off our feet, which was nearly impossible. But over and again, we tried.

Girls and guys grabbed my hands in theirs, holding tight, laughing, and tumbling in the waves. It was the best time I'd had in... I don't know when. And I'd almost missed it. I reflected on the intense negative feelings that drove me to leave the house earlier. That's when it occurred to me that something had stirred up those feelings out of nowhere. It was my first awareness of a direct spiritual attack, driving me away from the wholesome fellowship I needed. Of course, countless similar attacks had occurred, but this was the first time I was aware of it.

Eventually, we were all battered and tossed about long enough. It was getting late, and we needed to call it a night.

"Thank you, Jesus," I whispered as I unlocked my car. "Thank you for telling me to come back."

One woman in the group that night caught my attention. Alice was beautiful, but I was especially drawn to her love and commitment to God. We started spending time together whenever our schedules matched up. I sensed this could be more than just a simple friendship. I wanted to open up to her. One day, I did just that. I told her my story and let her in on my life-long struggle with same-sex attraction, porn addiction, and even past sexual sin with other guys. I didn't share the explicit details, but I was specific.

Alice listened intently, without interruption. I couldn't read her well but I knew I needed to put it out there regardless of her response. She needed to know who she was getting involved with if our relationship was to progress any further. I had my doubts about that.

Alice thanked me for being so open with her and trusting her. She had a few clarifying questions, but not many. I figured that was the end of our friendship and expected no more contact with her when I returned to the cottage. But a few days later, Alice contacted me to see when we could connect again.

I hung up the phone. "Wow, God!"

I was sure she wouldn't want to spend time with me again. But apparently, she did!

After a group meeting and young adult fellowship at Alice's place and everyone had filtered out the door, I stayed behind to catch up with Alice. The house she was using belonged to a friend of the family who was happy to have her house-sit, and it had a spectacular upper deck and view of the bay. We made ourselves hot tea and grabbed a couple of light blankets - a little campsite (without the fire) under the stars that night.

Alice surprised me when she said, "I want to tell you my story."

"I'd love to hear it," I replied.

We cradled our steaming cups of tea, carefully sipping from the edge.

Alice began her story and shared it late into the night. She was willing to be equally vulnerable in sharing her shame and pain. She hadn't lived the kind of life I indulged in and became enslaved to, but she had her baggage, too.

When she finished, I sincerely thanked her for letting me know these parts of her experience – the regretful details and the joy. Jesus had rescued her life. After this, our relationship progressed rapidly. It would be weeks before we officially started dating, but we spent as much time together as possible.

I could hardly believe how blessed I was. How did God accomplish all this in such short order? How could I be so lost as a kid who grew up in church, a Christian family, and went to Bible school? How could I have wandered through all kinds of addiction and madness as a young man? Yet, be where I am today by God's unfathomable grace?

My heart was overflowing with gratitude. Each new day seemed like a gift that I couldn't wait to live – seeing what God was up to and how He would bless and use me in meaningful ways.

Questions for Self-Reflection / Journaling / Group Sharing

1. Have you truly surrendered your life to Jesus, or like me, were you praying for eternal fire insurance?

2. Have you surrendered your sense of identity as well?

3. Have you ever experienced God interrupting your worldly plans?

4. What was the situation?

5. How did you respond to Him?

6. What are some ways that you need the Body of Christ to come alongside you for encouragement and accountability?

7. How can you become an authentic encourager and visionary for others?

CONCLUSION

S ince my highway revelation, the temptation toward porn, masturbation, and even the desire to act on same-sex attraction was nearly non-existent. I knew this was attributable to what God had done in my heart that day on the side of the highway and what He was doing each day that followed. I wanted nothing to come between me and Him.

I had been seeking and pleading with God to take away my same-sex desires forever. But this encounter with Jesus considerably shifted many areas of my heart. And that included a change in the power of same-sex attraction to control my thoughts and actions.

But also, I was unclear at this time about the various roots of my attraction to other men. I didn't have a clue that, while it seemed my compulsion to seek out men to sleep with had been broken when I gave my life to Jesus, the underlying, unhealed wounds of rejection and early childhood developmental experiences were still areas that needed to be touched and healed by Jesus.

For example, the envy of other guys and the comparison of my shortcomings resulted in harsh attitudes toward myself and even self-hatred at my perceived lack of self-worth. These were just some of the core issues that created the environment within me where same-sex attraction could develop and eventually take over my life, feeling foundational and bedrock as identity. Except it wasn't my true identity. It never had been. I turned certain men and characteristics of men into idols. Sex with these men was a form of idolatry and worship of what I once believed I was lacking.

While my compulsion to have sex with men and pursue romantic relationships with them had been broken, I was clueless about how vulnerable I remained with these open wounds still festering within. I didn't even understand how I was wounded. I felt more liberated than ever before. But God would reveal how deeply my wounds were ingrained over a decade later.

I also want to be clear that it wasn't that I didn't still have an attraction to men – I had reinforced that attraction and craving over and over again countless times. Rather, I now didn't want to (or need to) act on those attractions.

I didn't just "pray the gay away," as this intentionally demeaning and mocking phrase implies, although prayer is always a central ingredient in a Christ-follower's life. Instead, the out-of-control drive and compulsion to act on these desires was broken. That was freedom. I was no longer a slave to my attractions.

I wanted God to flip my desires, but He had something better in mind. He had a journey of discipleship He wanted to take me on. For the longest time, I didn't want the journey. I just wanted a fix. But in my surrender to Him, my surrender of acting out with men, and growing into manhood, my natural desires as a man made in God's image slowly emerged. The order and design of caring for another, extending protection, and covering for the *other* (woman) began to take root.

It wasn't in the eradication of all same-sex attraction that opposite-sex attraction emerged but in my surrender and obedience to God. I'm also convinced that God-given attraction isn't merely intense desire or infatuation. It isn't an insatiable need. And it certainly isn't the Hollywood romance version of happily ever after—one that lasts until the honeymoon fades and one dumps their spouse/partner for a newer model that makes them feel good for the moment.

No, God-given attraction is rooted in the differences between and the correspondence of male and female – welcoming the fact that God designed us to fit perfectly together (body and soul,) a union from which new life can be produced. This is untrue of same-sex sexual union – no life can be created.

Godly attraction exists within the healthy and beautiful boundaries God designed for sexual expression between one man and one woman within the commitment and covenant of marriage. It springs from a desire to bless the other, having an overflow of life and inner abundance that longs for this *other* to share it all with – to pour in and help secure and correspond to the other.

Of course, there's a powerful sexual and romantic component to God's design, and that's perfect. But it isn't the primary thing. It's the bonus. The tip of the iceberg above water is sustained and supported by the much larger commitment and emotional connectedness of the ice mountain below the waterline. Godly attraction is much more than just heart-pounding gymnastics in the bedroom. God-given attraction and design are about making and keeping our commitments – even when (especially when) desire fades or dips for a season(s). True love is something that we work to maintain and grow. Godly attraction has to do with the whole person, not only the exterior or mere body parts we may be turned on by. Godly attraction is about another – wanting to bless, secure, cover, and strengthen. A worldly appeal is all about self–wanting to *be* blessed, secure, protected, and supported.

* * *

Coming full circle to the title of this book, *Am I Gay*? Many reading my story might believe I was or that I still am. Over the years, I have heard from people who have accused me of living in a perpetual state of self-hatred or denial. I do understand these perceptions and critiques. After all, living in a culture that has come to celebrate LGBTQ+ as the highest form of self-expression firmly, it's no wonder that many people disagree with and even hate the story of my life. Not only mine but also countless others who have left an LGBTQ+ identity for a far better eternal identity found through faith in Jesus Christ.

No, I am not gay. I never was. I was a confused boy and young man, desperate for love and belonging, with a particular gap in my heart related to my gender. Left to figure out life independently, I drew various inaccurate conclusions about who God was and who I was in relationship to Him. I lived and identified as a gay man because, in my brokenness, that label and way of life made sense to me. But homosexuality isn't an identity (contrary to current popular opinion). It's a behavior rooted in desires and confusion that can reinforce one's identity.

I don't in any way deny my former life as a once self-identified gay man. But today, I am so immeasurably thankful that God has brought me to my true identity – a man made in God's image – a man bought with the precious blood of Christ with a new life as an adopted son of God. Today, I also get to be a husband to my wife, Melissa, and father to my two incredible sons. But those treasures are not my identity. My identity is in Jesus Christ alone.

When we let Him, God is more than able to make all things new.

I am well into writing the second half of my story. The most significant difference between my life in the first and second books is the surrender in the final chapter of book one. Going into book two, I am a new creation. I am no longer biblically defined as merely a sinner but as a saint who still struggles with sin. There has been a metamorphosis. The worm went into the tomb of his chrysalis and was made into something entirely new by the finished work of Jesus on the cross.

However, in this life, even saints still struggle with sin. We can also completely lose our way for a season(s) of life. The Apostle Paul addresses rebellion and warns of carnal Christianity in I Corinthians 2 and 3.

In this book, I have vulnerably unpacked and shared my struggles from childhood into adulthood – early adulthood, and most importantly, about coming into an authentic relationship and surrendering to Jesus Christ. This was a fight and a seemingly crazy and circuitous way of arriving at the Kingdom of God.

The theme concerns my search for belonging in this first half of my story. While that basic and essential God-given need continues to be refined and affirmed, the second book of my story (which will be out very soon as a companion to the first) will be about discovering meaningful Kingdom purpose – another essential God-given need for humans made in His image uniquely as male and female.

I hope this first book has both encouraged and given you hope that no one is ever too far beyond the reach of the God who passionately loves them and gave His own life to rescue them from death, darkness, and the power of sin.

I welcome you to join me in the second half of my story – and, more accurately, God's story and merciful work to develop and mature me beyond anything I once thought possible. It's been His doing through the use and ministry of His church poured out in my life. Our only responsibility is to yield and obey. And He even gives us grace for that.

QUESTIONS /
JOURNALING / GROUP
SHARING

T hese questions can also be found at the end of each chapter. This section can be a quick reference for group-led discussions or individual personal reflection.

***

Chapter 1

1. What was your parents' upbringing and childhood like?

2. How might their own experiences, both positive and negative, have influenced the way they parented you?

3. What were the cultural and societal factors that may have influenced the way your grandparents raised your parents?

4. How might these factors have shaped their beliefs, values, and behaviors as parents in raising you?

5. What cultural and societal factors influenced your parents' parenting style during childhood?

6. How might these factors have shaped your beliefs, values, and behaviors?

7. What were some of your parents' sacrifices and efforts to provide for your well-being and upbringing?

8. How can you appreciate and acknowledge their dedication and love, even if you sometimes feel frustrated or misunderstood?

***

Chapter 2

1. What are you aware of in your story of conception through birth?

2. What was your relationship like with your primary caregiver, typically your mother, during the first two years of your life?

3. Are there any recurring patterns or themes in your current relationships that may be related to your early childhood experiences?

4. Do you see any opportunities in which you can use your insights about your early childhood experiences to deepen your relationship with God and others?

5. How might these situations have shaped your view of God's love and care for you?

6. How might God be inviting you to heal and grow in these areas?

***

Chapter 3

1. From a Christian perspective, what does it mean for fathers to "train up" their children? How have you experienced this kind of guidance in your life? What did you experience?

2. Children need different interactions and styles of play with mom and dad. Was your dad engaged in physical play with you? Did you experience fun, rough-and-tumble interactions with him? How did the presence of this interaction (or lack of it) impact you?

3. In what ways have you seen the adverse effects of absentee or uninvolved fathers in the lives of those around you or in your own life? How has this impacted your views on fatherhood?

4. How can we cultivate a culture that values and supports fathers actively involved in their children's lives? What role can the church play in this effort?

5. What biblical examples can we look to for guidance on the importance of fathers in the family unit? How can we apply these lessons to our own lives and relationships?

6. In what ways have you seen God's love reflected in the love of a father figure? How can we better understand God's fatherly love through our experiences with earthly fathers? Or, has your experience with your earthly father tainted your ability to experience the love of your heavenly Father?

7. How can we pray for and support fathers struggling to balance their roles and responsibilities within the family? How can we encourage and empower fathers to be better parents? How do you specifically need encouragement as a father?

***

Chapter 4

1. What are some things that have prevented you from opening up about your painful peer experiences in childhood?

2. How can we overcome these obstacles and take the risk of sharing our stories?

3. How can we support and encourage others struggling to share their experiences?

4. How can our past experiences help us learn to open up to others in our lives today?

5. Who are some people in your life that you trust and feel safe talking to about anything?

6. How can we identify safe and supportive people to share our stories with?

7. How can we create a safe and supportive environment for them to share their stories?

***

Chapter 5

1. How has your early pornography exposure affected your view of sexuality and intimacy?

2. Have you experienced guilt or shame due to your early exposure to pornography, and if so, how have you coped (or not) with these emotions?

3. Have you ever felt like a fraud and feared exposure? Explain.

4. How has your faith or belief system impacted your understanding of sexual sin and your ability to forgive yourself for past mistakes?

5. Have you sought professional help or counseling to address any adverse impacts of early pornography exposure on your mental health and well-being? Has this been helpful?

6. How can you use your experience to help educate and guide others, especially younger generations, about the potential risks and harms of pornography use and sexual sin?

7. What steps can you take to promote healthy sexual thoughts and behavior in your marriage, healthy attitudes, and abstinence in singleness?

***

Chapter 6

1. Has there ever been a time when you have given up or wanted to give up on Christianity? If so, explain.

2. Have you ever been disappointed or angry with God? If so, explain.

3. What were some of your struggles launching from high school into college? If you grew up in a Christian home, was your faith challenged in college?

4. What unhealthy behaviors have you relied on to cope with disappointments, doubts, or challenges?

5. Have you ever received professional or pastoral counseling? If so, did you find it to be helpful? If so, how?

***

Chapter 7

1. Did you ever develop patterns of quitting or escaping challenging or complex situations? If so, explain. How has that impacted your life – in the past/in the present?

2. Or, have you developed an achieve-at-any-cost mindset? If so, explain. How has that impacted your life – in the past/in the present?

3. Have you experienced disappointment or even abuse in some way – verbal, spiritual, or sexual by someone in spiritual authority? How did that impact you?

5. Have you worked/prayed through those experiences with a counselor or mentor?

6. How might that experience still be affecting your life and relationships today?

***

Chapter 8

1. Have you ever been in a situation where you had to figure it out on your own and didn't feel like you had the tools to know where to begin?

2. How did that feel to you?

3. What was the outcome?

4. Did you grow through the experience?

5. Are there secrets you've been holding that you don't want anyone else to know?

6. What are those secrets?

7. Are you willing to find someone to share them with now?

8. Have you considered counseling or a support group to help you process unhealed issues? What are your options for support?

9. Have you ever felt like you've struck out and disqualified yourself from God's grace or His plans and purposes for your life?

10. Have you recovered from that sense of loss? How?

11. Might you need to revisit that for more profound healing and to rediscover God's plans for you?

***

Chapter 9

1. Has a Christian leader ever violated your trust? If so, how?

2. What has the impact of that been? Have you ever genuinely forgiven him/her?

3. Do you experience mistrust of leaders/Christians?

4. Do you need help in moving forward and beginning to trust again? If so, what are your options for support? Will you take action?

5. Have you ever used a bad attitude or behavior as a cry for help? Pause and pray - really consider this question. If so, how?

6. What would you have wanted someone to say or do to help you? Are you willing to seek help now?

7. Have you ever rejected what you knew was true to justify what you wanted? If so, how?

8. What kind of impact have those decisions had on your life and relationships?

***

Chapter 10

1. Have you experienced God sending a messenger to you in your life of sin?

2. Recount that experience/s

3. How might you better prepare to be a messenger of God for someone else?

4. Including both love and truth is essential as we approach a prodigal. Does your approach lean more toward mercy or sharp rebuke?

5. How might you build up what's lacking?

6. How have you been unhealthily emotionally dependent? Is this an area you still need and are willing to grow in? Explain.

7. Have you struggled with sexual sin or addiction? In what ways?

9. Is this still an area you need support in?

10. What are your options for support?

***

Chapter 11

1. Have you truly surrendered your life to Jesus or just prayed for eternal fire insurance like me?

2. Have you surrendered your sense of identity as well?

3. Have you ever experienced God interrupting your worldly plans?

4. What was the situation?

5. How did you respond to Him?

6. What are some ways that you need the Body of Christ to come alongside you for encouragement and accountability?

7. How can you become an authentic encourager and visionary for others?

ACKNOWLEDGMENTS

T hank you, Jesus, for setting this prisoner free.

Thank you, Melissa, for being my amazing wife and partner. I'm so grateful that I get to do life with you. Indeed, God makes all things new – in ways I could never have hoped nor imagined.

Thank you to my boys who encouraged me in writing this book, sacrificed time with me, and prayed that it would one day be finished.

Thank you, PK Hrezo, for your incredible insights and tireless work in editing this manuscript and making it a much better read than it would have been.

Thank you to all those who had a role in reading, editing, and making this book so much better than it would have been without you.

Thank you to the *Love & Truth Network* board of directors for all of your encouragement and support.

Thank you to my assistant, Jeremiah, for all your day-to-day work and support of *Love & Truth Network* and for keeping everything operating smoothly. Thank you for your friendship, as well.

Thank you to pastor John Hawco for preparing and leading a church that made room for me (and others) while I was very much a mess, and walking alongside me as I repented and learned to surrender to Jesus more fully. Thank you for giving me a chance I never expected - that led to twelve years of working with you and an incredible team in pastoral ministry at a local church.

Thank you to all the brothers and sisters who have been the hands and feet of Jesus to me when I desperately needed community. I am so thankful for mentors who discipled me – especially when it wasn't easy.

Finally, I am so grateful for my mom and dad who have stepped out of this life and into heaven. I miss you both and look forward to our reunion.

ABOUT THE AUTHOR

G arry Ingraham is a son of God, husband to Melissa, and father of two incredible young men.

He served on a church pastoral staff for twelve years and was later ordained. In 2013, Garry and Melissa founded Love & Truth Network, a national, non-profit ministry that equips Christian leaders to develop safe and transformational environments to restore sexual wholeness and biblical identity.

Garry teaches, equips, and writes about restoring relational and sexual wholeness, as well as developing safe and transformational environments in our churches, because of his personal history of brokenness and God's relentless love in bringing him to genuine faith and meaningful relationship with Him.

Love & Truth Network website & podcast:

- Love & Truth Network – www.loveandtruthnetwork.com

- LTN Podcast – www.loveandtruthnetwork.com/podcast

Printed in Great Britain
by Amazon